The Townsend Lectures

The Department of Classics at Cornell University is fortunate to have at its disposal the Prescott W. Townsend Fund—established by Mr. Townsend's widow, Daphne Townsend, in 1982. Since 1985, income from the fund has been used to support the annual visit of a distinguished scholar in the field of classics. Each visiting scholar delivers a series of lectures, which, revised for book publication, are published by Cornell University Press in Cornell Studies in Classical Philology.

During the semester of their residence, Townsend lecturers effectively become members of the Cornell Department of Classics and teach a course to Cornell students as well as deliver the lectures.

The Townsend Lectures bring to Cornell University, and to Cornell University Press, scholars of international reputation who are in the forefront of current classical research and whose work represents the kind of close reading of texts that has become associated with current literary discourse, or reflects broad interdisciplinary concerns, or both.

CORNELL STUDIES IN CLASSICAL PHILOLOGY

EDITED BY

FREDERICK M. AHL ★ KEVIN CLINTON
JOHN E. COLEMAN ★ JUDITH R. GINSBURG
G. M. KIRKWOOD ★ DAVID MANKIN
GORDON M. MESSING ★ ALAN J. NUSSBAUM
HAYDEN PELLICCIA ★ PIETRO PUCCI
JEFFREY S. RUSTEN ★ DANUTA SHANZER

VOLUME LVII

Platonic Ethics, Old and New
by Julia Annas

ALSO IN THE TOWNSEND LECTURES

Artifices of Eternity: Horace's Fourth Book of Odes,
by Michael C. J. Putnam

Socrates, Ironist and Moral Philosopher,
by Gregory Vlastos

Culture and National Identity in Republican Rome,
by W. R. Johnson

*Horace and the Dialectic of Freedom:
Readings in "Epistles 1",*
by W. R. Johnson

*Animal Minds and Human Morals:
The Origins of the Western Debate,*
by Richard Sorabji

*Ammianus Marcellinus and the Representation
of Historical Reality,*
by Timothy D. Barnes

Platonic Ethics, Old and New

Julia Annas

Cornell University Press

Ithaca and London

First published 1999 by Cornell University Press
First printing, Cornell Paperbacks, 2000

Printed in the United States of America

LIBRARY OF CONGRESS CATALOGING-IN-PUBLICATION DATA
Annas, Julia.
  Platonic ethics, old and new / Julia Annas.
      p.   cm. — (Cornell studies in classical philology ; v.
  57. The Townsend lectures)
  Includes bibliographical references and index.
  ISBN 0-8014-3518-8 (cloth : alk. paper)
  ISBN 0-8014-8517-7 (pbk. : alk. paper)
    1. Plato—Ethics.   2. Platonists.   3. Ethics, Ancient.   I. Title.
  II. Series: Cornell studies in classical philology ; v. 57.   III. Series:
  Cornell studies in classical philology. Townsend lectures.
  B398.E8A56   1998
  170'.92—DC21   98-30418

Cornell University Press strives to use environmentally responsible suppliers and
materials to the fullest extent possible in the publishing of its books. Such materials
include vegetable-based, low-VOC inks and acid-free papers that are recycled,
totally chlorine-free, or partly composed of nonwood fibers. Books that
bear the logo of the FSC (Forest Stewardship Council) use paper taken
from forests that have been inspected and certified as meeting the
highest standards for environmental and social responsibility.
For further information, visit our website at
www.cornellpress.cornell.edu.

    1   3   5   7   9   Cloth printing   10   8   6   4   2
    1   3   5   7   9   Paperback printing   10   8   6   4   2

CONTENTS

[v]

PREFACE

I was greatly honored by the invitation to give the Townsend Lectures in spring 1997, but understandably daunted by the prospect of producing rather unorthodox views on Plato at an institution famous for its rigor and scholarship. The experience, it turned out, was as intellectually stimulating and challenging as I expected, and also very enjoyable. For this I have to thank the warm hospitality of Cornell's Classics Department, especially Jeffrey and Caroline Rusten, Pietro Pucci and Jeannine Routier-Pucci, Charles and Harriet Brittain, Danuta Shanzer, John Coleman, and Laura Purdy. I am also very grateful to members of the Philosophy Department, just up the stairs, who also made me welcome, especially Norman and Barbara Kretzmann, Jason Stanley, Scott and Jane Mac-Donald, Carl Ginet and Sally McConnell Ginet, and Zoltan Szabo. I owe special thanks to Terry Irwin and Gail Fine and to Charles and Harriet Brittain for all their help and friendship, and for making my time in Ithaca so enjoyable.

Nancy Sokol and Miriam Zubal helped me find my way around a new institution and cope with computer problems and the like with great patience, good humor, and extensive knowledge. Nancy organized the actual giving of the Townsend Lectures and the initial reception with amazing equanimity, for which I feel gratitude and admiration.

The audience at the Townsend Lectures gave me many points to think about, and so did the members of the Townsend seminar. Terry Irwin and Charles Brittain came faithfully and gave me many probing and thoughtful responses. I am sure that I have not met these to their satisfaction, but they have greatly deepened my understanding of the material and the issues. Among the other seminar members, I would like to mention Travis Butler, Todd Ganson, Stephen Gardiner, Keith McPartland, Lisa Rivera, and Kate Woolfitt, who contributed in one or another way to my final reworking of the lectures. Peter Aronoff was an excellent and energizing research assistant as well as a participant in the seminar. I would also like to thank Tim Bayne for help with the index.

I am very grateful to the Getty Center for supporting me as a Getty Scholar for the year during which the foundations for this book were laid. The Center provided the ideal atmosphere for encouraging research into what was for me an unexplored area, and I am most grateful to the then director, Salvatore Settis, the other Scholars, and the Center's helpful and supportive staff.

I am also grateful for discussion and comments on the material at various points, including the penultimate version, from John Armstrong, Paul Bloomfield, Tom Christiano, Dale Cooke, Daniel Farnham, Cindy Holder, Scott LaBarge, Mark LeBar, Kurt Meyers, Daniel Russell, and Jennifer Ryan. I am sure that there are other faculty, visitors, and graduate students at the University of Arizona from whose comments I have benefited; I apologize if I can't at this point distinguish your contribution.

I am particularly grateful for written comments at a late stage from John Armstrong, Christopher Bobonich, David Brink, Brad Inwood, Terry Irwin and Charles Kahn. Jan Opsomer's splendid work *In Search of the Truth: Academic Tendencies in Middle Platonism* (Brussels, 1998) came too late for me to take account of it, especially of its thorough treatment of Plutarch's first Platonic Question, a work I also see as important for our understanding of the relation of skeptical and doctrinal approaches in later interpretations of Plato.

The jacket picture shows an Athenian official of the second century A.D., a period when some of the later Platonists discussed here were writing. Despite his rather unintellectual job of running the city gymnasia, he chose to have his portrait assimilated to the standard likeness of Plato.

As always, I am greatly in debt to my family for their support, and particularly in this case for not only doing without me for four months but being so supportive at a distance, and for not minding that e-mail communication seemed to make no impact on the phone bill. The book is dedicated to my husband, David Owen, and our daughter, Laura, with love as always.

JULIA ANNAS

Platonic Ethics

INTRODUCTION:
DISCOVERING A TRADITION

The title of this book tries to bring out the point that, with respect to Plato's ethics, when we take a look at the interpretations of the ancients, we find something which is not just old, in the sense of being an object of historical study, but also new, in the sense of giving us a new insight into Plato's ethical thinking.

By "the ancients" here I mean in particular the so-called Middle Platonists. This is not their own self-conception; like people in what we call the Middle Ages, they did not think of themselves as being in the middle of anything. In the ancient world they were just Platonists. Modern scholarship has called them Middle because they come between the period when Plato's own school, the Academy, was skeptical and the period of "Neoplatonism," beginning with Plotinus. (Chronologically, they come somewhere between the first century B.C. and the second century A.D.) The "Middle" Platonists are not a unified school; they are a set of rather different people producing interpretations of Plato's ideas, taken to be a unified set of doctrines. About some of them, such as Plutarch, we know a fair amount; but most of our important philosophical texts have authors who are mere names to us, and whose dates are utterly uncertain. For us the tradition of Middle Platonism is basically a set of texts—perhaps appropriately, since these are the first philosophers in a Platonic tradition to see their task as that of interpreting Plato's own texts systematically.[1] Earlier, Aristotle had interpreted Plato as holding doctrines, but not in order to present them as a Platonic phi-

---

[1] I draw from the work of Alcinous, Arius Didymus (not himself a Platonist, but an author who shares some sources with Alcinous), Apuleius, Albinus, Plutarch, Philo of Alexandria (who is relevant although he would not see himself as a Middle Platonist), and the Anonymous Commentator on the *Theaetetus,* as well as from some other ancient authors.

losophy to be argued for or against; rather, Aristotle presents Plato as just one among many philosophers contributing to the ongoing discussion of philosophical problems later given their more adequate formulation by Aristotle himself. As a result, Aristotle's accounts of Plato's ideas appear notoriously strange to us, because Aristotle is openly drawing on Plato for his own purposes, with no pretense of trying to produce a just picture of Plato's own ideas.

It may seem odd, and will certainly be unfamiliar, to approach the interpretation of Plato in a way that emphasizes a work like Alcinous's *Handbook of Platonism* more than Aristotle's account of Plato. Whether it is fruitful will emerge from the book taken as a whole. I certainly think that it is worth looking at a fairly extensive way of considering Plato's ethics in the ancient world, one which for the last two centuries has played almost no role in our own way of reading Plato. A few words are needed to indicate why I consider it not just a (literally) old interpretation of Plato's ethics but also new, one that can give us fresh insight.

First, the ancient Platonists remind us of how Plato was read in the ancient world—that is, for some hundreds of years; and this may at the very least give us some perspective on our own assumptions in reading Plato, which, familiar as they are to us, are not nearly as well established as a tradition. Thus they can help free us from the parochialism that threatens an uncritical reliance on a familiar way of looking at things. Merely this awakening to approaches other than the ones familiar to us is surely useful, in alerting us to what we have missed, and to what we find obvious that others do not.

But more substantially, ancient writers belong to the same ethical tradition as Plato. They are eudaimonists—they hold that each of us has a final end, which is *eudaimonia,* or happiness, and for which we seek a substantial specification. Common sense specifies happiness as a conventionally successful life, with health, wealth, and other recognized goods; reflection, developing into explicit ethical theory, directs us instead to some aim like virtue or pleasure, as a constraint on or organizing principle for our pursuit of conventional goods. Whatever our own substantial modern ethical position, it is likely to be remote from eudaimonism.[2] In the ancient world, by contrast, eudaimonism, which we can see surfacing as an explicit theory in the works of Democritus and Plato,[3] becomes after Aristotle the explicit framework within which ethical theories are presented and debated.[4] Thus the ancient Platonists, when they read Plato, saw his ethical ideas within the same tradition within which he produced them.

[2] This is obvious for forms of utilitarianism and Kantianism; but even modern versions of "virtue ethics" tend not to accept eudaimonism in anything like its ancient form.

[3] With Democritus the situation is complicated by the fact that we possess only fragments of his work. See my article "Democritus and Eudaimonism" (forthcoming).

[4] For detailed support for this claim, see Annas 1993.

When we see the easy way in which they describe Plato in the terms of explicit eudaimonism, we might be tempted to say that they are assimilating Plato to later ideas. But this would be a mistake. It is true that later writers do this in some areas—they unhesitatingly ascribe to Plato large amounts of later (Aristotelian and Peripatetic) logic, for example, and this is pretty clearly anachronistic; they assimilate an implicit use of some forms of reasoning to a later explicit awareness of those forms. But with ethics their use of explicit terminology picks out a framework which can be found there in partially explicit form (as has been increasingly recognized in recent work on Plato). Rather than see this as a form of bias or later projection, we should welcome the insight we get from looking at interpretations produced by people who did not, as we do, have to work into Plato's ethical thoughts from the outside, but already found his framework to be the familiar and natural one.

As we shall find, the ancient Platonists do not just see Plato as a eudaimonist (this would for them be trivially true); they also see him in terms sharpened by later debate. In particular what is important for them is the debate between the Stoics and Aristotelians on the place of virtue in happiness. (This is one thing that makes their writings more valuable on this issue than those of Aristotle, who is himself a eudaimonist, but is rather uninterested in Plato's ethical position, or in seeing Plato as here contributing to a tradition which they share.) Writing from a standpoint in which issues have been clarified by discussion, the later Platonists do not hesitate to enroll Plato on the side of the Stoics; they describe his ethical views in Stoic terms, since they take it that Plato regards as central the points that the Stoics do: the difference of kind between the sort of value that virtue has and the value of everything else, and the sufficiency of virtue for happiness. Though we may be startled by this at first, it is worth following the idea up and looking at its basis in Plato's texts (particularly since at least some Stoics themselves agreed that they were in harmony with Plato in ethics). A careful look at the texts reveals, I argue, that ancient Platonists and Stoics are right to see Plato as akin to the Stoics on some basic issues. Plato, however, has not been forced by debate to sharpen the issues that arise, and as a result he is often unclear or indeterminate on points where later Stoics had been forced by argument to come to a definite conclusion. So this ancient way of looking at Plato, far from being uselessly anachronistic, alerts us to the importance of the issues that got sharpened between Plato and the Stoics, and to Plato's contribution to them. It focuses our attention in the right place, one we might be less alive to were we to ignore the advantages of the eudaimonist perspective.

Another major point emerges rapidly when we read ancient interpretations of Plato; they are utterly indifferent to the methodological approach which has been important to us since the nineteenth century, and has been dominant in the last half of the twentieth century, namely a developmental approach. By far the majority of work on Plato, both scholarly and popular, assumes that Plato's philosophical thought underwent an overall development, sometimes taken to correspond with stages of his life. In his ethical thought Plato is generally taken to have started with an attempt to "define" ethical terms in the shorter, "Socratic" dialogues and to have moved on to a bolder, more "positive" ethical theory in the *Republic*. It is generally assumed that the *Republic* is the apex of Plato's ethical thought, and that in it Plato has moved from an early, tentative stage to a confident stage, one where ethics is connected with metaphysical and political theories. This is sometimes identified as a move from a phase which reflects the position of the historical Socrates to a phase where Plato is producing his own views, but even if we leave the historical Socrates out of it, we usually find the picture of an early, "Socratic" ethics and a later, "Platonic" one.[5] This development is seen as a change in two ways: Plato is seen as moving from a rigorous, "Socratic" theory that virtue is sufficient for happiness to a weaker claim, the claim that the virtuous person is happier than the vicious, but may not be happy if external circumstances are bad; and Plato is also seen as moving from a concern solely with ethics to a conception of ethics as supported by metaphysics and situated in a political context.

This framework for reading, teaching, and discussing Plato is so familiar that it may come to seem inescapable. It is a presupposition of discussion and research rather than something to be discussed itself. Yet if we are to take the ancient perspectives on Plato seriously, we should detach ourselves from this familiar context, and see whether doing so leads to interpretations that we should consider alternatives to our own. For, if we take the long view of Plato interpretation, the developmental view which we find so familiar is a mere blip on the radar, unheard-of before the nineteenth century. Nobody in the ancient world undertook to explain what we find in Plato's works via the idea that his thought underwent radical changes, or took the dialogues to be classified into "early," "middle," and "late." Rather, they read the dialogues, in a variety of orders, and looked for Plato's ideas; in modern terms they are "unitarians."[6]

I think it is fair to say that in modern Plato scholarship unitarianism is not taken very seriously. I do not propose to put forward a full-blown unitarian interpretation but merely want to examine the ancient non-developmental view of Plato's ethics, and some of its implications. If successful, this will of course

[5] This is most clear and explicit in Irwin 1995.

[6] Developmentalism and unitarianism are not the only alternatives; we could read each dialogue separately, making no claims about the connection of ideas between them. The only person to have done this rigorously is Grote (1888). I do not consider this option, because it has been historically uninfluential.

have implications for developmentalism in other areas of Plato's thought, but that is a different and far more ambitious project.

To the ancient Platonists, Plato holds that virtue is sufficient for happiness. I explore this first in dialogues which are conventionally considered early, where the thesis is not controversial, to see how well the ancient interpretation holds up as a general claim, and against the detail of important passages. The ancient Platonists, however, find the same position in the *Republic* and the *Laws,* and this is, to modern scholarship, definitely controversial. Nevertheless, when we look in detail at these works, the ancient claim holds up better than we might have expected. And this provokes some reassessment of other things that we tend to take for granted.

Central here is the privileged position of the *Republic* in Plato interpretation. For us the *Republic* is Plato's major work, the one most important for displaying his thought; it is widely regarded as the apex of a development beginning in the "early," Socratic dialogues, and as committing Plato to a political context and a metaphysical foundation for ethics. The ancient perspective is startlingly different. The ethical theory of the *Republic* is not seen as any kind of development from an "earlier" phase, and the *Republic* itself is not privileged as the central, most important dialogue. (In the ancient world, if any dialogue held that position, it would be the *Timaeus*.) Further, the ethical theory is not seen as being closely dependent on the political or metaphysical themes of the *Republic*. Nor is the moral psychology of that work seen as a radically new departure from the moral psychology of the "Socratic" dialogues—again, contrary to modern preconceptions. Looking at these issues with a fresh set of assumptions enables us to learn from the ancients—Stoics here as well as Platonists—to see central Platonic ideas in a fresh light. We have read the *Republic* in our familiar way only since the nineteenth century, and the context for doing that may well now appear no longer compelling.

Thus a serious look at the ancient interpretation of Plato's ethics leads us not merely to adjust some details of our own interpretation, but to look hard at the way we read the dialogues, our priorities among them (for example, in the prominence we give to the *Republic*), and the way we standardly assume that there is an *overall* development—that the *Republic,* for example, displays an advance in ethical theory, metaphysics, political thought, and moral psychology. The alternative view that we get on all these issues gives us the beginnings of a new approach to many aspects of Plato's thought.

The final topic of this book is another one where we find a striking improvement in our understanding when freed from the pressure of the developmental model. Plato's thoughts about pleasure have always been recognized as various, and as hard to make consistent. The developmental model forces a chronological approach on us, and thus imposes a path through the dialogues in the order in which they are conventionally thought to have been written. The ancient approach gives us an alternative path, suggesting different ways of joining and of dividing Plato's various discussions of pleasure. We are left with work to do, but with a promising line of interpretation.

The ancient Platonists can point out to us an aspect of Plato which we have missed or underestimated. This happens conspicuously with the stress they lay on the idea that for Plato our final end should be being virtuous and thus "becoming like God." This theme displays the greatest distance between ancient and modern readers of Plato. For the ancient Platonists it was one of the most important and stressed features of Platonic ethics. For modern readers it is invisible. It has dropped out of accounts of Plato's ethics, despite its prominent occurrence in several texts. Here the ancients help us to rediscover something that should not have gone missing in the first place. But their way of treating it also alerts us to a weakness of their mode of interpretation. Accounts which unify may give up too soon, leaving differences as fundamental or assigning them to different phases of development. But they may also go on too far, unifying ideas which can be held together only by ignoring or downplaying real difficulties. In this case the ancient Platonists, in treating the thought that virtue is becoming like God as merely a variant on Plato's main thoughts about ethics, paper over a deep problem.

In discussing this issue I have, for the only time, gone beyond the period of the officially Middle Platonists, and brought in the discussion of this problem that we find in Plotinus. This may seem slightly arbitrary, since I don't otherwise deal with Plotinus and the way he and Platonists after him saw their relation to Plato. I think that with the issue of virtue as becoming like God, however, Plotinus's special interest lies in the way in which he explicitly lays out the problem which his predecessors had not really faced. Further, in his solution he indicates the radically different way in which Platonic ethics has to be interpreted, if we hang on to virtue as becoming like God and also take a unifying approach. Here Plotinus enables us to look back on the Platonists before him and see the limitations of their unifying approach, as well as to appreciate their openness to a theme in Plato that the twentieth century has virtually ignored.

It is a cliché that all interpretation takes a set of assumptions for granted, and we should not be surprised to find alternative interpretations for which different things are taken for granted. But even in the modern situation of ongoing debates about many aspects of Plato's ethics, and with far less agreement assumed about Plato than about other ancient authors, such as Aristotle, it can still be a shock to find out just how different are the ancient assumptions about Plato from our own. Some readers of this book may value the shock effect and its result in making us more self-aware about our own presuppositions, but may not be convinced that in the end the ancients have a more fruitful interpretation than we do. Others may come to think that they do on some points and do not on others. My own interest in the ancient Platonists arose from a concern to see whether Plato could justly be considered a eudaimonist or not, and the thought that a good place to start would be with ancient eudaimonists, who saw him as being in that tradition. I have ended up convinced that Plato is a eudaimonist and that the ancient Platonists give us the best lead as to the kind of eudaimonist he is. In the process I have found more and more to doubt in the orthodox modern ways of reading Plato, not just on ethics but in general. I have found the results exciting, and a spur to further research. There are many signs that the orthodox, developmental reading of Plato is crumbling in places and losing its unquestioned dominance. This is surely a good thing, and a sign of vigor in scholarship. I suspect that Plato studies are likely to become less settled, more uncertain, and more open to wide differences of approach. I think it would be a good idea to have the ancient Platonists join us in this exciting new development.

[I]

MANY VOICES: DIALOGUE
AND DEVELOPMENT IN PLATO

"Plato has many voices, not, as some think, many doctrines." He is *poluphōnos*, of many voices, but not *poludoxos*, of many opinions or doctrines. This is a view of Plato which we read in Arius Didymus, court philosopher to the emperor Augustus,[1] in his *Introduction to Ethics*.[2]

Many views have been expressed about Plato over the centuries, and it may seem perverse, when beginning a study of Plato's ethics, to hark back to an obscure ancient author who figures marginally, if at all, in our books about ancient philosophy. Modern philosophers concerned with Plato have not on the whole been very interested in the perspectives taken on interpreting him in the ancient world. For much of the twentieth century, for example, the way in which Plato was interpreted by his own school, the skeptical Academy, was ignored. In the last twenty years or so this tradition has been recovered by

---

[1] On Arius, see Hahm 1990 and Kahn 1983. Göransson (1995) argues against many of their conclusions, and also, in chap. 10, against the conclusion reached by the nineteenth-century scholars Meineke and Diels (restated by Hahm) that Arius Didymus the doxographer is in fact identical with Augustus's philosophical friend Arius. Göransson reminds us that the identification is a conjecture, not a matter of fact, but fails to show that it is not a reasonable conjecture. See Inwood 1996.

[2] Preserved in Stobaeus *Eclogae* 2, along with long passages on the ethics of the Stoics and Peripatetics. Göransson (1995) argues in chap. 11 that, although we should accept Diels's and Meineke's attribution of the two latter passages to Arius Didymus, the "introduction to ethics" is too different from them to be also so attributed. This would be a good argument only if we had more precise independent knowledge as to exactly what works Arius wrote, though Göransson shows up faults in arguments designed to prove that all three passages *must* have the same author.

the work of several scholars,[3] and we are now familiar with the idea that for some time Plato's own school interpreted him as holding no opinions, but as putting forward a model of philosophy consisting of arguing against the positions of others without having any positive position himself. The result of this recovery of the skeptical tradition has been that we are now able to see some aspects of Plato in a wholly different light, particularly the ad hominem arguments of Socrates in the early dialogues. Moreover, we can now appreciate a philosophical rationale for Plato's use of the dialogue form, a topic which for much of the twentieth century has been the subject of indecisive literary squabbling. By writing in the dialogue form Plato is able to distance himself from the positions presented and the arguments put forward for them. He does not present his positions from an authoritative position, but puts forward arguments in a way which leaves the reader inevitably thrown back on her own resources for understanding what has been proposed. This way of proceeding privileges argument and rational support over the mere statement of a position.

I suggest that, just as our understanding of Plato's methods has been greatly helped by recovery of the ancient skeptical tradition of Platonism, our understanding of Plato's ethics may be aided by our turning also to other ancient traditions of interpreting him. Prominent among these is that of the so-called Middle Platonists. In the ancient world they were just Platonists;[4] it is modern history of philosophy that has seen them as lying in the middle between Plato's own Academy on the one hand and Neoplatonism on the other. There are other ancient writers whose interpretation of Plato converges with that of the Middle Platonists without their being Platonists themselves. Arius Didymus, for example, with whom I began, was not a Platonist; he seems to have been a Stoic.[5] He may in fact have been one of a number of philosophers in the ancient world whose interest in Plato and Aristotle was quite like ours; it did not stem from a prior commitment to the truth of the position. However, Arius's presentation of Plato commended itself enough to later Platonists that bits of it— or possibly its source—turn up verbatim in a later *Handbook of Platonism* by the Platonist Alcinous.[6]

[3] Notably, Jonathan Barnes, Gisela Striker, Michael Frede, and especially Myles Burnyeat.

[4] See M. Frede 1987 and Donini 1990.

[5] If, that is, Arius Didymus is to be identified with Arius the court philosopher of Augustus.

[6] See Whittaker 1990 and Dillon 1993. Göransson (1995) argues that, far from Arius being Alcinous's source, the dependency is the other way around, and that Arius may be much later than we assume. Göransson's detailed arguments are not, in my view, convincing, but in any event, as far as concerns the parts relevant to Plato's ethical thought

After the end of the skeptical Academy we find a period where there is convergence between Platonists and others: Plato should be interpreted as holding doctrines. The interpretations we find naturally embody the methods, themes, and priorities of philosophy as that had taken shape after Plato. By the time the skeptical Academy died out, in the first century B.C., any philosopher interpreting Plato could not but use concepts and theories that had developed after Plato wrote his dialogues. This fact is often, indeed, thought to render them unhelpful for us, for we have direct access to Plato, so we do not need them, and their own preoccupations might seem to make them an obstruction for us, rather than a help, in understanding the dialogues.

It is a real question why we should take an interest in ancient traditions of Platonism at all, if our main concern is Plato. Perhaps these people are interesting in their own right, but what do they have to do with *our* attitude to Plato? Shouldn't we just read Plato for ourselves, and produce the best philosophical interpretation that we can in our terms, and only then, if at all, turn to the quite secondary question of how other people, in other times and circumstances, have interpreted him? This is a common view, and partly accounts for the low level of interest among Platonic scholars in the ancient Platonists' interpretations. So we might think that turning to later Platonists and others to help us to interpret Plato is interpreting the more by the less interesting.

What *do* we get when we turn to ancient doctrinal traditions of interpreting Plato? We find a view which is stimulatingly different from our own. We also get a salutary lesson in disengaging ourselves from our own modern assumptions about how to read Plato. Discovering an interpretation in a tradition which takes quite other things for granted than what we do, or questions what seems obvious to us, lights up points that we ignore and alerts us to what we are presupposing unawares. It might be objected that we can get this just from looking at the variety of interpretations of Plato produced in the twentieth century. But there is a drawback to this. Superficial variety may conceal deep agreements, which show up only by contrast with a tradition which is further away; the current controversy may be so gripping that we fail to notice how local it is.[7]

What insight do we get about Plato from the ancient doctrinal interpreta-

---

(which Göransson treats very cursorily), it does not matter to my thesis whether Arius is a source for Alcinous, or whether both are using a common source, or even whether Arius is using Alcinous, since Arius is writing from a viewpoint which does not aim to further the agenda of any particular philosophical school. Excessive concentration on the question of who said something first has often hindered appreciation of the philosophical interest of ancient interpretations of Plato.

[7] Also, anyone who now gets deeply interested in Plato is likely to be already involved in a particular tradition, and her attitude to other contemporary traditions is likely to be

tions? Among other things, we may be led to question, or at least to think about, one assumption in particular which goes very deep in twentieth-century reading of Plato. This is that there is such a thing as the overall *development* of Plato's thought; Plato's ideas change over his life. This assumption goes so deep that its operation is pervasive and often unnoticed, and it is often assumed to be the only sensible interpretative assumption.

It would seem unreasonable to deny that Plato's thought develops at all. On some points the different positions that we find in the corpus certainly suggest that he changed his mind or tried out different approaches. An interpretation presenting Plato's thought as a completely unchanging system either runs into implausibility or has to stay at a very unspecific and general level. So much, however, is compatible with recognizing false starts, different approaches to the same problem, and change of mind on one theme coexisting with unchanged views on another. It is a far cry from this to the assumption that there is a development in Plato's thought which is systematic and linear, changing from one position to another where the two cannot be held simultaneously. It is this much stronger assumption which is often found, and one sign of this is the related assumption that there is such a thing as *the* order of the dialogues, that is, that the dialogues can be placed in a single definitive order reflecting the development of Plato's thought. Disputes over the ordering of dialogue A and dialogue B are disputes about the nature of that development. Typically, they take the form of showing that A and B contain positions which are not simultaneously tenable, so that they can be held only successively; the dispute then turns to showing which is best regarded as coming first.

I question this assumption of overall, linear development. One impetus for doing this comes from reading ancient accounts of Plato's ethics—for what I say is limited to Plato's ethics and is not a claim about the whole of his thought, though I realize that it is already controversial to think that one can separate the ethics from other aspects of Plato's thought in this way, and I have something to say, in the fifth chapter, in defense of the claim that it can. This is important, since it would be perverse to claim that the ancient Platonists are the best guides to all aspects of Plato's thought. Sometimes their approach is clearly marked by their own contemporary concerns in a way that lacks resonance in Plato, as when they ascribe to him Aristotle's and Theophrastus's logic, on the grounds that arguments in the dialogues can be analyzed using these forms. But where the ethics is concerned, we are not faced by hopeless anachronism. For the later

---

already colored by attitudes of conflict. The fact that we are not academically in competition with the Middle Platonists makes it easier for us to appreciate them even when we are in disagreement.

Platonists are eudaimonists, as is standard in the ancient world; they take the basic concepts of ethics to be those of *eudaimonia,* or happiness, and virtue. When they interpret Plato as a eudaimonist, they take themselves to be bringing out explicitly the structure of ethical thought that is implicit in him. In this they are right, and they have the advantage of us in that they stand, in a way that we do not, in the same tradition of ethical thought as Plato.

What does Arius have in mind when he says, as he does twice, that Plato has many voices?[8] In the first passage where he says this Arius is discussing Plato's view that our end in life is "becoming like God" (a startling idea, to which I shall return). Plato, he says, discusses this according to the parts of philosophy: in the way appropriate to physics in the *Timaeus,* ethics in the *Republic,* and logic in the *Theaetetus,* as well as in book 4 of the *Laws.* But, although the style is varied to achieve eloquence and grandeur, the doctrine is consistent: Plato means living according to virtue. In the second passage Arius says that Plato makes different divisions of goods in different places: there is a twofold division of goods in the *Laws* (between divine and human goods); a threefold distinction among goods of the soul, goods of the body, and external goods; a fivefold list of goods in the *Philebus;* and so on.

The first passage might lead us to think that Arius is merely contrasting variety of style or expression with sameness of idea. But in the discussions of our final end in the dialogues *Timaeus, Republic,* and *Theaetetus,* the very same expression "becoming like God" occurs in all three. What differ are the contexts and the method employed: in the *Timaeus* we are doing physics, in the *Republic* ethics, and in the *Theaetetus* epistemology, treated as part of logic. Different kinds of argument are employed, but we are not dealing with different ideas.[9] Similarly, in the second passage Arius mentions a number of different ways of dividing up goods, which occur in different contexts, and claims that they are consistent, for these different numbers result from different principles of division, and these do not clash. What concerns him, then, is what we have called

---

[8] The phrase occurs at 55.5−7: *Platōn poluphōnos ōn, ouch hōs tines oiontai poludoxos.* At 49.20 is the phrase *to de ge poluphōnon tou Platōnos,* and Wachsmuth follows Heeren in adding ‹*ou poludoxon*›, thereby making the passage come into line with the later one. Stephen White in his translation omits the supplement and translates 49.20 as, "Variety of expression is typical of Plato." However, though it is true that Wachsmuth is heavy-handed with his improvements to the text, and the textual reasons for making the emendation are not strong, the examples in both passages are sufficiently similar so that even in the earlier passage the contrast between *poluphōnon* and *poludoxon* is appropriate.

[9] Nor do we have the claim that one area, such as physics, discusses something which is a basis or foundation for ethics; the significance of this becomes clearer later.

since Shorey the unity of Plato's *thought*. What might prevent us from appreciating this, Arius holds, is not the idea that Plato's thought must have changed—something that never crosses his mind—but the fact that Plato has "many voices." Whatever this means, it is not best taken to refer merely to difference of verbal style. Arius seems to have rather strange views about Plato's style anyway.[10] Twice he praises him for beauty and clarity of style, and alarmingly both of these references are to the *Laws*.[11] So it is not at all clear what features of style he would have in mind.

What is the force of the word that Arius uses—*poluphōnos*, "many-voiced"? It is a not uncommon word in later writers, and has a variety of meanings, all of which, however, spring clearly from the two ideas of *polu*, a lot of, and *phōnē*, voice.[12] It can be used of noisy animals, particularly frogs,[13] which produce a large volume of sound, or of people who produce a lot of sound in the sense of starting and not stopping; thus it is used of drunks going on and on, and prolix books.[14] Its commonest use, however, is to indicate many *different* sounds; it is used of birdsong[15] and musical instruments, particularly the *aulos*, or double pipes, which has a large range of notes.[16] It is used of human voices that sound different, as in polyphonic harmony or different languages.[17] It is used, in talking of literary works, of Hypereides, who "has more voices" than Demosthenes, and most notably of Homer, who is repeatedly said to be the author who most

---

[10] This may, however, be an unfair impression derived from the way the passage has been shortened in transmission.

[11] 49.23–25; 54.10–12.

[12] One reference in Alexander of Aphrodisias (*De mixtione* 216.6) is to a difference of philosophical opinion (among the Stoics), but this is an exception: other uses of *poluphōnos* maintain Arius's contrast between an opinion and the way it is expressed.

[13] John Philoponus, in his commentary on Aristotle's *De anima* (377.26), usefully comments on this, saying that the term is used even of insects such as crickets which produce a lot of noise, even if it is not strictly speaking *voice* because not produced through the vocal organs.

[14] Drunks babbling on: Plutarch *On Talkativeness* 504b1, *Table-talk* 645a11, 715a5. Prolix books: Basil *Letters* 244.3, 265.2.

[15] This use is very frequent and can be found in Aelian, Aratus, Aristotle's biology, Basil, Diodorus Siculus, Eustathius, Plutarch, and the Scholia to Aeschylus.

[16] Musical instruments: Clement of Alexandria *Protrepticus* 1.5.3, Dio Chrysostom *Orations* 2.56, Nicephorus Gregoras *Historia romana* 432.17, Plutarch *Quaestiones conviviales*, 674e10. The *aulos*: Pseudo-Plutarch *De musica* 1141c3 ff., where this feature of the *aulos* is discussed at length; Scholia to Pindar's Pythian Ode 12, scholion 31.

[17] Polyphonic harmony: Clement of Alexandria *Protrepticus* 9.88. Different languages: Diodorus Siculus *Histories*, bk. 29, 19.1; Josephus *Jewish Antiquities*, bk. 1, 117.3 (the Tower of Babel).

exhibits *poluphōnia*.[18] Homeric language, enthuses Eustathius, is a "many-voiced thing" (*poluphōnon ti chrēma hē Homērikē glōssa*).[19]

We can hardly help being struck by the fact that Arius uses this word for a feature of Plato's way of writing. For, while Plato has no particular attitude to birds, the *aulos* and Homer are two things that he is famously against, and for just this reason, that they display too much attractive variety, and so confuse and distract the soul, which ought to be intent on rational simplicity. In particular, Plato's view of education in an ideally just state is dominated by the idea that we should not vividly identify with many different people, or with the results of radically different circumstances, if we are to be properly virtuous.[20] This leads to censorship of both Homer and the *aulos*.

Moreover, in this context Plato shows hostility not just to the expressive variety of having many voices, but to variety or variation in itself, *poikilia;* yet just this is another feature of his own style which Arius praises.[21] What Arius is indicating here is a feature of Plato's works which has exercised many in the twentieth century: his own way of writing displays a characteristic variety which, when he is writing about it, he downgrades and criticizes.

One would have to have a tin ear not to notice that sometimes the way Plato writes is at odds with what he is saying. Most famously, in the *Republic* he insists that the method of true philosophy, correctly carried through, will be highly abstract, based on practice in and using the methodology of mathematics, not at any point relying on appeal to the empirical world. Moreover, he insists on the sharpest separation of philosophy and its methods from literature and its appeal

---

[18] Of Hypereides: [Longinus] *On the Sublime* 34.1. Of Homer: Dionysius of Halicarnassus *De compositione verborum* 16 (Homer is the most *poluphōnos* of poets), Strabo *Geography* 3.2.12, Eustathius eleven times (*Commentary on the Iliad*, vol. 1, 702.14; vol. 2, 25.3, 175.21; vol. 3, 855.26; vol. 4, 52.4, 61.12, 193.20, 402.26, 547.3; *Commentary on the Odyssey*, vol. 1, 287.17; vol. 2, 317.43). Clement of Alexandria (*Protrepticus* 1.8.3) uses it of Christ's versatility in the ways he saves us (picking up on *Hebrews* 1.1 where God is said to speak in various ways through the prophets).

[19] *Commentary on the Iliad*, vol. 2, 25.3.

[20] *Republic* 392C–398B. It is in the *Republic* that Plato is most critical of Homer, in the well-known passages 378D, 391A, 393C–398B, 595A–608B. In other dialogues Plato often falls in with the common habit of quoting Homer to support a point (as for example *Phaedo* 94D and *Republic* 441C, where lines from the *Odyssey* support Plato's [different] divisions of the soul), but his references to and citations of Homer are frequently ironic or sarcastic. The *aulos* is discussed disapprovingly at *Republic* 399C–E, where what is objectionable about it is precisely that it has a wider range of notes than any other instrument, giving it the widest expressive range.

[21] 50.2–4: Plato has elaboration of style (*tēn poikilian tēs phraseōs*) because of its eloquence and grandeur.

to the vividness of experience and ability to make us empathize with it. The *Republic* itself, however, is not only not an example of the abstract mathematical style of philosophizing; it is not anything that could be developed in that direction; it is full of examples, analogies, metaphors, and all the appeals to the imagination for which literature is so harshly condemned. Yet it would be obviously mistaken to find here a deep incoherence or split in Plato's thinking. For patently, the *Republic* is not itself an example of the kind of philosophizing that it talks about. Further, there are many reasons for Plato not to try to make it like this. By using literary devices whose use in other contexts he deplores, Plato is able to make two fairly straightforward points. One is that these devices can be used for good as well as bad, to point people in the right direction as well as the wrong. The other is that their use, even in the right contexts, is pedagogical; the *Republic* is written in a way that appeals to our imagination because we are beginners, and if we were really to get involved in doing philosophy, and do it at a higher level, it would be very different and far more abstract. Thus there is no great difficulty here in understanding what at first looks like a dissonance between content and presentation of content.

Arius appears to think of Plato's use of variety of style as pedagogical: vivid writing is needed to interest those unused to the joys of abstract argument. There is Platonic precedent: at *Phaedrus* 277C Socrates says that the philosophical orator must address varied language to a "varied" soul and straightforward language to the soul which is straightforward. We might also recall that in the dialogues we see plenty of folly as well as wisdom; versatility is needed to depict shiftiness and irritability, such as we see in characters we are meant to despise, like Hippias and the other Sophists.[22] The Middle Platonist Albinus in his *Introduction* to reading Plato says that in the dialogues the philosophical types should be represented as appropriately straightforward, and the sophistic types as appropriately varied and fickle.[23] It is thus likely that Arius may have the pedagogical role of literary versatility in mind. (At any rate, we can hope that he is not thinking in the same way as the source of Diogenes Laertius 3.63, who tells us that Plato uses varied expressions to make his position hard for the uneducated to understand.)

In the twentieth century a variety of sophisticated approaches have been used to explain how Plato can condemn philosophically one of the most notable fea-

---

[22] At *Republic* 604E–605A the mimetic artist is said to go for imitating the "irritable and varied" character, which lends itself to imitation better than noble straightforwardness.

[23] Albinus, *Introduction,* chap. 2: to the philosopher what is appropriate by way of character is *to gennaion kai to haploun kai to philalēthes,* to the Sophist *to poikilon kai to palimbolon kai to philodoxon.*

tures of the way he himself writes. One comparatively simple explanation, the one that apparently seems obvious to the ancient Platonists, has seldom been taken seriously: the idea that its use might be pedagogical, that Plato might write in different ways for different audiences. This is in spite of the fact that the dialogues do differ in this way; the appropriate audience for the *Ion* does not seem to be the appropriate audience for the *Parmenides*. One factor here may be the hold of the overall developmental view, which demands that there be one proper order for the dialogues, and thus lessens the importance of differences of level or style. If it is part of our understanding of the Socratic dialogues, for example, that they come before the *Republic,* then we will regard differences of style as indicating stage of development. If, on the other hand, the differences are regarded as a matter of pedagogy, nothing follows about development.

So much for variety. But there is more than this to the idea of many voices in Arius. Whatever the literary suggestions of the word, what Arius mentions is the same issue as that is discussed in different dialogues, which he takes to be representative of the different "parts" of philosophy: logic, physics, and ethics. That is, starting from philosophy as it is practiced in his own day, he claims that treating Plato thematically, in what for him is a contemporary approach, does not reveal different positions in different dialogues, merely different "voices," different methods and approaches. This is, I think, an interesting idea, which challenges us because it is so different from the way in which we have got used to reading Plato. When we read dialogues which differ greatly in theme and approach, we reach first for the assumption that we have different positions which can be arranged in a linear fashion, not for the assumption that we have a single position and different treatments which can be thought of as different ways of voicing it.

There is one difference which has greatly exercised twentieth-century philosophical interpreters of Plato. Arius may or may not have had it in mind as coming under "many voices," but if he didn't, he certainly should have done. It exercised at least some Middle Platonists,[24] and it arises for any interpretation of Plato which tries to see his thought as a unity. It is that between the aporetic, negative Socratic dialogues, nowadays generally considered early, and the far more positive, content-proclaiming dialogues which have been traditionally grouped as "middle." Here the difference seems to be radical. In the aporetic dialogues Socrates appears as a questioner who challenges his interlocutors to show him that they really understand what they so confidently pontificate about. He makes a great display of not having knowledge himself, but merely testing the knowledge claims of others. In the more ambitious dialogues Socrates has

---

[24] Plutarch and the Anonymous Commentator on the *Theaetetus,* as we see later.

taken on a new role, that of a person with positions to put forward, sometimes quite insistently. Socrates seems to have moved from being the negative questioner of others to being someone with positive, dogmatic positions which the reader is apparently supposed to evaluate as claims to the truth—claims, indeed, which are hard to match in philosophy for their boldness.

In the twentieth century most of us, certainly those of us in the analytical tradition, have tended to take as part of our background the assumption that this difference should be accounted for developmentally: *first* Plato presents Socrates as an ad hominem questioner, and *then* he presents him as an expounder of doctrine. I shall return to the arguments for and against this approach shortly, but now I shall put forward an example containing problems for it. Here is an extreme statement of Socrates' role as the questioner of others' pretensions, with no position of his own:

The common reproach against me is that I am always asking questions of other people but never express my own views about anything, because there is no wisdom in me; and that is true enough. And the reason of it is this, that God compels me to attend the travail of others, but has forbidden me to procreate. So that I am not in any sense a wise man; I cannot claim as the child of my own soul any discovery worth the name of wisdom.

And here is an example of Socrates as the expounder of doctrine in his own person:

Let us try to put the truth in this way. In God there is no sort of wrong whatsoever; he is supremely just, and the thing most like him is the man who has become as just as it lies in human nature to be. And it is here that we see whether a man is truly able, or truly a weakling and a nonentity. . . . If, therefore, one meets a man who practices injustice and is blasphemous in his talk or in his life, the best thing for him by far is that one should never grant that there is any sort of ability about his unscrupulousness. . . . For they do not know what is the penalty of injustice. . . .There are two patterns set up in the world. One is divine and supremely happy; the other has nothing of god in it, and is the pattern of the deepest unhappiness. This truth the evildoer does not see.

These passages certainly give us a contrast, pointing up very sharply the contrast between the inquiring, non-dogmatic Socrates of the aporetic dialogues and the confident Socrates of the more ambitious dialogues. But both passages come from the same dialogue, the *Theaetetus*.[25]

We could scarcely have a more striking contrast than the Socrates who argues ad hominem against the views of others without expressing any of his own and the Socrates who presents a highly contentious view of his own. But Plato cannot have failed to notice that there is a contrast here, and we can hardly appeal to a development in Plato's thought to render consistent passages that occur with fewer than thirty Stephanus pages between them.

There are, of course, ways of construing the two passages to show that they are consistent. One is the skeptical interpretation, which held sway for some time in Plato's own Academy. In the first passage Socrates is describing himself as a midwife like his mother, but, like all midwives when practicing, he does not give birth himself. He has no philosophical ideas himself, but merely extracts them from others by questioning and then tests the results. Thus all his argument is ad hominem, directed against the claims of others. This is an attractive view, and we can see how it might be put forward as an interpretation of the position of the Socrates of the early dialogues, so keen to test the claims of others, so reluctant to substitute his own. An ancient commentator on the *Theaetetus*, unfortunately anonymous to us, relates an interpretation (which he does not himself share) that "some think, on the basis of passages like these, that Plato is an Academic, having no beliefs."[26]

On the skeptical interpretation, Socrates is simply describing his own practice in the midwife passage. He always argues against the claims of others, without bringing any of his own into it, because that is the best way to argue if you are seeking truth. People who are convinced that their own position is true are dogmatists; their fault is that they have made their commitment too soon, failed to realize that to base arguments on a position of their own renders them vulnerable to objections that can be raised against that position—objections which will certainly be raised by those inquirers who are really in search of the truth. On this view, when Socrates lays out a seemingly dogmatic position, it is put forward not as a position which he defends, but rather as something which commends itself to him, but is not to be philosophically defended in the present context. And indeed in the *Theaetetus* the passage is clearly marked—three times—as a "digression" from philosophical argument. On this view, there is no inconsistency within the *Theaetetus* itself.

There are disadvantages in generalizing this as an account of Plato more

[25] *Theaetetus* 150C–D, 176C–E, trans. M. J. Levett, rev. M. F. Burnyeat (Indianapolis: Hackett, 1990).

[26] *Anonymous Commentator on Plato's Theaetetus,* col. 54.38–43 (*Corpus dei papiri filosofici greci e latini* vol. 3 [Florence: Olschki, 1995], pp. 410–13).

widely. It is true that in the early dialogues Socrates argues against the claims of others and does not argue for his own. But he certainly expresses many positive opinions which seem to hang together; there is controversy as to how they do so, but few who have interpreted the dialogues doctrinally have done it so austerely as to find no ethical theory there at all. On the skeptical view, these positive assertions are all like the *Theaetetus* digression: views put forward for discussion, but not argued to or from in the context.[27] This severs the actual practice of argument from the positive statements that we find; and since there is so much in Plato by way of positive statement, this appears to be an unbalanced way of interpreting Plato.[28] Moreover, we may think that a genuinely skeptical approach to Plato is bound in the end to develop the practice of skeptical argument in other contexts rather than devoting much time to the interpretation of Plato, judging from the skeptical Academy, who argued against their contemporaries, the Stoics, rather than devoting themselves to the interpretation of Sun, Line, and Cave.[29]

If Plato is interpreted doctrinally, how can we reconcile these passages? Ancient Platonists hold varying interpretations of the dialogue as a whole,[30] but they unite in thinking Plato committed to the views expressed in the digression, particularly since in some respects these recall the *Republic*.[31] How then can Socrates

[27] Sextus Empiricus seems right here (though admittedly he has an ax to grind, since he wants to distinguish Pyrrhonism sharply from Academic Skepticism): "Even if Plato is aporetic about some things, he is not a Sceptic; for in some matters he appears to make assertions about the reality of unclear objects or to give certain unclear items preference in point of convincingness" (*Outlines of Scepticism,* bk. 1, 225, trans. Julia Annas and Jonathan Barnes [Cambridge: Cambridge University Press, 1994]).

[28] Grote (1888) notably claims that the negative argument in Plato and the positive doctrine are quite distinct and come from different sources. Moreover, Grote goes further than most interpreters in considering each dialogue separately, rather than approaching Plato thematically.

[29] We don't know their interpretations of any of the more obviously doctrinal dialogues. The fascinating fragment 215(a) of Plutarch tells us, in the context of discussion of the theory of recollection in the *Phaedo:* "That it is untrue that that which can be known is the cause of knowledge, as Arcesilaus maintained, since if this is so lack of knowledge will turn out to be a cause of knowledge" (Sandbach translation). It is unclear, however, whether Arcesilaus is defending the relevant view, as Sandbach thinks, or concurring with the view as Plutarch retails it. In any case it is hard to see how this relates closely to the *Phaedo.* And it is possible that the fragment comes from the later Plutarch of Athens; so our access to Arcesilaus here is frustrating. It is a tiny indication, however, that the skeptical Academy may have discussed dialogues such as the *Phaedo.* (I owe this reference to Charles Brittain.)

[30] Sedley (1996) discusses the interpretations of the skeptical Academy, Alcinous, and the Anonymous Commentator.

[31] Though there are differences as important as the similarities, which we explore in Chapter 3.

say that he has no ideas of his own? Unless this is not seriously meant (in which case it is highly misleading), Socrates' lack of position must be understood to be relative to the context of teaching: he has no doctrines *when eliciting other people's views*, since if he did, this would interfere with the process of getting views out of them, but this does not mean that he has no positions of his own which can be discussed in a different context. As David Sedley has pointed out, this is the view of the anonymous ancient commentator on the dialogue, which can be summed up as, "Qua teacher Socrates is barren; qua philosopher he is not."[32] Indeed, Anonymous goes on to suggest that Socrates' teaching method here should be considered in the light of the teaching passage in the *Meno*, in which Socratic teaching leads to *anamnesis*, or recollection; for you to learn something is for you to come to understand it from within yourself—an idea imaginatively rendered as the claim that when you learn something, your soul recollects what it knew in a former life.

It may seem that if you think that Plato holds doctrines, then the figure of Socrates as a barren midwife can be understood only as applying to a stage prior to the doctrine—eliciting it—or to a stage after it—teaching it—but not at the crucial stage of holding it. This kind of resolution will probably strike us as unattractive. It seems to give too little weight to the critical activity of arguing and testing the views of others; if our emphasis is on the doctrines, then it sounds as though Socrates' arguments against the views of others are dispensable to the philosophical enterprise. But this is too swift. Nobody could be a firmer doctrinal interpreter of Plato than Plutarch, and yet he respects the skeptical Academy, uses many of its arguments,[33] and makes some comments on the midwife passage which show how a doctrinal interpretation can regard Socrates' practice of ad hominem argument.[34]

Plutarch makes several points, most of them about the benefits to the learner of Socrates' way of arguing as he describes it in the midwife passage. If Socrates argues with you, he says, in the familiar way in which he uses only your premises and not his, eliciting your ideas and testing them rather than discussing his own, then this first enables you to distinguish Socrates, the real philosophical article, who wants to improve you and test your ideas, from the sham one, the Sophists who want only to win arguments. Second, having your ideas tested and rejected improves your judgment about ideas; you get less inclined to cling to your own idea just because it's yours, and more open to accepting the best idea even if it

[32] Sedley 1996, 100. Cf. shortly afterward: "Midwifery does not require having no brainchildren of one's own, just not revealing them" (p. 101).

[33] Plutarch's critical works, particularly the anti-Stoic and anti-Epicurean ones, are generally held to derive from Academy arguments. Similarly, Antiochus's dogmatic system probably relies on Academic arguments against the Stoics (cf. *De finibus*, bks. 4 and 5).

[34] In *Platonic Questions* number 1.

wasn't originally yours. These are reasonable common-sense points, but then Plutarch gives us something more important. Whether knowledge is possible or not, he says, Socrates' practice of arguing ad hominem is valuable. If knowledge is not possible, as the skeptical Academy think,[35] then Socrates is doing you a service in ridding you of your false beliefs, like a doctor curing your body of diseases. If, however, knowledge is possible, and there turns out to be only one true view (the Platonist view, of course), then you can acquire it by learning—you don't have to discover it yourself—but the best learner is the person who is not convinced beforehand that he has knowledge. Only when you appreciate the shortcomings of your own views can you be ready to see that another view is in fact true. Plutarch adds the analogy (rather unpleasant to us) of a person with no children of their own, who adopts a child, and is able to take the best offered— whereas the person producing their own child is, presumably, stuck with what they have. Plutarch concludes by reminding us that Socrates produced no ordinary kinds of knowledge, such as mathematics or Sophists' doctrines; he was concerned only to produce philosophical wisdom, and for humans this is not something that can be produced or discovered, but only brought forth by "recollection." That is, it has to come from within yourself; you have to do it for yourself in your own case. No ordinary teacher can produce it, only the midwife who makes you produce your own thoughts.

Plutarch is indicating that Socrates as the barren midwife has a role for the doctrinal Middle Platonists as well as for the skeptical Academy. We don't have to choose; we don't have to hold that Plato had no doctrines or, on the other hand, give up the idea that Socrates really is a barren midwife. Even if you think Plato has a doctrinal position, Socratic ad hominem argument has a role. When we read the dialogues, we can see that Socrates does not directly argue for positive positions, but argues against alternative views which his interlocutors hold. This alerts us to the point that even if we accept those positive positions as our own, we will not be doing so in the proper Platonic way if we just take them over on authority, or try to fit them on to our own views without reflection. They have to become *our* views, and for this to be the case our own views have to be tested to the point where we can genuinely appreciate, for ourselves, that the Platonic views are the true ones. The skeptical Academy doubted whether we would ever get to that point, and went on testing; the doctrinal Platonists

---

[35] At 1000C the supposition is that "nothing is apprehensible and knowable" (*katalēpton* and *gnoston*), an unmistakable allusion to the skeptical Academy. Moreover, the analogy that follows of the philosopher curing the person by the removal of false beliefs, like the doctor curing the body by removing diseases, perhaps echoes the use of this analogy by Philo, the last head of the Academy (the passage is in Arius Didymus ap. Stobaeus 2.39.20−41.25).

were more optimistic, and thought that a point comes when we can reasonably commit ourselves to Platonic doctrines. Skeptical Academics have to regard doctrinal Platonists as underestimating the problems that have to be overcome before we can finally commit ourselves to the truth of Platonic doctrines. Doctrinal Platonists have to think that the skeptical Academics overestimate these dangers. But each side can in principle respect what the other is doing.

Plutarch's little work shows us how a doctrinal Platonist can have a role for Socrates' negative ad hominem arguments, and how a Middle Platonist can respect and have a use for the work of the skeptical Academy.[36] But, of course, if you interpret Plato in terms of doctrines, you *need* not take this line; you can just concentrate on the doctrines, and ignore or downplay Socrates' role as barren midwife. This is what some ancient Platonists did. Those who temperamentally are drawn to positive doctrines rather than exploration of our grounds for holding them ignore the skeptical Academy, and some, like Numenius, positively hate them. In his work *On the Revolt of the Academy from Plato* Numenius reduces the skeptical Academy (amusingly, it must be admitted) to a series of disreputable renegades whose efforts had nothing to do with Plato's true legacy. In general, a range of options is available to people interpreting Plato doctrinally. We go from Plutarch's position of accepting the role of ad hominem argument in forcing you to think for yourself about Plato's doctrines, to an attitude like that of Numenius, which accepts the doctrines in a dogmatic spirit and has no use for ad hominem argument.[37]

There is here, I think, a strong contrast with the best-known modern "unitarian" interpreter of Plato, Paul Shorey. In his *Unity of Plato's Thought*[38] Shorey talks constantly of Plato's "fixed faith" in various ideas, representing him as concerned to convey an "ethical and religious spirit" in a way that is sometimes indifferent to argument and careless even about self-contradiction. In Shorey's view the central ideas come before any concern with reasons for them, and the unity of Plato's thought is a unity of spiritual conception, not of mutually sup-

---

[36] Cf. the Anonymous Commentator on the *Theaetetus* (46.43 ff. and 47.44 ff.), who insists that, though Socrates has doctrines, he does not teach these to the pupil, but rather articulates the pupil's "natural conceptions"—conceptions that we are born with, but need to articulate and clarify through argument and reflection in order to understand them properly. We have always been capable of bringing this understanding from within ourselves, but need Socrates to provoke us to reflect. Hence the model for achieving understanding by reflection is recollection: getting understanding from within yourself.

[37] We should remember that Plutarch's pupil and friend Favorinus appears to have cast himself as a supporter of the skeptical Academy (and is attacked by Galen for so doing) although by this period the Academy did not exist as a formal institution. See Ioppolo 1993, 1994, and 1995.

[38] Shorey 1904.

portive arguments.[39] In much of twentieth-century discussion of Plato, Shorey's legacy has lingered unremarked in the assumption that real philosophical concern with Plato's arguments is more likely to lead to a developmental than to a unitarian view of his ideas. But perhaps Shorey has foisted a false dichotomy on us; finding the same idea in widely different contexts of argument need have nothing to do with faith as opposed to reason. Shorey represents the dogmatic, Numenius end of the interpretative spectrum; we have failed to notice other options for the non-developmentalist.

As I emphasized, I chose an example of contrast within one dialogue, since in this case there is a reasonable assumption that we should interpret the dialogue as a whole. But, of course, the same problem recurs on a larger scale between dialogues, for Socrates the uncommitted questioner is the most obvious feature of the so-called Socratic dialogues, whereas Socrates the committed opinion holder is the most obvious feature of the traditionally "middle" dialogues. Platonists and other non-skeptics in the ancient world take the same line here: the negative argument plays a variety of roles vis-à-vis the positive claims, but they can be interpreted in terms of a single set of ideas.

In the twentieth century this kind of unifying approach has been very much out of fashion, and one major reason for this is that we have got used to an overall developmental approach to this, as to other difficulties and inconsistencies in Plato's works. It usually goes so deep as to be unquestioned that the dialogues of negative argument are early, and represent a different stage of Plato's thought from the positive, dogmatic middle dialogues. It goes so deep, in fact, that we tend to forget that it is only relatively recently that Plato's works have been interpreted as though the dialogues marked stages in a developing intellectual biography. This historicist view has had such an overwhelming success since its introduction that even today it requires some effort to read sympathetically the ancient doctrinal interpreters of Plato, to whom it never occurs to read the works in this way. The difficulty of thinking away an overall developmental view of Plato's thought is the main barrier we face in learning from the ancients about

---

[39] Cf. p. 6: "Expositors of Plato . . . treat as peculiar defects of Plato the inconsistencies which they detect in his ultimate metaphysics after they have elaborated it into a rigid system which he with sound instinct evaded by poetry and myth." P. 25: "Plato is not always overnice in the arguments by which the skeptic is refuted. It is enough that the 'wicked' should not have the best of the argument." P. 26: "It would be a waste of time to cavil on minor fallacies or rhetorical exaggerations with which Plato burdens the argument in his eagerness to make a strong case" (this clearly identifies strength of case with literary effectiveness rather than with rational strength). P. 36: "Their presentation [i.e., the arguments against Forms] in the *Parmenides,* then, does not mark a crisis in Plato's thought calling for a review of his chief article of philosophical faith. He does not and cannot answer them, but he evidently does not take them very seriously."

Plato. I try to do this, in the case of Plato's ethics, mainly because I have come to think that the ancients, being in the same ethical tradition, have a good understanding of Plato's position, and the fact that they do not see change and development in Plato's basic ethical ideas may indicate that our standing assumption that there is such a thing is in need of examination.

One influential modern tradition holds that there is a development in Plato's ethical thought because the short Socratic dialogues are intended as a representation of a real person, the historical Socrates, son of Sophroniscus, whereas the traditionally "middle" dialogues represent Plato's own views, though still through the persona of Socrates. Much printers' ink has been spilled in the twentieth century over this "external" Socratic problem: how does Plato's version of the historical Socrates relate to the historical person himself and the presentations that we find of him in others—Xenophon, Aristophanes, Aristotle? Much of this debate has proceeded on the assumption that with literary accounts of Socrates that are fairly close to him in date, we can come to a conclusion as to which is nearest to the original. In my view this underestimates a phenomenon which is clearer in later philosophers who also regard Socrates as an important figure for philosophy. Stoics, Cynics, and Academic Skeptics all appealed to their own version of Socrates as an inspiring figure, though aware that other schools, with views opposed to their own, claimed him as a similarly founding figure. Socrates was clearly well fitted to serve as a figure of the ideal philosopher, whatever form that might take; having crucially written nothing himself, he was available to inspire a variety of competing schools. But there is no reason to think that such plasticity was a feature only of later interpretations of Socrates; indeed, we can tell from the fragments of the so-called minor Socratics, who wrote Socratic dialogues like Plato's and Xenophon's, that right from the first Socrates was seen as an adaptable figure, serving as an ideal of the philosopher, vaguely specified as to his ideas and seen mainly in terms of his unconditional commitment to the life of philosophy at the expense of conventional rewards, even of his own life. Thus it is not enough to select some figure such as Aristotle as a control on Plato's version.[40] The historical Socrates right from the first greatly underdetermined all the different Socrateses of philosophy.

However, even if we are skeptical as to our getting enough independent hold on Socrates to find a development from the historical Socrates to Plato, and take

[40] As Irwin does, for example in chap. 1 of 1995. Field, in 1924–25, examines the later biographical tradition and the later Platonic tradition, claiming that it supports Aristotle's view; but he ignores the Skeptical, Stoic, and Epicurean interpretations of Socrates and their relation to the works of Socratics other than Plato. On these, see Long 1988 and the recent collection of articles in Vander Waerdt 1994.

it that Socrates in Plato is just that, Plato's Socrates, there still remains, for us modern interpreters, an internal Socratic problem: there might still be a transition from Plato's version of Socrates to Plato's own ideas. And this is, I think, the currently orthodox view, if any can be called orthodox: many scholars believe in the development of Plato's thought from the early to the middle dialogues, without necessarily taking a stand on the external Socratic problem. Commonly, some dialogues are seen as early, and as discussing problems to which later dialogues offer solutions. On this view, after writing large numbers of dialogues apparently to advertise the fact that he had failed to solve any problems or convince anybody, Plato turns to making bold positive claims instead. Plato's development becomes, among other things, a development in Plato's self-confidence.

This view depends heavily on the assumption that we can read the transition from early to middle dialogues as an advance in Plato's intellectual biography. It is as though there were a line, the development of Plato's thought, on which dialogues can be pegged in the order in which they reveal that development. There is a problem here, of course: why should we think that this order, if there is one, has anything whatever to do with the order in which they were written? Of course, if we had some independent way into the order in which they were written, we could see whether or not this order tracked a development in Plato's thought. And it is not accidental that the twentieth century has seen so much time and effort devoted to scientific, computer-based attempts to establish an order of the composition of the dialogues, in the hope that this would enlighten us about the development of their content. But not only have all hopes of establishing such a scientific ordering failed to materialize;[41] even if it were established, it is not clear that it would be any real use in establishing the development of Plato's thought, unless we accept a strong and very disputable assumption, namely that Plato writes in a way which amounts to giving us his intellectual autobiography: in any dialogue, what Socrates[42] says is just what Plato believes at that time. The vast computer-based efforts to establish a chronology of the composition of the dialogues do not even have a hope of establishing anything interesting unless this assumption is true—unless order of composition does precisely track development and maturation of thought.

It has been noticed by some, particularly in recent years,[43] that this assumption requires reading the dialogues, particularly the Socratic dialogues, in an odd

[41] See Keyser 1991, 1992. Keyser discusses the entire history of stylometric attempts to establish a chronology of Plato's dialogues, and points out, from specialist knowledge, that all attempts to do this with any precision have been technically flawed.

[42] Or, in "later" dialogues, the main speaker other than Socrates.

[43] Cf. Kahn 1981, 1996. The latter came out after the substance of this work had been written, and I was pleased to note extensive mutual support, from different directions, for skepticism about a developmental approach to Plato.

way. Periodically, literary critics have pointed out that treating Socrates simply as a conduit for whatever Plato thinks at the time trivializes and flattens the literary power of the works. But, even apart from this, there is a philosophical loss, since we lose the capacity of the dialogue form to distance the author from the arguments, something which surely played a motivating role in Plato's adopting the dialogue form in the first place. If we can track Plato's thought just by looking at what Socrates says, then the dialogue form loses any advantage over the treatise for making the reader think about what is said rather than taking it on authority.

Ancient ways of reading Plato contrast with modern ones. Albinus, for example, tells us that there is no one definite starting point for reading Plato's philosophy, since it is like a circle, where there is no one definite place to begin either. Where you start reading depends on facts about you: how much you already know, how gifted you are, how interested you are in Plato's philosophical, as opposed to literary, side.[44] It seems that for the ancient Platonists there was no such thing as *the* order of the dialogues; there were many orders, and the differences between them were seen as significant only from a pedagogical point of view. We do find attempts to order the dialogues chronologically, but they are quite unlike ours.[45] One is an ordering of the dialogues in terms of their dramatic dates, and one is a chronology of Plato's composition of them. But the latter bears no resemblance to our modern, stylometry-based versions; the *Phaedrus* is taken to come first, because in it Plato raises the question of fixing philosophical discussion in writing in the first place.[46] We do not find an ordering of the dialogues which is taken to reveal the development of Plato's intellectual biography.

[44] Albinus *Prologos,* chaps. 4 and 5. Cf. Diogenes Laertius 3.62 for alternative reading orders.

[45.] Anonymous *Prolegomena to Plato's Philosophy,* ed. Westerink, 24.1–19. Also interesting is 25.10–29, where the author criticizes the arrangement in "tetralogies" deriving from Thrasyllus, and still to be found in the Oxford Classical Texts. He particularly attacks the first tetralogy of *Euthyphro, Apology, Crito,* and *Phaedo* (still to be found in many translations), pointing out, very reasonably, that there is no resemblance to a tetralogy of three tragedies and a satyr play, and that in any case the four dialogues have very diverse aims which do not obviously belong together.

[46] The passage in the *Phaedrus* (277E–278B) where Socrates is made to complain that any written work is inferior to the living interchange of actual conversation has been overinterpreted in a number of ways, but even a minimal interpretation has to see it as a claim that in philosophy a written work is better seen as an occasion for further discussion than as the last word, the outcome of discussion. Though not directly connected, this fits well with Plato's preference for the dialogue form, as being a form which would tend to fend off the attitude that regards a written text as an authoritative expression of the author's views.

I would like to focus briefly on this idea of Plato's intellectual biography implicit in the standard developmental interpretation of Plato's philosophy. If it matters *when* a dialogue was written—if, for example, it is important whether the *Protagoras* was written before the *Gorgias* or vice versa—then we are relating the ideas in it not just to ideas in other dialogues but also to a supposed stage in what I call Plato's intellectual life. Now, one reason that it comes easily to us to do this is that we are used to the idea of being able to compare an author's life on the one hand with his or her works on the other, and in the twentieth century we are used to being able to interpret the works by way of the life, and to use biographies to shed light on literary and intellectual works. In the case of an ancient writer, however, we have almost no facts about the life in question. Although we have ancient "Lives" of Plato, they are not biography in the modern sense, and they crumble at the touch into collections of later moralizing anecdotes, very few of which preserve what we would call facts.[47] Twentieth-century philosophical interpreters of Plato have tended to be credulous, indeed often gullible, about our ability to see Plato as embedded in a particular biographical narrative. I say something more about this in the fourth chapter, in connection with our tendency to overstress the *Republic* in our interpretations of Plato; here I just baldly state that we do not have a full enough historical biography of Plato to be able to provide a firm intellectual biography usable as a reference point for interpreting the dialogues. Moreover, the biography that we do have is so sparse, and has come through so many filters of prejudice, hagiography, and sheer chance, that it is quite arbitrary what facts we do have about Plato's life, and connecting any of them to the texts is as likely to be misleading as illuminating.

It may be retorted that we do not need to have a solid historical biography. The development of Plato's intellectual life can be seen as a product of philosophical interpretation of the dialogues, and in that case it does not matter if we cannot tie it down to any but a few dates and events in Plato's actual life. This is a viable position, but it does not seem to suggest overall development more readily than some form of unitarianism. Philosophical interpretation of the dialogues will turn up contrasting positions, but unless we are already biased in its favor—for example, by belief in a solid historical biography—there is no prior reason why we should turn to a developmental rather than some form of unitarian interpretation.

Traditionally, it is unitarian interpretations which have been thought prone

---

[47] Cf. the following comment by Jonathan Barnes (1995): "Ancient biographies are not cordon bleu concoctions of fact—they are crude stews, the rare of gobbets of fact swimming in a sauce of dubious inference and unreliable anecdote" (p. 1).

to overlook or minimize inconsistencies and difficulties in Plato's thought. But reflection shows that overall developmental views are in principle no less likely to do this. I argue, for example, in the third chapter, that there is a split in Plato's ethical thought between two different ways in which virtue affects the agent's attitude to conventional goods: in one of these, she makes the right use of these goods; in the other, she turns from and "flees" them. Mostly, Plato emphasizes the way virtue transforms a human life, but sometimes we find a more un-worldly strand, in which virtue is associated with escaping the conditions of human life altogether. A unitarian interpretation of Plato might well flatten out or neglect this difference; but, equally, an overall developmental view tends to flatten out or neglect it, too. Indeed, it is arguably *more* likely to do so, especially since it cannot be associated with any traditional grouping of dialogues or tra-ditional chronology. On a developmental view, there is, so to speak, nowhere to put it. If we suspect that Plato's thought, while generally a unity, contains dis-continuities, we are more likely to succeed in doing justice to these if we do not make a prior commitment to an overall developmental interpretation.

The Platonists, we may note, were saved from a tendency to historicize Plato's development by the fact that from early on they did not think of him as an or-dinary historical person anyway. Our oldest biographical "fact" about Plato, which goes back to his nephew Speusippus, is that Plato's real father was Apollo. The god kept Ariston, Plato's earthly father, from Plato's mother until after the birth, rather like the way in which the angel keeps Joseph from Mary until af-ter Jesus' birth in Matthew's Gospel (a point of comparison which did not es-cape the notice of ancient Christian writers).[48] Right from the start Plato was seen as someone special, a genius, someone not to be interpreted in the pedes-trian kinds of way appropriate to ordinary people. Since a robust idea of Plato's historical life was thus not as important to them as it has been to us, they were not as tempted as we have been to find in him a line of thought with a histori-cal shape.[49] Plato is, for them, the intellectual voice speaking in this corpus of texts—or rather, the intellectual unity in the many voices that we hear from them. Rather than try to embed Plato's texts in a developing history, they re-sponded to them in their own terms, as to a set of ideas.

I have obviously not given a full or nuanced account of the unitarian/ developmental debate as that has dominated twentieth-century Plato studies. I

[48] Cf. Riginos 1976, 9–32 , esp. 11, for reference to Origen and Jerome, who see clear parallels between the story in, for example, Diogenes Laertius 3.2 and that in Matthew 1.18–24.

[49] Cf. Dörrie and Baltes 1990–96, 2:365: we sometimes find interest in which is the first and which the last dialogue, but no interest in tracing a biographical trend through them.

have not even mentioned the great dispute over development (or not) in the theory of Forms, which has been for many the motor of the debate.[50] I hope I have said enough to suggest why it might be worthwhile putting this debate aside and seeing what we get from listening to the ancients, who discerned many voices in Plato rather than many positions successively occupied.

[50] The role of Forms has motivated the claim of a development between the "middle" and the "later," "critical" dialogues (here the work of Gwylim Owen has been influential). It also underlies many of the differences claimed to exist between the "early" and "middle" Socrates in Plato (Vlastos 1991, for example, lists ten alleged differences, most of them involving the metaphysics of Forms).

[II]

TRANSFORMING YOUR LIFE:
VIRTUE AND HAPPINESS

Modern Plato scholars often refer to "the Socratic dialogues." In theory, this should be a uselessly vague reference, since Socrates appears in all Plato's dialogues except the *Laws*. In practice, the reference is always understood to be to a group of dialogues which are nowadays considered "early," that is, composed relatively early in Plato's intellectual career. The dominant assumption is that first Plato presents Socrates as putting forward the views of the historical Socrates, or as putting forward an early version of Plato's own ideas, and then goes on to use him as a mouthpiece for his own, different ideas.

Sometimes this difference is associated with the point that in these dialogues Socrates often engages in argument against the views of others without drawing a positive conclusion himself. This can lead to the interpretative claim that Plato first presents Socrates in a negative, aporetic role and then shows him boldly producing Platonic positive ideas, where this is taken to mark a change in Plato's own thought: first *he* puzzles about some questions, then he provides answers to them. This claim urgently needs to answer the question why Plato would write several elaborate dialogues to advertise to the world the fact that he had failed to answer the questions. But it also runs up against a more important point.

Despite the argumentative tone, the traditionally early dialogues do contain a number of positive claims which Socrates puts forward. Moreover, they are claims of a bold and revisionary kind. A good person cannot be harmed; virtue is all that is relevant for happiness; it is better, if you have done wrong, to be punished than to get away with it—these are positive claims indeed. Socrates argues against other people in these dialogues, but there is no doubt that he has a strongly expressed position of his own.

The orthodox interpretative hypothesis for much of the twentieth century has still been that there is a marked shift between the "Socratic," traditionally early dialogues, and other dialogues, notably the *Republic,* which are considered to be "middle," and that this shift consists (among other things) in a change of ethical position: the ethical ideas that we find in the Socratic dialogues are systematically distinguishable from those of the *Republic* and other, middle and later, dialogues.[1]

It is startling, when we turn to the ancient Platonists, particularly to an accessible author like Alcinous, author of a *Handbook of Platonism,*[2] to find this assumption completely absent. In his chapters on Plato's ethics Alcinous takes it for granted that there is a single ethical position to be found in Plato's dialogues, in explication of which he twice cites or refers to the *Euthydemus* and *Laws*—dialogues which we do not usually consider together. Moreover, he claims that Plato's ethical position "is presented in very many of his works, but particularly in the whole of the *Republic.*"[3] Alcinous writes in the eudaimonist tradition of ethics, as indeed do all ancient philosophers, with the exception of one school.[4] Moreover, Alcinous interprets Plato's ethical position in terms of the Stoic claim that virtue is sufficient for happiness, and the related claim that only the fine (the aim of the virtuous person) is good. This latter makes the point that virtue has value in a way radically different from the way in which other things have value; there is a gulf between the kind of goodness which virtue has and the goodness of other kinds of thing, and we are mistaken to try to compare them or combine them as though they were good in the same way. Ancient Platonists (and others)[5] found it natural to see Plato's ethical thought in this way. Because we do not read Plato from within a eudaimonist tradition in which the Stoics are a natural point of reference to interpret and sometimes to clarify Plato, Alcinous's interpretation (which is not peculiar to him, but shared by most ancient Platonists)[6] may seem strange. In this and the following chapters I make a case for our taking it seriously.

In this chapter I examine the eudaimonist interpretation of Plato's ethics, and

---

[1] The clearest and most influential statements of this interpretative position (although they differ on some aspects of it) can be found in Vlastos 1991 and Irwin 1995.

[2] See Whittaker 1990 and Dillon 1993.

[3] Alcinous *Handbook,* chap. 27 (trans. Dillon).

[4] The Cyrenaics; for this general claim about ancient eudaimonism, see Annas 1993.

[5] As we shall see, the Stoics themselves accepted that their position on ethics (though not on many other points) was like Plato's.

[6] Among the ancient Platonists, only Plutarch and Calvenus Taurus seem to reject the idea in their own right (and so, presumably, as an interpretation of Plato), but we are not well informed as to why. What is striking is the unanimity of other Platonists on the interpretation in Stoic terms. See Dillon's commentary on Alcinous's chapter 27, and his (1977) on the ethical positions of the various Platonists.

particularly the legitimacy of seeing him in terms of the basic Stoic ideas that virtue has value of a kind different from that of other things, and is sufficient for happiness. I begin by considering dialogues other than the *Republic,* most of them (but not all) those generally considered "Socratic." In the next chapter I look at an important strand in Plato's ethics which, while stressed in the ancient world, has been completely neglected in modern interpretations, and ask how consistent it is with the position reached so far. I then, in the fourth chapter, turn to the question whether the position which can be found in these dialogues can really also be found in the *Republic.* The answer to this raises other questions as to the way in which we should read the *Republic,* and its relations to other dialogues.

When we read *Apology, Crito,* and *Gorgias,* we are struck by a feature which they notably share and which, while it might be implicit in other dialogues, is loudly explicit in them. The views on moral matters which Socrates puts forward in them are radical. Most people's values, he holds, are quite mistaken; they care up to a point about virtue, but they also care about health and beauty, money and prestige, things later to be called "external goods." But it is no good valuing virtue only up to a point, Socrates insists: virtue matters far more than people think it does, and he goes around trying to persuade people to change their values. "Aren't you ashamed," he says to the Athenians, "that you pay attention to making as much money as possible, and also prestige and honour, but pay no attention and do not care about wisdom and truth and making your soul as good as possible?"[7] If he is right, people should utterly revise their priorities.

Moreover, Socrates is uncompromising about the results of holding such different priorities from other people. In his defense speech in court he refuses to make any concessions whatever to the values of the jury. He defends his life in terms of what he claims to be right, even though he is aware that this constitutes a confrontation with their values, which he regards as simply wrong. In reply to an imagined critic who faults him for behaving so as to be risking death, he says that we should not consider the consequences of our actions at all, even death, but only the issue of whether the action is just or not;[8] behavior which others see as provocative he represents as simply forced on him by considerations of right and wrong. When the jury find him guilty, and he has to propose a penalty, he comes up with the conventionally outrageous suggestion of a high civic honor, not to annoy (though he is quite aware that it does annoy) but simply because he cannot consistently judge himself by their standards.[9] When he is condemned to death, he declares that no harm can come to a good person,

[7] *Apology* 29D–E.
[8] *Apology* 28B–D.
[9] *Apology* 36B–D, and cf. 37A.

and urges the jury to behave to his sons as he has behaved to them—that is, to criticize their values and tell them to live differently.[10]

In other dialogues, Plato keeps us aware of Socrates' fate in order to underline his uncompromisingness about values. In the *Gorgias,* for example, where Socrates' fate is insistently in the background, he declares that he will stand by his views even when they bring him into conflict with the majority of people. Being moral, he claims, matters so much more than other things that it is better to be wronged than to do wrong; the wrongdoer is harming himself more than his victim. He realizes that most people regard this as an absurd view, but is unmoved by their opinion.[11] In the *Crito* Socrates is shown rejecting a chance to save himself from death, on the grounds that this would be doing wrong, and that no outcome makes wrongdoing worthwhile. "If it becomes clear that such conduct is unjust, I cannot help thinking that the question whether we are sure to die, or to suffer any other ill-effect for that matter, if we stand our ground . . . ought not to weigh with us at all in comparison with the risk of acting unjustly."[12]

If we ask ourselves what kind of moral position is being suggested here, we are, I think (if we detach ourselves from the overfamiliarity with these passages which we may suffer from), most likely to make sense of it as a deontological position. For Socrates certainly seems to be insisting that what matters is morality, regardless of consequences. No gains or losses of conventional goods can make any impact on the issue of whether a course of action is morally right or wrong, and nothing other than this is relevant to the question of how one should act.

In the *Apology* and *Crito* this point is underlined by the fact that in these dialogues virtue has a special deliberative role for Socrates. In the *Apology* he compares himself to Achilles, who did not hesitate to prefer death to dishonor,[13] and to a soldier obeying orders.[14] He seems indifferent as between the locutions "because it seems best to him" and "in obedience to orders"; confusing the value of virtue with that of conventional goods is seen as a failure to appreciate the force of the demand that virtue makes.[15] Virtue is not merely one good among others,

---

[10] *Apology* 41C–E.

[11] *Gorgias* 469A–474C.

[12] *Crito* 48D, trans. H. Tredennick and H. Tarrant (London: Penguin, 1993). Cf. *Apology* 28B–D.

[13] 28B–D. Many have been surprised by the self-comparison to Achilles, whose values were very different from Socrates', but the point of the analogy is the structure of the reasoning: other things, even death, have no weight once it is clear that honor (for Achilles), virtue (for Socrates) is at stake.

[14] *Apology* 28D. Socrates also appeals to his own past actions as an Athenian soldier under orders.

[15] When Socrates says that he knows that it is bad to do wrong and disobey one's superior (29B), this is not a mysteriously isolated piece of moral knowledge, but a claim to know something about moral wrongdoing: it is like disobeying orders. It is thus compa-

but a good which makes an unconditional demand like that of the orders which a soldier must obey.[16] In the *Crito* this attitude is repeated. Socrates there switches unselfconsciously from the language of good and bad to the deontic language of "ought" and "should" in a passage emphasizing that we should never do wrong.[17] We should not do wrong because it is bad; but its badness seems to be explicated by the fact that we should not do it.[18] Socrates recognizes that most people do not consider the matter so straightforwardly; they weigh considerations of conventional good and evil against doing right and wrong. But they are mistaken; virtue makes a special kind of demand, which has to be obeyed no matter what.[19]

Such an uncompromising position is, whether we agree with it or not, fairly easy to understand. The problem comes when we put this together with something else that we find in Plato's dialogues.

In a passage in the *Euthydemus*[20] Socrates is impressing on an intelligent but unformed young man the need to be serious about philosophy, and to treat it as important, not as a game, as the Sophists do. In this passage, which became fa-

rable to the claim in the *Meno* (98B) that Socrates knows at least that there is a difference between knowledge and true belief. Socrates in the *Apology* represents himself as ignorant of much about virtue, but he knows enough to know how to think about virtue: it is not just one factor in deliberation, but makes a demand that must be obeyed. (This attitude to virtue gives Socrates' uncompromising stance in the *Apology* the "Kantian" aspect mentioned above.)

[16] What of 37B, where Socrates regards some conventional evils (alternative penalties) as things he knows to be bad? His reaction shows that he regards them not as bad in themselves, but only as impediments to his philosophizing. The only penalties he accepts are those which he does *not* regard as doing himself harm (a provocative stance to the jury).

[17] *Crito* 49A–B. We go from deontic language (the gerundive *oudeni tropōi adikēteon*) to what looks like a restatement of the point in terms of good and bad—wrongdoing is bad and shameful for the wrongdoer—to the claim that *therefore* (*ara*) we should not (*dei*) do wrong.

[18] At 47D–E Socrates seems to regard the conventional evil of illness as really bad. However, this passage can be regarded as simply producing an analogy for goodness and badness of the soul, not as a considered claim about illness itself. Even if read literally, the passage can be taken as a forerunner of the Stoic idea that loss of health is a reason for leaving life, because it renders the living of a virtuous life impossible.

[19] In the *Crito* Socrates underlines (49D) the fact that most people think differently about virtue from himself and those who agree with his previous deliberations (mentioned, but not explicated): those who disagree on this must despise one another's deliberations, and they have no common decision. As in the *Apology,* Socrates knows enough to know the right, as opposed to the wrong, way of thinking about virtue, but it is not made clear how he knows this.

[20] *Euthydemus* 278–82, the "Socratic protreptic" passage. At 273E3 what is introduced is *eu prattein,* or "doing well," rather than happiness itself, but it is clear from 280B6 (as well as Aristotle's discussion of the point in the first book of the *Nicomachean Ethics* [1095a18–20]) that this is regarded as synonymous with *eudaimonein,* or "being happy."

mous as a "protreptic," or exhortation to choose philosophy as a way of life, Socrates begins by laying out a set of assumptions. These are supposed to be obvious; they are common ground to Socrates and the Sophists, and the young man Cleinias is to choose between the very different ways in which they interpret them. Everyone, claims Socrates, wants to be happy; in fact, it's a silly question to ask, since it would be absurd to deny it. Further, being happy requires having many good things—it would be just as absurd to deny that—and these good things must benefit us. Socrates does not envisage querying any of these assumptions. It is obvious from the context that they are regarded as widely shared without disagreement. Moreover, they are regarded similarly in another passage, in the *Symposium*.[21] Cleinias has quite conventional ideas about what the good things must be that are needed for happiness—things like health, beauty, power, and influence; he adds in the virtues, but not prominently. Socrates corrects him, but not (and we shall shortly see the importance of this) by attacking the shared assumptions about happiness. Rather, in a short and controversial argument he sharply revises the content of happiness: it is to be found in wisdom and virtue, he claims, not in conventional goods as Cleinias thinks. Socrates prefers to go against the everyday intuitions that health and wealth are good things, rather than against the formal points that in everything we do we seek happiness, and that happiness comes from the possession (and, it turns out, the proper use) of good things.

It has been noted that the assumptions that Plato has Socrates accept are strikingly like those that Aristotle lays out in the first book of the *Nicomachean Ethics,* where he argues that we are all committed to a *telos,* or overall final end, which is "complete" and "self-sufficient." That is, we can see everything else that we do as a means to or way of achieving it, while we do not see it as a means to or way of achieving anything further, and it does not leave out anything of importance to our lives overall. At the everyday level we all agree that this overall end is happiness, though this does not actually settle much, since there is disagreement as to what happiness is.[22] Aristotle's account is, of course, more formally developed than that in the *Euthydemus,* though there is also an interesting parallel in another dialogue, the *Philebus.* There Socrates sets forward as acceptable, without need of argument, the idea that a good life must be complete and self-sufficient, and shows that this consideration on its own serves to rule out some candidates.[23]

---

[21] *Symposium* 204E–205A. It is there emphasized that happiness is intuitively an ultimate goal; nobody asks why you want to be happy, since the answer that you are doing something in order to be happy "has an end (*telos*)." Moreover, it is equally obvious that the happy are happy "by obtaining good things." Cf. *Gorgias* 472C, *Republic* 352D.

[22] *Nicomachean Ethics* 1.7, esp. 1097a24–b21.

[23] *Philebus* 20B–23A, 60A–61A. Pleasure and knowledge are each ruled out as a candidate for the good life, since it turns out that each on its own produces a life lacking

The passages in the *Euthydemus* and *Philebus* enable us to see Plato as right in the mainstream of ancient ethical theory, for he clearly emerges as a eudaimonist, someone who holds that ethical questions are centered on the question of what happiness is and how best to achieve it. Moreover, he proceeds as ancient eudaimonists do, in starting from the shared assumption that we all seek happiness in what we do and in sticking firmly to this even while producing a theory which greatly revises our specification of what happiness is. The more mainstream we see Plato as being in this regard, however, the harder it becomes for us to make overall sense of his theory, and the Socratic dialogues force the problem on us in the most pointed way. For assertions that you should never do what is wrong no matter what the consequences in terms of loss or death, or that it is better to be wronged than to do wrong, do not look much like assertions about happiness. Socrates says, in the *Apology*, "You are mistaken, my friend, if you think that a man who is worth anything ought to spend his time weighing up the prospects of life and death. He has only one thing to consider in performing any action: that is, whether he is acting justly or unjustly, like a good man or a bad one."[24] This does not look to us much like a suggestion as to how to achieve happiness by obtaining good things. We might be more likely to see it as a Kantian than as an Aristotelian thought;[25] and yet we have reason to see Plato as belonging in the eudaimonist tradition as much as Aristotle is.

If we are not to give up on finding an overall interpretation which will make sense of Plato's various positions about virtue and happiness, we must find a way of fitting Socrates' moral intransigence into a theory of happiness. The first major obstacle to this lies in our own assumptions about happiness.[26] For us, both at the everyday level and in more theoretical discussions, happiness figures in a rather different way from the ancient conception, so that, although there is no better translation for *eudaimonia* than happiness, we find some of the moves that are made in the ancient discussions surprising or hard to accept, and have to be aware of this in order to understand why Plato proceeds as he does.

There appears to be an immediate point of similarity: it is fairly easy to get people nowadays to see the point of the idea that everything we do is done for the sake of happiness; even when they don't agree, they generally do not have diffi-

---

in something important, and so is not complete. At 20D the good is said to be adequate, or *hikanon*, suggestive of Aristotle's condition of being *autarkes*, or self-sufficient, and also *teleon*, or complete, again suggestive of Aristotle (indeed, the insistence that it is "most complete," or *teleotaton*, calls to mind Aristotle's comments at *Nicomachean Ethics* 1097a25−30).

[24] *Apology* 28B (trans. Tredennick and Tarrant).

[25] Kantian in its anti-consequentialist insistence; of course there is no parallel to other features of Kantian ethics.

[26] I have developed these thoughts more fully in Annas 1997.

culty in understanding the idea and its appeal. Philosophers who teach elementary ethics classes, for example, generally report that students initially welcome the idea that happiness is what directs even altruistic behavior and self-sacrificing lives—even Mother Theresa figures are taken to be aiming at happiness in some way. But the apparent similarity at once opens up a real discrepancy, for the thought does not play the same role. In particular it is not a robust thought for us, by which I mean a thought on the basis of which we reject other thoughts. We can see this if we look at the *Philebus* passage; formally, this is an argument about the good, but it is clearly said that what is being sought is what will make a human life happy.[27] Socrates is defending the claims of reason to be the good which everything seeks to achieve a happy life. His interlocutor, Protarchus, is at this point a hedonist defending the claims of pleasure to be what makes a life complete and self-sufficient. The argument hinges on the fact that both accept that if the good is complete, then nothing need be added to it for it to make the good life good. For Socrates shows Protarchus that the life of pleasure unaccompanied by any form of intellectual activity, far from being complete and self-sufficient for us, would be the life of a clam, whose pleasures come and go without any consciousness or memory of them. Nor can the life of reason be a life which is obviously right for a human to choose, as opposed to a god, for humans need a life which is in some way made up of pleasure *and* reason. Here an important conclusion is reached directly by appeal to ordinary intuitions about the completeness of happiness, and the result is treated as decisive. It does not occur to Protarchus to avoid the argument by claiming that a final end need not be complete.

It does not seem that modern intuitions about completeness would be as robust, or that an analogue of this argument would go through so straightforwardly. A modern version of Protarchus might indeed respond as he does, that if as a candidate for happiness pleasure turns out to lack something, then there must be more to happiness than pleasure; but he might equally well respond that what it shows is that pleasure *is* indeed the best candidate for happiness, but that there is more to life than happiness. Indeed, if he is a hedonist, he is most likely to respond that the life of pleasure is the best candidate for happiness, and that what Socrates' argument claims is that we should care about the life of reason rather than happiness. (He might then argue that we should not be narrow-minded about the kind of happiness available to clams.) At any rate a modern hedonist is unlikely to be persuaded by this argument that hedonism, as a theory of happiness, is a non-starter.

---

[27] Cf. *Philebus* 11D4−6. But it is an oddity that the *Philebus* says so little explicitly about virtue and happiness, though the discussion covers issues which in other dialogues are discussed in those terms.

Our intuitions here, then, are less robust than those of the ancients. And there are two other ways in which our central views about happiness diverge also, and which stand in the way of our finding it at all easy to understand Plato's view. One is that there is great appeal to us in the idea that happiness is subjective. The point is well illustrated by an example of L. W. Sumner's,[28] of a woman who is happily married for ten years and then discovers that all that time her husband had another partner. Are we to say that she thought she was happy, but now discovers that she was not? Sumner calls this "Orwellian" rewriting of history, and claims that we incline rather to say that she was indeed happy before, though she now sees that her happiness rested on falsehood and that there were thus many ways in which her life was going badly. In my experience, any audience will divide about fifty-fifty as to whether to take this view or to hold that the woman was not in fact happy, though she thought she was. There is no consensus here, and this indicates that our views on happiness may well be confused and divided.

Further, at the level of theory rather than intuitions we find another difference. Our conception of happiness is what I call rigid,[29] that is, it does not tolerate much shifting of content. Rigidity is not a matter of being tied to one particular content; there are currently many candidate accounts of happiness—welfare, desire-satisfaction, and many more. Rather, once we have decided on an account of what happiness is, we are resistant to allowing that that content could be greatly modified or redefined while still allowing that it is happiness that we are talking about. The ancients assume that we begin with an intuitive, confused, and partly mistaken conception of happiness; ethical theories give us competing candidates for the correct specification of happiness, which will revise and overturn much of the original intuitive content. We, by contrast, find it problematic that the content of happiness might alter while it retains the same role, our final overall goal.

It is this point which is the most important one for us to bear in mind—or at any rate in the back of our minds—when we go on to explicate the way in which Plato's Socrates proceeds as though he were obviously concurring in the way everybody thinks—seeking a correct specification of the happiness that everybody is looking for—while maintaining the uncompromising attitude that we have seen him hold about virtue. We have already seen, very briefly, that Socrates, in the *Euthydemus,* goes along with Cleinias and the Sophists in accepting that everyone wants to be happy, but hopes to move Cleinias from his common-

[28] In Annas (forthcoming).
[29] I have used this term in Annas 1993, chap. 22, and in Annas 1997. I have not seen the idea much discussed in modern moral philosophy, but this difference seems to me to be even more important than the modern subjective conception of happiness in making ancient views of happiness appear alien and remote from us.

sense assumption that happiness is constituted by things like good health and riches to the idea that the only thing that matters for happiness is the wisdom of the virtuous person. This is a radical shift indeed, but nobody questions its propriety. When we explicate the argument, we are at once struck by the claim that virtue is the only thing that matters for happiness, and may think that our difficulties with the argument stem from this idea; but it is worth bearing in mind also the point that we may be finding a problem with the argument itself, quite apart from the particular claim about happiness. It is difficult for us to begin from happiness as an ordinary starting point and then go on to revise the content in accordance with a philosophical theory which implies that we were wildly wrong, and still accept that we are talking about happiness. We are more at home with arguments which press the claims of virtue *as opposed to* happiness. But the indications that Plato is a eudaimonist are unmistakable. We must, then, try to see how Plato can see the Socrates of the *Apology* as a seeker for happiness.

The *Euthydemus* argument, short and outrageous as it seems, is invaluable for showing us what is going on. After starting, as already noted, with the shared assumptions that everyone seeks happiness in everything he or she does, and that we become happy by acquiring good things, Socrates proceeds to make a claim which has two parts, one of which can be seen as arising from common sense while the other cannot.[30]

First,[31] he makes the point that good things don't benefit us if we just have them lying around, any more than a workman is benefited by his tools and materials if they are just lying around, rather than being put to use. They have to be used, and used correctly. The application to happiness is acceptable enough: happiness cannot consist just in things or in having stuff—riches, reputation, and so on—but must rather consist in what you do with these things, the use you put them to. Happiness lies in what you make of your life and its share of conventional goods, rather than in the conventional goods themselves. This is a point which emerges out of common sense; we find it in untheoretical contexts, and it suggests that it does not take more than everyday reflection to see what is wrong with the suggestion that Cleinias throws out, namely that happiness just comes from "having present to one" the conventional goods of beauty, riches, and power. Most people might initially get no further than this idea, but a little thought[32] shows that happiness requires not just goods but the recognition of

---

[30] Here I do not discuss the puzzling section of argument from 279C to 280B, where Socrates claims that good luck, put in the list of conventional goods, is in fact superfluous if one has wisdom, since good luck just is wisdom, for wisdom always leads to success.

[31] 280B–281B.

[32] If only a little thought is required, why do we not find the idea more widely spread? Perhaps it is just that, as Housman put it, only two minutes' thought would be required, but thought is irksome, and two minutes is a long time.

priorities among them. We find this in an interesting passage of the *Menexenus,*
where Plato is parodying a jingoistic patriotic speech, and thus is, for once, presenting ordinary views at some length.[33] The fathers who have died for their
country tell their sons that conventional goods like wealth and strength are no
benefit without virtues like courage and justice; the outer goods can't be relied
on without the inner ones, since they may be lost (without courage one will lose
one's wealth to others), and also outer goods won't make up for lack of inner
ones, for these are more valuable. Without justice, for example, knowledge is
shown up as mere sharp practice rather than wisdom. It is not doubted that ordinary people value virtue more than conventional goods, on reflection, both
because the idea that virtue is the more valuable seems right and because they
accept a dependence of the value of conventional goods on virtue. Hence the
appeal even to unphilosophical people of the idea that happiness is self-sufficient,
or *autarkes*—the happy person needs virtue because the value to him of other
things depends on their being put to good use by virtue.[34]

Cicero[35] enthusiastically finds in the *Menexenus* passage an indication that Plato
held that virtue was sufficient for happiness. But this is far too hasty. Recognizing that the benefit to us—and thereby their contribution to our happiness—
of conventional goods depends upon their deployment by virtue shows only that
virtue is necessary for happiness, and, although this is certainly an advance on
the view of unreflective common sense, it falls short of the stronger claim. But
we find the stronger claim in the *Euthydemus.*

For Socrates goes on to claim[36] that without wisdom you are actually better
off with conventional *evils;* without the sense to use conventional advantages in
a way that will benefit you, you will be less unhappy being poor, weak, dis-
graced, cowardly, lazy, slow, short-sighted, and deaf than you would be with the
opposites of these. This is an idea guaranteed to bring us up short. But the point
is not just to startle, but to bring home a claim about how mistaken people are
in their view of the place of conventional goods in happiness. The argument,
says Socrates, concerns conventional goods, but not in respect of how they are

---

[33] *Menexenus* 246D8–247A4 and 247E5–248A7.
[34] The ideas in the *Euthydemus* passage also find resonances in Xenophon *Memorabilia*
4.2, and in Aristotle *Politics* 7.1, where he retails the view as intuitive and accepted even
without argument, that goods of the soul are more valuable than external goods, because
the benefit to us of the latter depends on the former, and the former set a limit to their
usefulness, but not vice versa. Aristotle represents intuition as drawing the conclusion that
happiness is exactly proportionate to one's possession of virtue; this is a hasty claim, and
far too strong, like Cicero's (below).
[35] *Tusculan Disputations* 5.34–6.
[36] 281B–E.

in themselves and by nature good: [37] for it turns out that they are not good or bad in themselves at all; their value depends on the use made of them by virtue or vice. This is a radical claim, and presented as such; it revises the values that most people have. Conventional goods are not, as we think, valuable in their own right, and thus make no contribution to happiness themselves; rather, the value they have depends on the kind of life that they form part of.

Socrates' claim is thus a two-part one: the value of conventional goods for happiness is dependent on their use by virtue, and most people are mistaken in holding that conventional goods contribute to happiness, and conventional evils subtract from it, no matter what, whether in a good life or a bad. Socrates' second claim goes far beyond the idea that the value of conventional goods depends on their use by virtue, for that would leave it open that, though virtue was necessary for happiness, conventional goods still could add to the happiness of the virtuous person. This would allow that the virtuous person with money would be happier than the virtuous person with none, money being always a good no matter what. We can see that Socrates intends something stronger than this from what he says about the vicious. For conventional goods lack the power to add to the happiness of the vicious, and conventional evils lack the power to subtract from it. Rather, conventional goods are *bad* for the vicious, and conventional evils are *good* for them. How can we make sense of this? How can being poor and deaf *increase* your chances of happiness if you are vicious? We can understand this only if we are prepared utterly to revise our conventional valuations of things and accept that in their own right these things don't have value. They can, presumably, encourage and sustain virtue by facilitating virtuous action, but they do not add to the happiness of the life of the virtuous in their own right. And the only contribution they can make to the happiness of the wicked is by retarding wickedness, by diminishing its scope, and enabling the person to become virtuous. They can't produce or remove happiness in their own right; only virtue and vice can do that.

What role then do they have? In Plato there seems to be a deafening silence on this, a silence filled by the clamor of competing modern interpretations. [38] Alcinous makes an interesting suggestion, in a sentence with verbal reminiscences of both the *Euthydemus* and the *Laws*. "As for those things that are called good by the many, such as health, beauty, strength, wealth and suchlike, none of these,

---

[37] Does this phrase imply that there is a sense in which they really are good in themselves (as, for example, Waterfield's translation implies [Harmondsworth: Penguin, 1987])? I doubt that it does, since the conclusion of the argument implies that most people are just wrong about this. I take it that Socrates is mentioning the view he takes to be wrong and setting it aside, before going on to give the preferred view, introduced by, "But, as it seems, it's like this."

[38] Among the best known is that of Vlastos 1991 (and cf. Brickhouse and Smith 1994).

he says, is ever good, unless their use is linked to virtue. Apart from this, they have the role simply of matter, and can come to be evils for those who make bad use of them. Sometimes he also calls them 'mortal goods.'"[39] At first this characterization as matter might seem less than helpful, but Alcinous is doing more than suggesting a metaphor; he is seeing Plato in terms that bring him close to the Stoics, by suggesting that for Plato conventional goods and evils have the role that "indifferents" do in Stoic ethics—for they are called "matter (or materials) for virtue,"[40] something quite natural if virtue is thought of, as it is in Plato and in the Stoics, as a skill exercised on materials.

In Stoicism, only virtue is good and vice evil, and all other conventional goods and evils are notoriously called "indifferents," although (at least in orthodox Stoicism) some of these are "preferred" (such as health and wealth) and some "dispreferred" (such as disease and poverty). The indifferents motivate us to pursue and avoid them; moreover, this is natural, since we are following our human nature in doing this. But happiness consists in virtue, and virtue consists in pursuing and avoiding these things in a virtuous way. Of course, spelling out what this virtuous way consists in would take us too far from Plato; but even from this we can see that it is reasonable for Alcinous to deal with a gap in Plato's account by indicating a later theory that produced an elaborate account of how to fill it—reasonable, that is, given that the special role of virtue is central to Plato's theory in a way relevantly similar to the way it is in the Stoics'. The indifferents—conventional goods and evils—have value for happiness only in being the materials for and context within which the virtuous life is lived. On their own they neither add to the happiness of a life nor subtract from it.

Although this interpretation, I believe, gets to the heart of what Plato thinks, there is a complication. For, lacking technical terms, Plato does say that conventional goods become "greater evils" than conventional evils are for a vicious person, and that conventional goods are "greater goods" than conventional evils are for a virtuous person.[41] And Alcinous in his explication of this point says that conventional goods and evils have the role of materials "when separated from

---

[39] Alcinous Handbook, chap. 27.

[40] The indifferents are called materials (hulē, materia) at Plutarch On Common Conceptions 1069e, 1070f–1071e, Cicero De finibus 3.60–61. It is interesting that the pseudo-Pythagorean ethical writings also contain this use of hulē: in pseudo-Archytas On Moral Education 40.22 Thesleff we find that the bad person will always be unhappy "whether he has material or not" —aite echei hulān (kakōs te gar autāi chreētai) aite spanizei. Here external goods are material for the person to make good or bad use of. In pseudo-Metopos On Virtue 119.8 Thesleff we find the related idea that the emotions are the material of virtue, since virtue is concerned with them—ta de pathea tās aretās hulā; peri tauta gar kai en toutois hā aretā.

[41] Euthydemus 281D–E.

virtuous use," and can, for the vicious, turn out bad.[42] It might seem, then, that conventional goods and evils can add something in their own right to the life of the virtuous person. They cannot make a person happy, but they might be able to make the virtuous, happy person happier. In that case, then, in later terms the theory implicit in Plato would be the theory of Antiochus, who claimed that virtue was sufficient for happiness, but that conventional goods could then add something valuable to the virtuous person's life and make him happier. Antiochus tried to combine the advantages of Stoic with Aristotelian ethics in holding that virtue was sufficient for the happy life, but not for the completely happy life, which contains virtue and also conventional goods.[43]

However, while this might seem neater as an interpretation of Plato, closer to his actual use of the words "good" and "bad," there is a severe cost to holding it. For Plato emphasizes that conventional evils are good for the vicious—good, of course, in a completely non-conventional way, since they can benefit the vicious only by serving to make him less vicious and so more capable of becoming happy. This is stressed in order to drive home how mistaken ordinary views of happiness are. But if conventional goods add to the happiness of the virtuous happy person in a conventional way—add to her happiness in their own right— then Plato would be switching around between radically different ways in which conventional goods and evils can play a role in virtuous and vicious lives. The view would go: In the life of the vicious, the value of conventional goods is the opposite of what people think—rather than being conventionally advantageous, they take the person further from happiness, by encouraging vice and discouraging virtue. But people are right about the role of conventional goods in the life of the virtuous—they are in fact good for him, and add straightforwardly to his happiness in the conventional way. This is an implausibly convoluted view to read into Plato. It is simpler to interpret him as holding a Stoic line, namely that virtue is sufficient for happiness and that conventional goods and evils have the role merely of indifferents or material for the virtuous and vicious life. Passages where he uses the word "good" in ways that strictly go beyond this are officially improper ways of conveying the idea the Stoics later conveyed more rigorously.[44]

Moreover, this is not only a simpler interpretation; it shows that there is good

---

[42] Alcinous, chap. 27, 180.9–16.

[43] Antiochus's view is explicated in Cicero De finibus 5.

[44] It is also implausible that Plato would hold a theory which emerges as a compromise between two types of theory (Stoic and Aristotelian) developed in detail far beyond what we find in Plato—a theory, moreover, which was not influential in ancient ethics. The use of "good" and of comparative forms of language (virtue being "better than" other things) by Alcinous and others should therefore not be taken as legitimating the ascription to him of an Antiochean view. Rather, it reproduces Plato's own use of terms,

reason for interpreting Plato in the Stoic terms of virtue's being sufficient for happiness. Plato and the Stoics both display, in contrast with Aristotle, a concern with the special role and value of virtue, its difference from conventional kinds of good. Plato's grasp of the implications of this radical thought is not as firm or precise as that of the Stoics, and he has not rigorously thought through the implications, for the role of external goods, of holding that virtue is the only truly good thing, and is sufficient for happiness. This is not surprising; Plato is pioneering a eudaimonistic theory, and the Stoics have the benefit of explicit discussion such as Aristotle's. But this should not obscure the real similarities.[45]

When, in this passage, then, Plato commits himself to saying that only virtue is good (and, since happiness comes from obtaining good things, all we need for happiness), this does, as we have seen, chime strikingly with later Stoic ideas about virtue.[46] But the idea does not depend for him on the verbal point of calling only virtue, but not conventional goods, good. We can also see this from two passages in the *Laws*. The *Laws* is generally held to be Plato's last dialogue, left unfinished at death, and if we assume a developmental view, we would not even expect to find in it a position substantially the same as that of a "Socratic" dialogue. Alcinous in his *Handbook of Platonism,* however, cites both dialogues together to illustrate the same idea, and, when we look at them, he seems to be right. In an early part of the *Laws* Plato has the Athenian say that goods are of two kinds, divine and human;[47] the human kind, illustrated by health, beauty, strength, and wealth, are dependent on the divine ones, which are the virtues,

---

but within a firm statement of the thesis that virtue is sufficient for happiness these terms are not taken to introduce a radically non-Stoic way of comparing virtue and conventional goods. Later authors such as Alcinous could recognize that, while the Antiochean view might seem to answer better to the surface of some passages, the Stoic view gave a much better, and simpler, understanding of the basic position.

[45] There is an interesting contrast here with the pseudo-Pythagorean ethical writings. Pseudo-Archytas *The Good and Happy Man* 8.29–9.6 Thesleff puts forward the frankly Theophrastean view that happiness requires prosperity (*eutuchia*) as well as virtue, and thus depends on chance. However, pseudo-Archytas *On Moral Education* 40.19–41.7 Thesleff has a different view, more in the spirit of Antiochus: virtue is sufficient for non-unhappiness, but for happiness the person must be able to use, not merely possess, virtue. Although the pseudo-Pythagorean writings are Platonic in spirit in many ways, ethically they are far more conservative. The Stoic kind of interpretation that we find in the Platonists presumably comes from their taking it as a requirement that they pay attention to Plato's actual words.

[46] I have discussed this aspect of the passage, and the connection with the Stoics, in Annas 1994.

[47] *Laws* 631B–D. Alcinous quotes from this passage, though with a slight mistake (*ditta* for *dipla*) which he shares with Arius Didymus's reference to the passage at Stobaeus *Eclogae* 2.54.12. This may indicate that he is quoting from a source shared by Arius rather

which are here led by, rather than being identified with, the wisdom of the virtuous person.

In the *Euthydemus* the dependence of conventional goods and evils for value on virtue is emphasized in order to encourage a promising but unformed boy to choose to live virtuously. This is an individual effort, and it is hard to see how the bare argument is to continue to influence him independently of the effect of Socrates himself.[48] In the *Laws* the emphasis has shifted to social and cultural influences. Because conventional goods are dependent on and ranked by nature behind the divine good of virtue, the lawgiver, an abstract figure standing for society's enforcement of its norms, must ensure that education of every kind tends to produce and encourage beliefs that fit in with this. Citizens are to be molded by praise and blame, pleasure and pain, to consider virtue to be what matters, rather than conventional goods and evils. The point made in both dialogues is that people are right in holding that they aim at happiness, and in thinking that it matters; where they go wrong is in thinking that conventional goods should be unproblematically sought, and conventional evils avoided, in their own right. In the *Laws* most people are said to live in a fog on this matter, which it takes the lawgiver to dispel.[49]

The *Laws* sustains not just the dependency thesis, but the view that unreflective people are completely wrong about what contributes to happiness. A slightly later passage brings this out.[50] The Athenian says that most people are flatly wrong in their view of the conventional goods, and again this emerges most dramatically with the vicious. For the wicked, conventional goods are actually bad

---

than directly from Plato; but this is not certain—there might be a variant in the early textual tradition, or either or both may be citing the text from memory carelessly.

[48] One striking difference between the *Euthydemus* and *Laws* passages is that in the former we get a ground for the dependency claim in the idea that virtue is a kind of skill of using other things, which are material for it. In the *Laws* there is a statement of the dependency claim, but no grounds are given for it. This shows that the dependency claim does not itself depend on the analogy of virtue with a skill. Plato's reasons for dropping the analogy between the two dialogues are discussed in Annas (forthcoming).

[49] *Laws* 663B–C. There is a complication here; the Athenian puts forward a view about the role of virtue and conventional goods in happiness; when the Cretan is unconvinced, the Athenian produces an argument to show that what most people are wrong about (and need righting about) is the role of *pleasure* in happiness. However, pleasure has not figured in the discussion of conventional goods. The argument is relevant to the discussion if we value the conventional goods only for the pleasure they give us, but this is not said; the Athenian insists that we do find them pleasant (663A), but pleasure is said to be what we aim at in all we do (663B), not what we aim at in seeking conventional goods. On the role of pleasure, see Chapter 7.

[50] *Laws* 660E–663D, esp. 661A–E.

for them, and conventional evils good. Somebody with absolutely every conventional good, but no virtue, is bound to be unhappy; wickedness is sufficient for unhappiness, and conventional goods and evils make no impact on this (except through their potential to restrain or remove wickedness). Similarly, the virtuous person is happy, and conventional goods and evils make no impact on this—it does not signify whether he is tall, strong, and rich or small, weak, and poor. Human, conventional goods lack value in themselves for happiness. Plato does not seem to have changed his view that all that matters for happiness is virtue and all that matters for unhappiness is wickedness.

We might, however, think from other passages that the *Laws* has the weaker view discussed above, namely that virtue is sufficient for happiness, and that the value of conventional goods depends on it, but that nonetheless these can still add to or subtract from happiness themselves. Their having value is dependent on virtue, but, once you are virtuous, they can still themselves add value. There are several reasons why we might think this, but none is in the end persuasive.

First, at 661D the Athenian commits himself to the position that what are called evils are good for the unjust, but evil for the just, whereas (what are called) goods are truly good for the good, but evil for the vicious. This has to be interpreted in a way consistent with the major thesis that virtue is sufficient for happiness, which occurs insistently both before and after this sentence. The virtuous person, we are told, is happy whether strong or weak, rich or poor; the vicious person is unhappy even if he possesses all the conventional goods that he can. It might seem that Plato is inconsistent here. But we are not forced to hold this—for, after all, conventional goods and evils are bad and good, respectively, for the vicious not in their own right but in the impact they have on wickedness, either encouraging it or retarding it. So they can be good and bad, respectively, for the virtuous in the same way, namely not in their own right but only insofar as they have an impact on virtue by encouraging it or retarding it.

Nonetheless, it is remarkable that the Athenian admits that conventional evils are evil or bad for the virtuous. He can only mean, as we have seen, that they can be bad in having an impact on virtue, cramping its scope and making life difficult for the virtuous person. But this runs against the spirit of what we find elsewhere in Socrates' insistence in the *Apology* that a good person cannot be harmed, and in a passage at the end of the *Republic*[51] where it is said that in the case of the virtuous person "apparent evils" such as poverty and illness will be turned to some good; evil could come to him only from some previous fault of his own. Perhaps in the *Laws* Plato is more pessimistic about the power of circumstances to affect the virtuous person's character. Perhaps he has simply been

---

[51] *Republic* 612E–613B. This passage is discussed also in Chapters 3 and 4.

led by a rhetorically antithetical sentence to say something careless. At any rate it is not in keeping with his attitude elsewhere to the virtuous person's ability to deal with misfortune.

It might be objected that the radical division of goods into two kinds, the divine and the merely human, runs against a common division elsewhere in the *Laws* of goods into three kinds; if so, authors who greatly privilege the twofold division may be misleadingly stressing an untypical passage. Certainly Diogenes Laertius tells us[52] that Plato used to divide goods into goods of the soul, goods of the body, and external goods, and we can see passages in the *Laws* which support this.[53] But we also find that one of the passages that leads Arius Didymus to say that Plato has many voices concerns different divisions of goods, including the present two divisions, and Arius is confident that it does not indicate different positions.[54] And this is surely right. The threefold division is a commonsensical one; Aristotle presents it as such (which is perhaps why Diogenes says that Aristotle ascribed the idea to Plato), and it seems to be common property.

It might seem that the idea that virtue is sufficient for happiness is an unlikely one to find in the *Laws,* where Plato lays so much stress on the importance of material and social aspects of the life of the citizens. Why all the fuss and detail about legislation for the citizens' life, the insistence on education and molding by very definite institutions, if virtue is all that matters? However, the material and social advantages of life in Magnesia do not have to be considered as having value in their own right for the citizens' lives. They might be required rather to provide conditions propitious for the attainment of virtue. And this in fact is the spirit in which Plato discusses them. Someone who, like Plato, thinks that a city should do without walls in order to produce courage in the citizens, and who tries to counteract the trading advantages of a good site, is hardly someone who thinks that prosperity and security are valuable in themselves, and so he does not have to be considering them as adding value to the citizens' lives. Rather, he considers them the framework for the development of the citizens' virtue.

It is not surprising, then, to find a later Platonist like Alcinous citing both the *Euthydemus* and the *Laws* to support his interpretation of Plato's ethical thought in Stoic terms: that only the fine (or morally valuable) is good, and that virtue is sufficient for happiness. Plato's view indeed seems to parallel the basic Stoic insistence that the value of virtue is different in kind from the value of other kinds of thing, and that, once we properly understand this difference, we will see that virtue is sufficient for happiness, since other things do not in themselves

52 *Lives of the Philosophers* 3.80.
53 *Laws* 697B, 726A–E, 743E.
54 Arius ap. Stobaeus *Eclogae* 2.49.20.

have the kind of value that could contribute to happiness. This interpretation, moreover, seems to have been shared by at least some Stoics; one of the heads of the Stoa in the Hellenistic period, Antipater, wrote three books arguing that Plato's thought was in harmony with that of the Stoics in ethics.

But to return to the intransigent passages with which I began: how do we see them in the light of Plato's discussion of goods and happiness? In them Socrates goes to some pains to contrast his own values with those of other people. He sees things differently from other people. Certainly we find something which is presented in the *Laws* not only as a clearing of fog but as a change of perspective.[55] Perhaps we can best think of it as the idea that virtue has a transformative power; it transforms your view of happiness by transforming your values and priorities, so that you can see that the values and priorities of the unreflective are wrong, and correspondingly so is their view of happiness. Plato does not give us an account of virtue of the kind which Aristotle does, telling us that it is a stable state, built up by habituation and reflection, and sustained by good practice. This is something which the later Platonists present him with,[56] and, unhistorical though this may be, it reflects an awareness that for Plato virtue is something deeply rooted in the person, not just an isolated habit but an aspect of the person capable of transforming and molding other aspects.

Plato does not have a single word corresponding to "transformative,"[57] but we can, I think, see an idea that we could describe this way at *Apology* 29D–30B, the passage where Socrates says that if he could go free on condition of ceasing to philosophize, he would not do so, for he would obey the God rather than his fellow citizens. What the God commands him to do is to go about telling them that their values are the wrong way around—they care more for what is unimportant than for what is important. "Virtue does not come from possessions, but from virtue possessions and other things become good for people, all of them in private and public."[58] The things that most people think matter do not matter at all in the way that they think they do. The value they have for us depends radically on whether we are virtuous or not, and we should be misguided to follow

---

[55] *Laws* 663B–C.

[56] Alcinous *Handbook,* end of chap. 28, where good habits, way of life, and good practice are mentioned. Chaps. 29 and 30, on virtue and good natural dispositions, also mention habituation, and introduce the Aristotelian element of the mean. On this, see Chapter 6.

[57] Charles Kahn has suggested to me, however, that there is something like this idea in the "turning around" of the soul at *Republic* 518C–519A.

[58] On this translation, see Vlastos 1991, 219 n. 73, and Irwin 1995, sec. 41 n. 22. It is, of course, an example of the use of "good" that can misleadingly give the impression that Socrates holds the "Antiochean" view; he does not, after all, say that as a result of virtue wealth and other conventional goods become indifferent.

most people's estimates of the importance of conventional goods, for they may be exactly wrong—conventional goods, for example, are bad, not good, for the vicious.

This is a powerful idea. It is because he is so confident in the power of virtue that Plato can have Socrates put forward claims such as that it is not living that matters, but living well, where this means: living virtuously;[59] doing wrong is worse than suffering wrong because it harms you more, loss of conventional goods being as nothing compared with the loss of virtue;[60] virtue is sufficient for the happy life.[61]

This may strike us as a hopelessly optimistic view about the power of goodness. But, leaving that aside, it certainly has one feature which stands out when we are considering ethical theory. As a theory of happiness, it is very demanding. You won't have got your account of happiness right until you achieve the right perspective, and that will be utterly different from your initial standpoint. Becoming virtuous requires transforming your values and priorities; nothing short of this will do. All your valuations of conventional goods and evils will turn out to be wrong.

This suggests a second kind of objection: that as an ethical theory it is too demanding. A theory can be seen as too demanding if it has goals so lofty that it is clear that nobody can in fact achieve them. If we know in advance that most people who make the effort are going to fail decisively, then we may respond by finding fault with the loftiness of the goal. In the ancient world the most well known locus of this debate was the dispute between the Stoics and the Aristotelians on the nature of our final end. The Stoics, who hold that virtue is sufficient for happiness, can be seen as holding a view which is edifying but unrealistic. On the other hand, Aristotelians, who hold that happiness requires conventional goods as well as virtue, can be seen as making unworthy concessions to everyday prejudices. Later Platonists see this as the major issue arising between Plato and Aristotle, since they see Plato's ethical thought as converging with that of the Stoics. One of them, Atticus,[62] complains vigorously that Aristotle fell away from Plato's insight in not maintaining the proper measure of happiness and in failing to allow that virtue is sufficient for it. Aristotle, he complains bitterly, gave up on the power of virtue in allowing that it needed the goods of fortune to attain happiness, and in complaining that it would be helpless to give us happiness without them. Atticus is scornful about this "low and false view." "Aristotle's works on this," he tells us, "the *Nicomachean* and *Eudemian Ethics* and

[59] *Crito* 48C.
[60] *Apology* 30C–D, *Crito* 49B, *Gorgias* 479D–480B.
[61] *Gorgias* 470E, 507B–C.
[62] Atticus frag. 2 des Places.

the *Magna Moralia,* have ideas about virtue which are petty and grovelling and vulgar. They are the kind of thing that an ordinary person would come up with, an uneducated person, a child—or a woman." (In view of Aristotle's own views about women, this complaint is rather amusing.)

Personally, I find this outburst rather refreshing. It is easy for us, from the safe distance of the twentieth century, to drift into thinking that Plato is a great philosopher, and so is Aristotle, without seeing any conflict in these judgments, and it is bracing to be returned to a perspective from which this attitude is just a flabby refusal to take sides. But the Atticus passage is interesting in another way also. It illustrates the fact that the view we find in the Socratic dialogues, the *Euthydemus,* and the *Laws* is not one for which ancient readers felt the need to apologize. Those who admired Socrates' uncompromising stance in the face of conventional values expected to find it linked to a demanding view of what is required for happiness. If virtue transforms a life, then happiness has to bend a great deal to meet its requirements. We are used to a rigid conception of happiness and see difficulties, but for Plato, and for many in the ancient world, these were merely the difficulties to be expected by those who see a true account of happiness.

So, if we have problems seeing Plato as a eudaimonist, because of the revisionary and demanding nature of his theory, perhaps what this points up is not a problem for Plato, but merely our own reluctance to expand the conception of happiness beyond what common sense initially gives us. We are used to moral theories that are demanding, but it is not easy for us to conceive of such a theory which is a theory of *happiness,* rather than of something else. But this is not an argument against a theory like Plato's. It shows merely that it takes a long intellectual journey away from common sense and conventional beliefs to achieve the wisdom of the virtuous person and thus to have your whole life, and your conception of happiness, transformed.

[III]

BECOMING LIKE GOD: ETHICS, HUMAN NATURE, AND THE DIVINE

Our final end, according to Plato, is to become like God. This is what Alcinous tells us;[1] Arius Didymus[2] tells us that Socrates thought this too, underlining the point that ancient Platonists did not see Plato's Socrates, at any rate, as holding a different view from Plato.[3] The reference to Socrates may reflect the point that the most famous passage for this idea comes from the *Theaetetus,* a dialogue which, although it is long and complex, is self-consciously Socratic, and presents Socrates emphatically as a barren midwife, someone who elicits ideas from others rather than presenting his own.

It is at first sight hard for us even to make sense of this idea of becoming like God. This is partly because we are more attuned to the alternative ancient tradition, that of Aristotle (in the main)[4] and the Stoics and Epicureans, who see

[1] *Handbook,* chap. 28.

[2] Stobaeus *Eclogae* 2.49.8–9.

[3] Arius says that in holding that our end is "becoming like God," Socrates and Plato were in agreement with Pythagoras, who held that our end is "following God." It is most likely that the reference to Pythagoras in fact is to neo-Pythagoreans of the Hellenistic period; we have a number of neo-Pythagorean ethical treatises, which discuss topics like virtue and happiness in Hellenistic terms (one—pseudo-Archytas, *On Moral Education*— makes a clear reference to Carneades' division of final ends) without any appeal either to number mysticism or to specifically Pythagorean ways of life. M. Frede (1987) suggests also that Plato as a Pythagorizer was a construct of the doctrinal interpretation of Plato, as opposed to the skeptical interpretation on the one hand and, on the other, the Stoicizing version of Antiochus.

[4] The passage which we read as the second half of "Nicomachean Ethics book 10" has some points in common with the Platonic idea of becoming like God; it is unfortunate that we know so little of its fortunes in the Hellenistic period. During this period the position of "Aristotelian" ethics is standardly taken to be that in which external goods are needed for happiness. At *De finibus* 5.12 Cicero refers to an Aristotelian work on

our final end as lying in the fulfilling of human nature, rather than in an attempt to become some other kind of thing. And in the first part of what we call the Hellenistic period theories of this kind dominated the field. When Carneades, head of the skeptical Academy, analyzed the various philosophical options facing persons reflecting about their final end, he came up with a framework which makes room only for theories which see our final end as referring to human nature.[5] But after the end of the skeptical Academy and the rise of doctrinal interpretations of Plato, the idea made a dramatic comeback; it is a formulation which Middle Platonists, and others who interpret Plato doctrinally, see as important and authoritative.[6]

Becoming like God, or assimilating oneself to God, is not meant as an alternative to the idea that we seek happiness; it is just a specification of what happiness is. Moreover, the idea is also not intended as an alternative to the idea that virtue is sufficient for happiness; for it is explicated, in many of the passages in which it occurs, by the thought that becoming like God is what becoming virtuous is. So we are still talking about the life of virtue. But whereas most of the texts already indicated contain the idea that virtue transforms a human life, by revising our values and priorities, we seem here to have the idea that virtue turns a human life into something different in kind.

Given its fame in the ancient world, the almost total absence of this idea from modern interpretations and discussions of Plato is noteworthy.[7] Partly, this may be due to the unconscious effects of our own classification of the dialogues; the *Theaetetus,* after all, is a dialogue about epistemology, and the claim about becoming like God occurs in a passage which is marked off as a "digression" from the main argument. Partly, it may be due to the fact that this idea is scattered through very diverse dialogues and does not correspond with a single phase of

---

ethics which some ascribe to his son Nicomachus; but if this is indeed our "Nicomachean Ethics," it is remarkable that no awareness is shown of the "book 10" passage which has attracted so much modern discussion.

[5] See Cicero *De finibus* 5.19–21. Antiochus also seems to have made use of this; interestingly, it turns up also in the pseudo-Pythagorean ethical writings (pseudo-Archytas *On Moral Education* 43.8–23 Thesleff) which are ethically more conservative and Aristotelian than Platonic.

[6] For references, see Whittaker 1990, 137 n. 451.

[7] There is no reference to the *Theaetetus* passage, for example, in Irwin 1995. More surprisingly, there is no reference in Morgan 1990, which discusses at length Plato's attitude to religion and his use of it in characterizing philosophy. Since writing the first version of this chapter, however, I have been able to read Sedley (forthcoming), which raises the issue of *homoiōsis theōi* as the recognized Platonic ideal in antiquity, neglected in modern interpretation. Sedley focuses more than I do on the passage at *Timaeus* 90B–D. I have also been aided by discussions with John Armstrong, who develops the idea somewhat differently in his Ph.D. dissertation.

any familiar developmental story. Partly, it may be due to genuine bafflement, even embarrassment; we are familiar with ways in which God comes into ethical theory, but this is not one of them, nor is it obvious to us how we are to make sense of it. So it may be tempting to write off the idea as fantastic, or rhetorical overstatement, something not worth philosophical attention. This would be a mistake, however; whatever we make of the idea, it points up a fascinating divide in Plato's thought on a topic of central interest.

The *Theaetetus* passage begins from a contrast between the philosopher and the litigious man, who operates in politics and the law courts. (It is tempting to call this type a "lawyer," and modern parallels are not lacking, but it would be misleading given that the Athenians, although famously litigious, had no professional lawyers.) The philosopher is self-motivated, whereas the litigious man has his life organized for him by the necessities of others: court timetables, deadlines, the consequences of the friendships and enmities his ambitious career has produced. While the litigious man gets his own way efficiently, at least in the short run, the philosopher is completely unworldly. He doesn't know the way to the agora or the law courts; he is oblivious to laws, to political struggles, and to personalities which fascinate others. He's not even aware of what he is missing; it is "only his body which lives and sleeps in the city" while his mind takes off and wings its way through the universe. As a result, he is helpless in practical matters; he is like Thales, who watched the stars and fell down a well. He becomes a figure of fun for his ineptitude, and what is perceived as his attitude of superiority to others. If he can get the practical man into a philosophical argument, he can make him feel inadequate; but he does not know how to convince him, since he refuses to appeal to his values, and, if put up against him in a law court, would not stand a chance.

It is in this context that Socrates says that in human life good and evil will always be mixed up, and it is useless thinking that evil will ever be eliminated; God, on the other hand, is never evil, but always just virtuous. "That is why a man should make all haste to escape from earth to heaven; and escape means becoming as like God as possible; and a man becomes like God when he becomes just and pure, with understanding."[8]

It is tempting at first to hold that this conception of the philosopher is closely akin to that of the philosopher in the *Republic,* and this is reinforced when Socrates goes on to lay out thoughts which recall the *Republic* on the true rewards of virtue and vice. The virtuous become like the "paradigm" of goodness, and the vicious like the paradigm of badness. Since, however, these are accessible only to intellectual reflection of a sort which the vicious don't undertake, the vicious

[8] *Theaetetus* 176A8–B2, trans. M. R. Levett, rev. M. F. Burnyeat (Indianapolis: Hackett, 1990).

fail to notice the awful nature of what is happening to them.[9] The intellectual paradigms sound rather like Forms in the *Republic* (though scholastic worries can be raised about the evil paradigm). But the philosophers of the *Republic* are rulers, indeed the best rulers that there are; they can hardly be identified with the inept klutz of the *Theaetetus*. An obvious response to this is that in the *Theaetetus* we see the philosopher in the real world rather than the ideal state; and in the *Republic* Plato says that the best that virtuous people can do in actual society is to shelter from the storm behind a wall.[10] But in that passage Plato is thinking of actual people,[11] not of ideal philosophers. Given the structure of the *Republic*, it is unclear that it makes sense to juxtapose ideal philosophers with actual society; ideal philosophers are ex hypothesi a product of the ideal society, where they are philosopher-rulers, and cannot be considered outside it.

Perhaps, then, the philosopher in the *Theaetetus* should, as we would expect anyway, be considered alongside Socrates of the Socratic dialogues. But there are insoluble problems here too. Socrates in the Socratic dialogues emphatically knows his way to the agora, indeed spends most of his time there, and fulfills his political obligations rather than being blithely unaware of politics. He takes on generals, sophists, and rhapsodes, trying to find out if they are experts in their purported subjects, rather than (as the philosopher of the digression does) rushing to the abstract universal as soon as possible, leaving particulars behind. In the *Theaetetus* itself Socrates is perfectly aware of who Theaetetus and his family are, indeed takes an interest in promising young men and their families.

From the much greater self-absorption of the philosopher in the *Theaetetus* flow a number of deeper differences. In the *Theaetetus* there is no stress on intellectual search; not knowing his way to the agora, the philosopher does not feel impelled to stop people and question them about their beliefs. In contrast to the Socrates of the Socratic dialogues, he is unconcerned with others' mistakes and wrongheadedness; he regards despots as silly and irrelevant, not as a real intellectual and practical menace. He lacks the motivation to engage with others to improve their intellectual state, and he seems to lack the thought that he would get anything out of engaging with others either. Many readers have been tempted to share the alleged view of the philosopher's fellow citizens, who consider him arrogant in his self-sufficiency.

So unattractive is this as an ideal of the philosophical life that there has been at least one attempt to deny that Plato is recommending it. Rachel Rue[12] has argued that the philosopher in this passage is meant to be the opposite of the liti-

---

[9] 176E3–177A8.
[10] *Republic* 496B–E.
[11] He gives the example of Theages.
[12] Rue 1993.

gious man, and that neither is satisfactory; the life that Plato is actually recommending is that of Socrates, which is envisaged as being in the middle, with more
practical engagement than the philosopher and more idealism than the litigious
man. Apart from other objections, if this were right then ancient Platonists
would have grievously misunderstood Plato's intentions here; but Rue is right
to press on our notice the problems that arise in this passage if we try to make
it consistent with either the Socratic dialogues or the *Republic*.[13]

There is a problem here, namely, the puzzling inconsistency of the account
of the philosophical life both with the portrayal of Socrates elsewhere and with
the account of the ideal philosophical life in the *Republic*, which the passage otherwise recalls. What is its source? We might at first locate it in the idea that becoming virtuous is becoming like God. Surely this is in itself an odd idea of
virtue: how could virtue lie in altering yourself into some other kind of being?
But if we look at some of the other passages that Alcinous mentions, we find
that the matter is more complicated.

Alcinous and Arius Didymus, probably drawing on the same source, refer to
the fourth book of the *Laws* for the idea that our final end is "following God,"
although the idea of becoming like God figures in the passage also.[14] "Following God" is regarded as a Pythagorean formulation, though the ancient Platonists seem to regard it as essentially a variant on "becoming like God," and do not
distinguish what could have been regarded as rather different ideas. This passage
of the *Laws*, much quoted and referred to in the ancient world, begins with the
resounding statement that God is the beginning, middle, and end of all things.
Happiness comes to the person who follows God and justice in a "lowly and ordered way."[15] God loves what is like himself, and since he is measured and moderate, he loves people who are temperate and just. The actions which are de-
manded by this are then spelled out: as often in the *Laws*, we find that what is
in mind are traditional forms of deference, deference in particular to the gods
and to one's parents. There is much that is disappointing about this passage. Virtue

---

[13] Rue points out the Socrates, unlike the philosopher he describes, cares for the
Athenians (more than the Cyrenians), knows who Theaetetus is, knows his way to the
agora, and so on. Apart from literary considerations about the two allegedly opposed pic-
tures of the sharp practical man and the philosopher canceling each other out, Rue focuses
on problems with the idea of becoming like God, a problem I am concerned with here
(and which, because of general neglect of the topic, Rue is almost alone in pointing out).

[14] Alcinous *Handbook,* chap. 28; Arius Didymus in Stobaeus *Eclogae* 2.49.23−25, where
special attention is drawn to the *Laws* passage, which goes from 715E to 718C.

[15] 716A: *tapeinōs kai kekosmemenōs.* It has been noticed that the word *tapeinos* is usually employed, by Plato as well as others, in a pejorative way, and that it is remarkable
that Plato presents it here as part of the happy life to be lowly.

seems to be seen in terms simply of behavior rather than in terms of achieving understanding about behavior; further, it is very traditional behavior at that, and the assumption does not appear to be questioned that performing traditional religious duties conduces directly to becoming virtuous. And God seems here to be depressingly punitive, interested chiefly in punishing people who get uppity and above their human station. It is at any rate very clear, however, that pleasing God by becoming like him just is being virtuous, where that does not have any implications of unworldliness or withdrawing from the world—indeed, here virtue is conceived of rather unreflectively and in a completely traditional way.

Another passage[16] gives us another idea again. At *Timaeus* 90 B–D we find the idea that human nature is such that we can either encourage and identify with our mortal aspect or try to share in immortality to the extent that humans can. This is identified with happiness, and with the final end in life, here said to be put before us by the gods. What Plato has in mind to explicate this is clearer from the preceding passage; the soul is tripartite, and the two lower parts of it are essentially connected with the body and thus are affected by what affects it. But the highest part, reasoning, can control the other two, and the best state of the person is where reasoning does this, and also is itself in the best state. This comes about when the person can engage in a certain kind of thinking, one which will bring our thoughts to the regular and stable condition of the movements of the cosmos. Plato has a curious physical picture of literally changing the form of our thoughts so as to make them conform to the regularity of the circle, the movement of the divine heavenly bodies. But apart from this, we can still see the general idea, though it is introduced here very abruptly and without argument. It is that of assimilating our thoughts to a form utterly different from the form they have when we are engaged in mundane ordinary thinking. What Plato calls our mortal aspect just is our life when engaged in thinking about the everyday business of living. But there is another kind of thinking, which we engage in when thinking about abstract matters which are independent of our own particular point of view. Plato represents this as thought actually becoming like its object: that is, taking on the independence of our particular human point of view which characterizes the movements of the cosmos. It is an imaginative representation of what Sidgwick was later to call more prosaically thinking from the point of view of the universe. What is most startling in this very startling passage is the identification of this kind of abstract, non-personal thinking with happiness for a human being. The form of the claim is clear enough: it is in transcending our

---

[16] It is mentioned by Arius Didymus, but not by Alcinous, though Dillon in his 1993 commentary makes the point that "verbal reminiscences of it abound in the latter part of the chapter" (p. 172).

human nature, not fulfilling it, that we find happiness. Moreover, we do this by thinking in an abstract and philosophical way.

The *Laws* and *Timaeus* passages seem to have disconcertingly little in common. One points us to traditional religious behavior, the other to abstract study of the movements of the cosmos. The idea they have in common is that they are thinking of virtue as produced by the dominance of the rational part of the soul. In the *Laws* this takes the repressive form of keeping down desires and refraining from self-assertion; in the *Timaeus* the rational soul is freed to engage in its own appropriate activity of thinking. Why would both these passages figure in later accounts of Plato's ethical thinking as examples of Plato holding that becoming virtuous is becoming like God? The underlying idea is that we can recognize in ourselves a rational and a non-rational aspect, and that we can recognize the rational aspect to be more truly ourselves; we can identify with it rather than with the non-rational aspect, and can recognize that this is appropriate for the kind of being that we are. More is said later about this side of Plato's moral psychology: the powerful and in many ways dangerous idea that we can and should identify with one aspect of ourselves, and by the same token regard the other aspects as external to the true self. Here what matter are two points: this identification with the reason in us can be seen, in an intuitive way, as productive of virtue, and it can also be seen as becoming like God in that reason is seen as divine.

At the end of the *Alcibiades,* in a passage which, perhaps surprisingly, does not turn up in ancient discussions of this topic,[17] we find that knowing yourself properly means knowing not your body but your soul, and especially the part of the soul in which its virtue, wisdom, resides. This part of the soul, which thinks and achieves knowledge, is its most divine part, and like God; so someone who takes care to look at this part will know God, and also know himself.[18] Here we find moves made so fast, and with so little pause for argument or explication, that they must be intuitively appealing. Knowing yourself is, properly speaking, knowing your mind. But your mind is the most divine part of you, and the part which is like God, so knowing yourself is, properly, knowing God.

We should notice that the conclusion, outrageous as it may sound at first, is actually fairly innocuous. The idea of becoming like God becomes considerably less exciting if what it is taken to mean is that you identify with your reasoning

---

[17] Although the ancients had no doubts about the genuineness of the *Alcibiades.* Perhaps its neglect in this connection is linked to the later Platonists' tendency to treat it as a simple, introductory dialogue.

[18] *Alcibiades* 133B–C. There follows a passage which is controversial, since it is not in our manuscript tradition but is in passages from the dialogue quoted by Eusebius and by Stobaeus. It further develops the idea of the god in the soul, but does not add anything lacking in the thought sketched above.

and thinking aspect rather than with your non-rational aspect. Indeed, we may suspect at this point that the idea of becoming like God is as vague as the idea of identifying with one's reason. The latter can mean a number of things, and could have reference equally well to the functioning of practical reasoning as of theoretical. In the *Laws* all it seemed to mean was keeping your desires and self-assertion down. However, it can also, as in the *Timaeus* and certainly in the *Theaetetus*, refer to reasoning which takes people beyond their own particular and personal viewpoints and gets them to think from the point of view of the universe.

This variety of meaning explains the fact that we find some Middle Platonists saying that we can achieve our end of becoming like God in the practical as well as the theoretical life. Albinus says that some things have reference to theory and the theoretical life, others to action and the practical life, but both have reference to becoming like God. Apuleius says something similar.[19] It might seem, disappointingly, that the seemingly striking and outrageous idea that becoming virtuous is becoming like God threatens to peter out into a vague cliché. This may seem to be confirmed when we find a passage like the following in Plutarch, a writer never afraid of a cliché. In *How to Listen to Lectures* he presents it as a commonplace that "you have often heard that following God[20] is the same thing as obeying reason." The context is that children need external sanctions on their behavior, but adults can replace external with internal rational constraints.[21] Following God just is following your own reason rather than having someone else's reason direct what you do.

But the *Theaetetus* passage is not a cliché, and there was a reason why it became so famous. In it the idea of becoming like God is associated with the idea that this is a *flight* from human life, from earth to heaven; becoming virtuous is an escape from the inevitable mix of good and bad that characterizes human life, to a state where there is no evil. "It is not possible, Theodorus, that evil should be destroyed—for there must always be something opposed to the good; nor is it possible that it should have its seat in heaven. But it must inevitably haunt human life, and prowl about this earth. That is why a man should make

---

[19] Albinus *Prologos* 6.151.2–4; Apuleius *De Platone* 2.23.253. Alcinous, however, disagrees (one more sign that he is not the same author as Albinus): in chap. 2 what he identifies as becoming like God is the state of the soul engaged in theoretical reasoning as opposed to practical (though, with a reminiscence of the *Phaedo,* he calls this *phronēsis*).

[20] This is of course presented as the more "Pythagorean" formulation, but there does not seem to be a great difference between this and the more "Platonic" formulation as far as concerns the implications they have (doubtless one reason Socrates and Plato are thought to agree with Pythagoras on this one).

[21] Plutarch *How to Listen to Lectures* 37d. Cf. *To an Uneducated Ruler* 781a, where it is presented as equally commonplace that God punishes those who imitate his thunderings, but is pleased by those who emulate his virtue and imitate the fine and philanthropic.

all haste to escape from earth to heaven; and escape means becoming as like God as possible; and a man becomes like God when he becomes just and pure, with understanding."[22]

This is a powerful passage, and we can see why it became so famous. The attitude it expresses can only be called unworldly, and it is this unworldliness—the stress on the need to escape the conditions of human life to be virtuous and so happy—which made it the important text to illustrate the idea of virtue as assimilation to God. It is an attitude which we do not find in most of Plato's work, where virtue is construed as a skill or expertise, a type of *practical* knowledge to be applied to the conditions in which we live. But it does have a striking parallel in the *Phaedo*.[23]

In the *Phaedo*, which presents a picture of Socrates as a virtuous philosopher instead of concerning itself with actual biographical details,[24] we find an account of philosophy which is the same in spirit, if not terminology, as the *Theaetetus* digression. "Other people may well be unaware that all who actually engage in philosophy aright are practicing nothing other than dying and being dead." Death is the separation of soul and body, and the philosopher "practices for death" by withdrawing his soul as much as possible from the body and its concerns. He distances his mind from desires that arise from the body, and from relying on the information provided by the senses. "The philosopher differs from

---

[22] *Theaetetus* 176A–B (trans. Levett).

[23] Alcinous refers to *Phaedo* 82A–B in his chapter on becoming like God as our final end, but appears to misunderstand the passage. This has drawn adverse comment, especially from Göransson (1995, p. 108 n.1, p. 132, and p. 191), who regards it as sufficient proof that the author (or rather compiler, since he regards the *Handbook* as a self-contradictory ragbag) did not understand Plato, or alternatively was unfamiliar with the *Phaedo*. It is true that the passage is ironic, and is listing people who do the best they can in a very inferior way, precisely to be contrasted with the true philosophers. However, although this carelessness is important, so is the fact that Alcinous refers to the *Phaedo* at all in this chapter, since the crucial phrase, "becoming like God," does not occur in it.

[24] See Gill 1973, pp. 25–28, for the point that Socrates' actual death is described in an actually impossible manner, to give a picture of the philosopher's death as the soul parting peacefully from the body. Some ancient commentators warn against approaching the *Phaedo* and other "death-of-Socrates" dialogues with an interest in the biographical details. Albinus (*Prologos* 4) objects to reading the tetralogy put together by Thrasyllus (and still to be found in popular translations of Plato), *Euthyphro-Apology-Crito-Phaedo*. People who do this, he complains, seem to order the dialogues "by the characters and life circumstances," and although this might be fine for another purpose, it is not suitable for teaching Plato with a view to understanding him. The anonymous author of a Prolegomena to Plato's philosophy also objects (24.1–19) to the tetralogy, with its analogy to groups of dramas. Plato attacks dramatists, he points out; the *Phaedo* is hardly light relief, as the fourth play of the groups is; and in any case the aim of all four dialogues is quite different. (The passages are 50.1 and 5a in Dörrie and Baltes 1990–96, vol. 2.)

other people in releasing his soul, as far as possible, from its communion with the body."[25]

Moreover, this affects his conception of virtue. In a tangled passage (which has perhaps caused unnecessary problems because of a desire to make the position in it consistent with what Plato says about virtue elsewhere) we find the idea that the philosopher's virtue is utterly different from that of everyone else, because of his commitment to wisdom. Most people, claims Socrates, are virtuous because they are seeking things they find pleasant or avoiding what they find painful. Thus the brave stand firm in battle because they fear dishonor more than death. They employ reasoning simply to work out which course will achieve what they already want. But the philosopher gives reasoning a different role, in which it is regarded as valuable in itself and not because of its convenience in allowing us to compare other things. True virtue is not "exchanging pleasures for pleasures and pains for pains" but exchanging them all in return for the one true coin, wisdom. Thus we have true virtue with wisdom "whether pleasures and fears and all else of that sort be added or taken away." Separated from wisdom, however, virtue is not true virtue, but merely slavish. Real virtue, on the other hand, is a purification from these things (pleasures, fears, and so on) and wisdom the purifying rite.[26]

True virtue, that is, is something to which the presence or absence of pleasures and pains is simply irrelevant. Plato claims that it is the everyday conception of virtue which is "odd," but in fact it is his own conception which threatens to be paradoxical, especially when we move on to the idea that true virtue is a "purification" from considerations such as those of pleasure and pain, an idea repeated later in the dialogue, where wisdom is called a purification and release from the body, and is available only to those who truly strive for philosophical understanding, as opposed to the many, who practice ordinary "civic" virtue, built up from mere habituation. True virtue is presented here as an escape from all everyday considerations such as pleasure and pain; the *Phaedo* presents it as a release from the body. What Plato means by the body varies in the *Phaedo*, correspondingly with the varying characterizations of the soul, and is not uniform; but there is a real similarity with the idea in the *Theaetetus* digression, that true virtue is a flight from, and a getting-rid of, the mix of good and evil in the world, toward another kind of state. Purification, insists Socrates, is the soul's every-

[25] *Phaedo* 64A–67E; I quote from the translation by David Gallop, World's Classics Series (Oxford: Oxford University Press, 1993).

[26] *Phaedo* 69A–D. The passage has caused much trouble, partly because of the fact that coinage serves, rather ineptly, as the metaphor both for the inferior attitude (weighing up pleasures and pains) and for the better attitude (turning to wisdom and ignoring the relevance of pleasures and pains).

where detaching itself from the body, and concentrating into itself, regarding the body as a mere prison.[27] Here we clearly find the idea of virtue as a flight or withdrawal from the world.

The *Phaedo* and the *Theaetetus* digression indicate a strand in Plato's thinking that arguably stands apart from the way he more generally conceives of virtue. His standard view could well be considered austere enough: virtue is sufficient for happiness, and conventional goods have no value except as contributing to a virtuous life. But a view of virtue which leads to intransigence in the face of suffering and death is different from a view which takes a uniformly negative view of the human condition generally. Why, for instance, should the virtuous person be uncompromising in the face of death, like Socrates, rather than re-garding death as irrelevant, neither here nor there? We return to this problem later, but first I want to consider two other passages which are mentioned in the chapter where Alcinous discusses the idea of assimilation to God.

One is from the final book of the *Republic*. "That man will never be neglected who is willing and eager to be just, and by the practice of virtue to be likened to God so far as that is possible for man."[28] The context is interesting. Socrates is restoring the worldly rewards and punishments which he took out of the argu-ment at the beginning, and he is going to insist that the virtuous in fact do bet-ter in worldly terms than the wicked, who start off strong but flag later. Before we get to the rewards from humans, we are told about rewards from the gods for the virtuous. But the gods' rewards are not quite what we expect; we are told about the virtuous person who suffers conventional *evils,* such as illness and poverty, and the gods' caring is illustrated by the way that the moral person can turn these things to good. We are familiar with the idea that conventional evils don't in themselves subtract from the happiness of a virtuous life, but here the power of virtue is just identified with the likeness to God which the gods no-tice and care about.

In this passage, although the strongest possible contrast is drawn between worldly and God-given rewards, virtuous assimilation to God is not said to be a flight from the world. Indeed, we find in the central books that the philosophers study the stability and order of the intellectual realm, and are then said to become as much like this divine realm as possible; but they are then immediately said to produce this order and structure not only in their own souls but in those of oth-ers; they are to do good to others who are imperfect, not to flee from them.[29]

---

[27] *Phaedo* 67C, 83A. Festugière (1954, chap. 4) associates these passages with the later idea of *anachōresis,* or retreat from the world.

[28] *Republic* 613A (trans. Dillon). The whole relevant passage is 612A–613E.

[29] *Republic* 500C–D. (Of course there is the complication that the philosophers will not want to "return to the Cave" from their own point of view; but the insight into virtue which they get from studying and assimilating themselves to the order and struc-

In the *Phaedrus*, however, the soul that follows God and becomes like him does seem to be escaping the conditions of human life. As the souls circle round in the form of chariots with their charioteers and try to get a glimpse of the "place beyond the heavens," it is the soul which likens itself to God which does best at this, thereby escaping reincarnation in human form (at least until the next time around) and association with a body, which is here likened to a shell enclosing the real person.[30]

The *Republic* and the *Phaedrus* have much in common, particularly their development of the idea that the soul is complex and tripartite. Both have, however, passages where the soul is contrasted to the body as a whole, and where its association with the body is characterized in a negative and abusive way. In the *Phaedrus* it is in the passage just mentioned; in the *Republic*, in a passage just before in book 10, where the tripartite soul is called a barnacled encrustation on the real soul, which is simple in form.[31] It seems that in the very dialogues where he explores with most detail the complexity of the soul's interrelation with the body, Plato also feels the pull of the simpler idea that the true form of the soul has nothing to do with the body, and expresses this idea alongside the other one. What matters here, however, is that in the *Phaedrus* this goes along with something like the flight idea, and in the *Republic* it does not.

So far, we seem to have found a measure of confusion. The idea of virtue as becoming like God can be interpreted in different ways, and Plato shows no awareness of the differences. Nor do the Middle Platonists; Alcinous, for example, puts various passages together as though they obviously supported a single idea. Before being condescending, however, we should reflect that the difference between these positions is apparent to us because we find the idea of becoming like God strange, and therefore probe the contexts where we find it in order to discover how to interpret it. To Plato and ancient Platonists, on the other hand, the idea that becoming virtuous is becoming like God, and the associated idea that becoming like God or the divine is living in a way that identifies oneself with one's reasoning, were clearly both intuitively obvious and emotionally compelling—two features that might explain why we do not find more sensitivity to the different forms the idea takes. (We should remember, after all, that when Aristotle is discussing the life of contemplation in the text that we

---

ture of the intelligible world makes it clear that they are not to escape the task of concerning themselves with others.) See also 383C, where it is said that the Guardians are to become, as far as is possible for humans, *theosebeis* and *theioi*. Superficially, it is hard to see how the same person can become both divine and god-fearing, but beneath the surface awkwardness we can see the idea that it is becoming virtuous which leads to becoming divine, insofar as humans can ever achieve this.

[30] *Phaedrus* 247C–249C.

[31] *Republic* 611B–612A.

read as the "tenth book" of the *Nicomachean Ethics,* he uses the idea of "becoming immortal" to explain commitment to the life of contemplation, not the other way around.)[32]

Part of the reason for this may be an indeterminacy here in the idea of God. If becoming like God is living according to your reason, then it need imply no more than a very ordinary, indeed traditional, practice of virtue, understood as a rational activity. God here is just reason, understood as the divine in us, with no implication that reason is actually different from what we already supposed it to be, namely something which can guide practice as well as theory. But if becoming like God is actually a flight from the mix of good and evil in our world, then God is being thought of rather differently, as something perfectly good outside human experience and not to be characterized in human terms, but which nonetheless it makes sense for humans to try to emulate. This is a conception better suited to monotheist than to polytheist religion, and it is no accident that the *Theaetetus* passage has its main afterlife among Neoplatonists, and in the Jewish and Christian traditions.[33]

A Platonist like Alcinous is vaguely aware of a difficulty here, which emerges in a worry as to which God the virtuous person is likened to. "The end would be likening oneself to God—by which we mean, obviously, the god *in* the heavens, not, of course, the God above the heavens, who does not possess virtue, being superior to this." (This is Dillon's translation, which obscures a nice point: Alcinous says that we do not liken ourselves, by Zeus, to the God above the heavens, and this brings up the awkward question of how Zeus fits into any of this.) The worry about what likening oneself to God means is answered by distinguishing two Gods—one the *Timaeus* craftsman creator of the world, who is in it, and one outside the world altogether. The Craftsman God of the *Timaeus* certainly has a mind and intelligence, and desires things to be as good as possible,[34] but this does not seem like much of a basis for acquiring virtues, so it can hardly be claimed that the problem has been satisfactorily solved; insofar as he is God, the problem of how we can liken ourselves to him by practicing virtue does not seem notably less than in the case of the God "above the heavens."[35]

---

[32] *Nicomachean Ethics* 10.7.1177b26–1178a8.

[33] The idea of becoming like God by identifying with your reason is attractive to Stoics, who have, however, no truck with the idea of fleeing the world rather than living in it and dealing with it rationally. It is tempting to see the flight idea as what marks off Platonists who want to distinguish their position from the Stoic one.

[34] *Timaeus* 30A.

[35] Moreover, the phrase "outside the heavens" recalls the "places outside the heavens" of *Phaedrus* 247C, which is just the place that the soul likening itself to God aspires to go. Göransson (1995) regards Alcinous's distinction as contradicting what has been said about becoming like God earlier in the work, and thus as proof of diverse sources; but it is un-

But the solution is of interest as showing at least awareness that more than one thing could be meant by "becoming like God."

We cannot, then, ascribe to Plato, or to the later ancient Platonists, a clear idea of the differences among the positions that can be covered by the idea that becoming virtuous is becoming like God. Nonetheless, we can see one major difference between the rest on the one hand and the *Theaetetus* passage and *Phaedo* on the other.[36] It is only in these that we find what I have called the unworldly strand, the idea the virtue is not a matter of coping with the good and evil that we find in our lives, but rather a matter of fleeing from the whole thing, escaping to a realm which is not human at all.

As I have already indicated, modern interpreters are not much interested in this, and a further reason for this might be that it has no resonance with us as any kind of model for ethical thought. The philosopher of the *Theaetetus* digression doesn't know his way to the agora, hasn't a clue as to how to achieve anything. There doesn't seem anything particularly admirable about this. Socrates can strike us as admirable when he refuses to compromise his values in the face of death, and tells us that a good person cannot be harmed. Would we admire him if he said that a good person won't notice whether he is being harmed or not?

Perhaps, it might be thought, the question whether we would admire someone or not is not the point here. If we take seriously the idea that becoming like God is moving to some quite other sphere than the ordinary human one, then ethical responses like admiration lose relevance, for they simply stay on the human level which the aspirant philosopher is trying to escape. What is required is rather the recognition of a reality which transcends our ordinary concerns utterly. If we follow through this idea, we might conclude that the attitude being sketched here is more like what we would call a religious or spiritual attitude than a moral one. Interestingly, we find the *Theaetetus* digression quoted and expanded on in a work, *On Flight and Finding,* by the Jewish philosopher Philo of Alexandria, who welcomes it in his exegesis of biblical texts.[37] Philo was more

---

likely that a compilator could be so stupid or forgetful, and the passage is better interpreted as an attempt to preserve unity in the idea of likeness to God.

[36] The *Timaeus* and *Phaedrus* passages also seem to belong with this strand, but implicitly, since they do not overtly contain the "flight" idea.

[37] Philo *On Flight and Finding* 63 and 82. Colson and Whittaker, in their appendix to the Loeb (p. 584), comment, "Each of [the quotations] is, I think, considerably longer than any citation from Plato to be found elsewhere, and the former is the only passage in this series of treatises in which he gives a reference to the dialogue quoted." Cf. also Philo *On the Special Laws* 4.73: humans resemble God most in showing kindness; *On the Creation* 146: humans are like the rest of the created world in body, but in mind like the divine reason; *On the Decalogue* 72–75: the impiety of those who worship images emerges if their prayers are answered to become like God, since they would become like the im-

influential in the Christian than in the Jewish tradition, and some of the Church Fathers, for example Gregory of Nyssa and Clement of Alexandria, take over the idea in a way owing much to Philo and to the Middle Platonists.[38] Later we find Augustine pointing to what looks like a reminiscence of the *Theaetetus* passage to indicate that Plato is the only pagan philosopher that Christians need take seriously.[39] At some periods there has been a tradition of seeing Plato as a philosopher with an essentially unworldly ideal, akin to unworldly versions of Christianity. Modern philosophical interpreters of Plato have repudiated this particular interpretative tradition so thoroughly that they have forgotten that it was getting at something.[40]

What, though, about the idea of becoming like God as an *ethical* ideal? We may be helped here by turning to what other later Platonists made of the *Theaetetus* passage in particular. Plotinus in his essay on virtues[41] quotes it and develops an influential position from it. He has noticed what must surely be an obvious objection to the whole idea: how can virtue be becoming like God, since God does not have the virtues, at least not in the way that we do? If our world is necessarily a mix of good and evil, then the virtues will be developed by our becoming able to cope with the evil as well as the good. Courage, for example, will develop from our ability to resist fear; temperance, from our ability to resist pleasant temptations; and so on. But this does not seem to transfer to God, or even the gods of Greek religion, if these are thought of in an ethical way. As Aristotle says,[42] there is something "vulgar" in praising the gods for justice and temperance, since they have no bad desires to learn to overcome. Such praise drags them down to our level, and whatever Plato intends, it's not that.[43]

Plotinus comments that this point makes it implausible that we are made like

---

ages; *On the Virtues* 8–9: the virtues make the soul self-sufficient and content, which likens it to God; 167–68: the good man will try to reproduce virtues in others, this being most appropriate to the rational nature, which should imitate God as much as possible.

[38] See Merki 1952, Lilla 1971.

[39] Augustine *City of God* 8.5. The reference is not very exact: Plato, he says, has declared that the wise person imitates, knows, and loves "this God" (i.e., God as conceived by true religion) and is happy "by partaking in him."

[40] One modern scholarly discussion is Festugière 1954, where Plato is treated as a philosopher "whose religious thought coloured the spirituality of all the centuries to come" (p. 7). Festugière's purpose "is to show what aspects of [Plato's] philosophy have influenced decisively the spirituality of later ages" (p. 42). He frequently refers to the themes of flight from this world and of *homoiōsis theōi*, treating them as a single idea.

[41] *Ennead* 1.2, "On Virtues."

[42] Aristotle *Nicomachean Ethics* 1178b8–18.

[43] The Aristotelian view is shared by the pseudo-Pythagorean ethical writings, which are in general more conservative than Plato. See pseudo-Archytas *The Good and Happy Man* 9.7–15 Thesleff, which distinguishes sharply between divine and human virtue.

God by practicing the virtues of everyday life, which he calls "civic" or "polit-ical" virtues. But these seem to be what is open to us to practice. He thus tries to make sense of the idea of becoming like God in practicing virtue by dis-tinguishing kinds or grades of virtue. In practicing one kind, the civic or so-cial virtues, we are preparing ourselves to develop a higher kind, very different from these. The problem of becoming *like* God is solved by distinguishing two kinds of likeness: that of one copy to another copy, where they are the same kind of thing, and that of copy to original, where this may not be true. Two houses, for example, can be like each other, being the same kind of thing. But a house can also be like the blueprint (and one house can be more like the blue-print than another) even though a house is not the kind of thing to *be* a blue-print—it is a different kind of thing altogether. So, Plotinus comments, there is no paradox in our becoming *like* God, although God is something completely different from us.

Hence, for Plotinus, practicing the civic virtues, which is what he finds in some of Plato's works, and particularly the *Republic*,[44] serves as a preparation for devel-oping the higher, purificatory or cathartic virtues. The reference to purification shows that he is thinking of the *Phaedo,* as well as the *Theaetetus.* Purification of the soul is, for Plotinus, a process of detaching itself from the body and its con-cerns, which enables it to turn to what is wholly good; it needs to be purified for this, since it is itself not good but merely capable of good and evil. The puri-fied soul which has escaped the world and the body is able to strive for a clear intellectual view of the Forms, the intellectual paradigms, and this is what the higher virtues consist in.[45]

What are these higher virtues like? The civic virtue of justice is, for Plato, "doing one's own," which makes essential reference to a plurality of people among which this constitutes a fair principle. But the higher virtue of justice is a kind of "doing one's own" which makes no reference to other people. Like the virtue of the moral person in the *Republic,* it consists in having one's soul in a certain state, but here it is a state purely of striving for intellectual intuition of the Forms. Similarly, the higher form of temperance is a turning toward in-tellect, and the higher form of courage is not being affected by things. At first we may think that virtue has been redefined in a way which removes its sense; courage, for example, just is a developed state of understanding and reacting ap-

---

[44] This is presumably where he gets the term "civic" (cf. 430C), although in the *Re-public* Plato intends this to distinguish an inferior kind of virtue, not the kind based on understanding. Plotinus seems to use it of virtue proper.

[45] Porphyry later tidies up the scheme, replacing the single contrast of civic and puri-ficatory virtues with a set of grades of virtue: civic, purificatory, theoretic, and paradig-matic. On this issue, see Dillon 1990, chap. 16, and 1996. I have also had my very ama-teur understanding of Plotinus helped by Bussanich 1990.

propriately to things that are fearful and damaging. How can not being affected be *courage?*

Here it is helpful to remember a move that we frequently find in Plato's Socratic dialogues, a move that is way further back on this road, and has the advantage of being familiar. When Socrates asks someone what a virtue, such as courage, is, the interlocutor sometimes replies by indicating types of action: courage is standing firm in battle, virtue depends on your social role and is different for men and women.[46] Socrates is not satisfied until he has uncovered what unites these different forms of action and explains why they are cases of the virtue in question: virtue turns out to be the intellectual state underlying these different types of action and providing the understanding displayed by the virtuous person. As such it is frequently characterized as a skill or expertise. Intuitively, a problem arises: how can *virtue* be identified with something as intellectual as a skill? We are being urged to redefine our idea of virtue, to direct attention away from the actions that we can see and think are unproblematic, toward the underlying state which grasps the point of and explains them. Plotinus's move can be seen as somewhat similar: the higher virtues are forms of striving for intellectual understanding, which intuitively is very unlike the idea we have of virtue. But, as with the move from variety of type of action to singleness of expertise, we have a move from what seems obvious in practice to the unobvious underlying intellectual unity.

There is one outstanding difference between the familiar move in the Socratic dialogues and what we find here. There the move to intellectual unity was still a move to an understanding of what goes on in practice, whereas here the intellectual paradigms which the higher virtues aim to grasp are explicitly not the kind of thing we find in practice. Is this degree of abstractness fatal to the idea that we have something here relevant to virtue? Not necessarily: we can find something similar in other kinds of moral theory, often with no other similarity whatever to any forms of Platonism. In some forms of utilitarianism, for example, what matters is a grasp of abstract and impersonal moral principles which explicitly cannot be themselves put into practice; nonetheless, grasp of them is supposed to guide the understanding of someone who is to be a utilitarian in practice.

With Plotinus, however, we unavoidably come across a further element, one which forms the main barrier to our seeing the theory as a moral theory with resonance for us. At the end of the treatise he raises the question, Will the person with the greater virtues—the purificatory ones, that is, which enable us to grasp the Forms—have the civic virtues also? The idea that the higher virtues

---

[46] *Laches, Meno.*

have an abstract intellectual tendency does not, one would think, preclude the lower activity of civic virtue. But Plotinus is adamant that, although the virtuous person might have the civic virtues potentially, he will not activate them. "For instance, he will not make self-control consist in that former observance of measure and limit, but will altogether separate himself, as far as possible, from his lower nature and will not live the life of the good man which civic virtue requires. He will leave that behind, and choose another, the life of the gods; for it is to them, and not good men, that we are to be made like."[47] Dillon remarks, "For instance, I suppose, the sage would tend to be the sort of person who would help old ladies across the road, if he happened to notice them, but he would in practice be most unlikely to do so."[48] We seem to be back with the problem of the wise person being oblivious to evil, rather than aware of it and refusing to give in to it (and, as Dillon's example brings out, this is likely to disturb us most in the case of being oblivious to evil happening to other people). Again, it is the idea of *flight* from the world which brings out the problem: a desire to get away from the messy business of controlling desires and fears and on to a less problematic state where you no longer have to worry about controlling them because you have risen above them.

It might be urged that this is an unsympathetic response. Perhaps what is meant is something more like this: the person with both the higher and the civic virtues will be alive to, and perform, the actions that civic virtue requires, but will not regard this as being his real *life;* his real life, in which he strives to become like God and achieve intellectual grasp of the world of Being, is lived on a different level, which accompanies the so-called life consisting of the activity of the civic virtues.[49]

---

[47] Chap. 7; translation by A. H. Armstrong, Loeb Classical Library (Cambridge: Harvard University Press, 1978).

[48] Dillon 1990, p. 100.

[49] Charles Brittain has interestingly suggested (in an unpublished paper) that the person with the higher virtues will perform the actions required by the lower ones because he will be reminded of the need to do so by a psychological mechanism consisting of "involuntary" movements of the soul, which are residues of the rational resolves of the person with the lower virtues and, because the higher virtues are enabled by previous training in the lower virtues, impinge on the attention of the higher self. Thus the person with the higher virtues will have the old lady's plight drawn to his attention by the effect of his previous training in the lower virtues. If there is a problem, it is not whether he will respond to her, but whether he will be in the street in the first place, since he will focus his life on contemplation rather than on virtuous activism. Brittain points out that, although the examples in Plotinus's own text suggest merely residues of the claims of bodily appetite, the idea was expanded by Porphyry and others to accommodate the claims of the lower virtues. It seems hard to see how this idea, however, could account for the

If so, he would have an overall resemblance to the ancient Skeptic, who like-wise performs the duties of civic virtue, but without the conviction that this is anything really worth doing. He is likewise detached from what he does because he does not find real value in it; but this does not mean that he ignores old ladies, or is oblivious to other occasions for the performance of civic virtue.

But there is a difference between the Skeptic and the later Platonist. Both of them have what we might call two perspectives on their lives: one from which you should of course help the old lady, and one from which this is not something that matters, not of real importance. But the Skeptic merely suspends judgment as to what, if anything, *is* of real value; his active, "civic" life is accompanied by tranquillity, *ataraxia,* as to whether anything is really important. And tranquillity does not compete for psychological energy with doing what civic virtue requires.

The later Platonist, however, precisely does have a commitment to something else's being of importance, indeed of overwhelming importance. It is hard to see how the higher and lower virtues are not to compete for psychological space and energy, since they have such divergent aims. Moreover, both are virtues—and a virtue is not just a perspective, or a state of tranquillity, but a reasoned and de-veloped state which determines the direction of the person's life. The higher virtues indeed are mutually entailing: if you have one, you have them all, and your life is thus thoroughly permeated and formed by one kind of sustained con-ception of what is worthwhile. How can a different set of virtues not compete with this? Presumably, this is why Plotinus tells us that the person with the higher virtues has to choose between two *lives,* not just two perspectives on the same life.

It is hard to see how one person can live two lives in this way—indeed, Ploti-nus does not envisage this; he thinks that the person will choose the life of higher virtue instead. But then we are back with the problem of whether this person would, in fact, reliably perform even the actions that civic virtue requires. Ploti-nus's attempt to reconcile the divergent strands in Plato, sophisticated as it is, cannot be said to succeed. There is a rift in Plato's thought, as he is torn between conceptions of virtue as, on the one hand, an uncompromising but committed engagement with the world and, on the other, a flight from and rejection of it.

We can sympathize with both the usual strand of thought about virtue in Plato, characterizing it as a practical skill exercised on the familiar materials of everyday life, and also with the unworldly strand, characterizing it as a flight from everyday life to something quite different. But it is not possible to com-

---

active, rather than merely reactive, aspect of the lower virtues, in particular for the rulers' obligation, in the *Republic,* to propagate the good rather than merely contemplate it. Moreover, if one recognizes an urge to action in oneself as merely the residue of previ-ous habituation, why would it not be irrational to yield to it, rather than something en-dorsed by the rational soul?

bine these strands in a single set of ideas; one or other will suffer too much strain. Much modern interpretation of Plato has solved the problem by ignoring the unworldly strand.[50] Once it is taken into account, the two can be reconciled as Plotinus does it, by locating them on different levels of the climb to virtue. But this will not solve the problem that they compete for precedence; and Plotinus's own solution, which firmly puts the civic virtues at a lower level and regards the life of true virtue as one lived on a higher plane, lacks resonance as an *ethical* theory, however much it may strike a chord as an account of certain types of religious life. In taking Plato's answer to the question "What is our final end?" to be "Becoming like God," but also regarding this as answering to the discussions of virtue in all the dialogues, the ancient Platonists showed more zeal for unity than sense of a philosophical problem.

The *Theaetetus* digression, striking as it is, thus contains a thought which takes ethical theory in a problematic direction. If virtue lies not in coping with the imperfect and messy world, but in rising above it, we run a risk of characterizing virtue in a way which loses the point of it. Aristotle is surely right when he says that a person would not wish the greatest good of all for a friend, namely becoming a god, for then he would no longer be one's friend, but someone else.[51] Someone who was familiar with the Socrates of the Socratic dialogues and then met the philosopher of the *Theaetetus* digression might well have the same thought.[52]

---

[50] The *Theaetetus* digression has been simply ignored, and the problems posed by the *Phaedo*'s thoughts about virtue have been underplayed.

[51] *Nicomachean Ethics* 1158b26–1159a11. Cf. *Magna Moralia* 2.15, where Aristotle insists that we are dealing with self-sufficiency for a human being, not for a god.

[52] I am grateful for comments from many people, in particular Terence Irwin and Charles Brittain.

[IV]

THE INNER CITY: ETHICS
WITHOUT POLITICS IN THE *REPUBLIC*

Since the mid-nineteenth century Plato's *Republic* has been the work which dominates most people's view of his philosophy. It or parts of it turn up in survey and introductory courses in philosophy, political science, classics, humanities, and literature. It is likely that the way it is most frequently taught is as a contribution to political theory. Outside specialists in ancient philosophy, there has not been a great deal of resistance to this way of reading the work,[1] and yet there is an obvious problem. The *Republic* is an extended answer to a question in moral philosophy: Why should I, an individual person, be moral? But it also brings in memorable proposals about the state: rulers should be philosophers, should have no private life, and so on. Which of these aspects should drive our interpretation? Crudely put, is the *Republic* about ethics or about politics?

This may seem an unpromising question, for surely there is an easy answer: it's about both. Indeed, it's also about art, literature, metaphysics, education, and a lot of other topics. But this bland answer does not relieve the pressure of the question about the ethical and political interpretations, for the *Republic* is not a grab-bag of topics; it is clearly intended to have an overall argumentative structure. From the first readers on, there has always been an interpretative issue of the status of the moral and the political elements in the work.

Why should we read the work as primarily a political one, making a contribution to issues in political thought? One answer is an ahistorical one: we can just see, from reading the work, that it contains great contributions to a timeless tradition of political thought.[2] I do not argue against this line of thought,

[1] See, however, Waldron 1995.

[2] This assumption has gone so deep for so long that it has become embodied in the Library of Congress cataloging system. Translations and studies of the *Republic* are shelved neither with Plato texts under PA, nor with history of philosophy under B; they are under

since it would obviously be hard to argue that the *Republic* contains no political ideas that we can find interesting. (It is worth pointing out, however, that the *Statesman* and *Laws* contain far more extensive and serious discussion of political ideas than the earlier work, and that overemphasis on the *Republic* has somewhat skewed accounts of Plato's political ideas and what he takes to be important.) I argue here against two different lines of thought which seem to me to underlie much discussion of the *Republic,* either singly or together, and which skew our interpretation by overemphasizing the political aspects of the work and by giving them a false role in it.

The first is what I call the historicized political interpretation. It is often taken for granted that the *Republic* was written in the context of, or even as Plato's answer to, contemporary problems of Athenian politics, in particular as Plato's answer to what he saw as the problem of democracy. This idea is, when one examines it, wholly anachronistic, and rests on a number of assumptions which are extremely questionable, and in some cases false.

The first of these is that we have a decently full idea of Plato's intellectual biography, and can use this as a firm basis for recovering Plato's own, personal, views, from which we can then set out to interpret the dialogues. This is to assume that we are in the position of a modern biographer who can compare "the works" and "the life." But our "biographical" information about Plato crumbles at the touch. Modern biographies of Plato are the products of uncritical rummaging-around in the ancient Lives of Plato to find bits of information which we find acceptable as "fact." The oldest "biographical fact" about Plato, which has a well-marked provenance and goes back to his nephew Speusippus, is that his real father was Apollo (and indeed we find in the ancient Lives that he was born on Apollo's birthday!), but modern accounts of Plato's life do not feature this, though they are happy to retail points that we find more believable, such as that he went to Sicily and tried to educate Dionysius II of Syracuse.

When the ancient biographical tradition is examined, as it has been in an excellent book by Alice Riginos,[3] it becomes patent that, apart from a few points such as the names of Plato's family,[4] the biographical tradition cannot be relied

---

JC, with texts in political thought. Thus the very way we have access to the books predisposes us to read the *Republic* in the context of works such as Hobbes's *Leviathan* rather than in the context of other dialogues by Plato whose theme is officially "moral" rather than "political."

[3] Riginos 1976.

[4] Though Plato's own name is far from certain. There is an insoluble puzzle arising from the fact that quite a substantial tradition gives his name as Aristocles (the name of his paternal grandfather), but has no good story about any change to the name Plato. (There are various fanciful derivations of it as a nickname, but Plato is not a nickname

on to preserve historical facts. It has been heavily infiltrated, right from the start, by ancient controversies (over Plato's relation to Aristotle, for example) and by influence from the dialogues. Most of the biographical anecdotes bear a relation to a passage in the dialogues, and it would be naive to assume that the anecdote preserves a historical fact which can be used to illuminate the dialogue. Often it seems far more likely that we have a factoid which has been produced precisely in the light of the dialogue. The number of cases where this seems more likely suggests that the most reasonable course is to suspend judgment as to the story's preserving any biographical facts, except where we have strong grounds not to. Thus we can choose to believe that Plato visited Egypt, to explain his references to Egyptian art, and we can choose to believe that he deliberately decided to live on a noisy street to explain why he inveighs against excessive sleep. Or we can regard the anecdotes as the product of a later tradition in the light of these striking passages. But clearly much the most reasonable policy is to suspend judgment: Plato may well have gone to Egypt, and lived on a noisy street, but it would be rash of us to claim either that he did or that he didn't.[5] The ancient Lives are just not the right kind of place for us to hope to find reliable deposits of fact. It is surprising that Riginos's work has not had more impact on Platonic studies.[6] Despite the occasional skeptical note,[7] ancient philosophers have remained surprisingly untroubled by the problems inherent in the ancient sources for Plato's life.

Nor does the tradition hold up any better for the supposed political interests of the Academy. This was known in the ancient world as a center for discussion of political theory, among other things, but was not seen as reacting to or as making a contribution to Athenian political life, and its well-known products were nearly all not Athenian.[8] We hear, among others, of a Corinthian farmer who came to the Academy after reading the *Gorgias*. We do not hear of Plato telling these people to go home, as the *Gorgias* and *Republic* were contributions to Athenian politics, and none of their business.

However, don't we have a source of information about Plato's interest in politics which is independent of the biographical tradition? This is the Seventh

---

but a perfectly good name of the period.) There is some mystery about Plato's name, but we are not in a position to ascertain the answer. See Riginos 1976, 35–38.

[5] On these two anecdotes, see Riginos 1976, 64–65 and 158–59.

[6] This is especially surprising given the impact of similar study of the ancient Lives of the Poets on study of the dramatic poets. The writings of Mary Lefkowitz have been influential here; see Lefkowitz 1981.

[7] Such as Boas 1948.

[8] Here I am simply relying on Brunt (1993), who conclusively demonstrates that the Academy was not, and was not in the ancient world seen as, a training ground for practical politicians. He concludes that the Academy's "influence on the history of states was nil" (p. 332).

"Letter." There has been a long-running debate on the authenticity of this "letter," to which I have nothing to add.[9] It is hard to see what could be supposed to count decisively for or against authenticity; factors such as style, philosophical content, and historical plausibility are all indecisive. Style is hopeless; if the *Protagoras* and the *Statesman* had come down to us without external indications of authorship, would it have seemed reasonable to think that they were by the same author? (Think of the *Lysis* and the *Laws,* the *Apology* and the *Parmenides;* there is no such thing as a central "Platonic style" to judge the "letter" against.) Philosophical content likewise cannot provide an independent criterion, given the intensity of debate as to what is the best interpretation even of those works that are undoubtedly by Plato. As for historical plausibility, it is sometimes argued that the "letter" must at least present a historically acceptable picture, or it would not have got accepted. This does not prove very much, however. The author of the *Axiochus* was not concerned to produce a historically plausible picture of Socrates; the author of the thirteenth "letter" does not seem to have been very concerned to produce a historically plausible picture of Plato. Why should the seventh "letter," which quite contradicts the assumptions of the thirteenth, be different? Again, the reasonable reaction is not to be assured that the seventh "letter" is spurious, but to suspend judgment; perhaps it represents some aspects of Plato's intellectual history, but it would be unwise either to assert or to deny this.[10]

Moreover, disputes over the authenticity of the seventh "letter" risk missing an important point, namely that the genre of ancient "letters" is not the right kind of genre on which to rely for accurate recording of a personal position. A literary letter is a public presentation and interpretation of a position, not a personal outpouring from one individual to another. Thus it is wrong to think that letters of dubious authorship, like the Platonic letters, must either be from Plato's own stylus or be forgeries by someone trying to pass themselves off as Plato. Writing letters in the style of various people became a standard exercise in the

[9] See Edelstein 1966 for arguments against authenticity; for arguments in favor, see von Fritz 1971. Tarrant (1983) points out the limited value of arguing about authenticity on traditional grounds. Tarrant's own thesis, that the philosophical digression in the "letter" represents Middle Platonist ideas, and that it was inserted at a late date, is tempting, but depends on an argument *e silentio* (writers like Plutarch clearly know of *a* "seventh letter" but surprisingly fail to mention the digression in contexts where we would expect this) which not all will find convincing. In any case, the "political" part of the "seventh letter" was clearly known at least from Cicero onward.

[10] It is worth pointing out, however, that there is something questionable about the widespread modern habit of assuming that the Seventh "Letter" alone can be genuine, although no scholar would hold that the whole corpus of thirteen "letters" could possibly be genuine, and then discussing it in a kind of scholarly void. In the absence of a convincing case that the seventh "letter" can thus be extracted from its context, the most we are entitled to is Brunt's point that if it is genuine this is despite the company it keeps.

rhetorical schools; thus producing a "Platonic letter" is better regarded as an exercise in a literary genre rather than as what we would call a forgery of historical evidence.[11] The seventh "letter" was not regarded in the ancient world as a unique glimpse into Plato's personality, one enabling us better to understand the dialogues; it seems to have been regarded as a literary production like the dialogues. Cicero refers to what is probably our seventh "letter,"[12] but he also refers to such works as a letter from Philip to Alexander (in Latin),[13] clearly thinking of such letters as a literary device, not an authentic personal document. A recent study of a later collection of "letters" from Plato's Academy calls it a "novel in letters," which is, from our point of view, what it amounts to.[14] The Platonist Alcinous accepts the "letters" as Platonic, but regards the seventh "letter" as stating one Platonic position to be compared with that of the *Republic,* not as stating a personal position which takes us behind the scenes.[15]

This point about the genre of the seventh "letter," if we take it seriously, stands in the way of any attempt to embed the *Republic* in some story about Sicily and Plato's successive attitudes to political change. Even if we are maximally concessive, and allow that the "letter" was written by someone building on some known facts about Plato's life (and since the seventh "letter" is the source

[11] On Greek letter writing, see White 1986, 187–220, esp. p. 190: "Students [in the rhetorical schools] engaged in the exercise of *prosopoeia* at an advanced level of training. This was the act of representing (imitating) someone, often a famous person, in sentiments and activities suitable to that person. . . . Even though it was essentially rhetorical in intent, *prosopoeia* is probably the primary source of the so-called 'forged' letters ascribed to famous ancient people."

[12] *Tusculan Disputations* 5.100 and possibly *De finibus* 2.92.

[13] *De officiis* 2.53.

[14] Konstan and Mitsis 1990, which calls the collection of letters about Chion of Heraclea a "philosophical novel in letters." Edelstein's (1966) suggestion that our Platonic "letters" were read as what we call historical novels has met with more resistance; more is at stake where the seventh "letter" is concerned for our interpretation of Plato. The Chion letters are marked as late by their style, whereas it is often urged that the Platonic letters cannot be much later than the Platonic corpus because their style is contemporary with it. But what this shows is rather that our Platonic letters were written by someone who could write convincing Platonic Greek, whereas the Chion letters were written by someone more concerned to have his characters appeal to contemporaries. These two styles of writing historical novels—accurate reconstruction of the past versus putting past people into modern style—are still with us.

[15] "Among constitutions, Plato declares that some are non-hypothetical, and these he has described in the *Republic.* . . . He describes other constitutions which are based on the presence of certain conditions, such as that in the *Laws,* and the emended one in the *Letters.*" Alcinous *Handbook of Platonism,* chap. 34. 1 and 4. I use Dillon's translation. It is worth noting that later Platonists refer to the "letters" and do not privilege the seventh; presumably, they regarded conflicts between the letters in the same way as conflicts between the dialogues: a problem to be addressed, not evidence about authenticity.

of the whole Sicily story, this is more concessive than some might like), we are still not entitled to infer from this to a detailed story about Plato's "actual," "real-life" intentions in writing the *Republic*. The large role played in twentieth-century *Republic* interpretation by the seventh "letter" reflects a naive assumption that here (at last) we find the "real" Plato, not hiding behind the dialogue form; but when we reflect on the literary genre of the "letter," we can see that, whether by Plato or not, it takes us no nearer to "direct access" to Plato's thoughts.

We should, then, take seriously the point that we have no evidence for situating the *Republic* in the context of Plato's supposed attitude to politics, and in particular his supposed disillusionment with Athenian politics. For we have no evidence of Plato's disillusionment with Athenian politics. As I have already stressed, the material we have does not give us good grounds against it either; given what we have, the reasonable course is to suspend judgment. We cannot contextualize the *Republic* in facts about Plato's life as we might for a modern author.[16]

If we take this point about the seventh "letter" seriously, then it is easier for us to accept another point, which is too seldom made. Athenian politics of the fifth and fourth century do not actually shed any light on the *Republic*. Seldom can a work have owed less to its political context. Plato goes to enormous lengths to stress the point that his sketch of the ideal state works from first principles, rather than tinkering with existing institutions. One aspect of this comes out strongly in books 8 and 9, where unideal states are discussed.[17] Plato gives them names like "democracy" and "oligarchy," but his use of these terms bears no re-

---

[16] Twentieth-century anglophone writers on Plato have been strikingly uncritical in their reliance on the seventh "letter" and the ancient Lives to give us a biography of Plato as background against which to study the dialogues. Among many popular books this is true of Crossman 1937, Field 1949, and Grube 1935, chap. 8 (it is notable that Grube appeals to the "life" behind the works for political philosophy, though not in other areas). Field 1930 is a good example of extreme naiveté about the seventh "letter"; according to Field, either it is a later "forgery" written to make money or it is an authentic document expressing Plato's own personal views, and we should accept the latter since we have no good evidence for the former (p. 199). Field constantly calls the seventh "letter" "direct evidence" or "direct statements" giving a "general account of his state of mind" (p. 61). Field also does not doubt that the "letter" puts us on "firm historical ground" about historical events (p. 14).

[17] These sketches are often misunderstood as indicating Plato's attitude to contemporary forms of government and their mutual relations. This kind of reading is trenchantly exposed as mistaken in D. Frede 1997. Frede's thorough discussion of the passage shows decisively that "Das Bild der verschiedenen Staatstypen ist nämlich so grob verzeichnet, dass man sie eigentlich nur als Karikaturen bezeichnen kann, die nur schwäche Ähnlichkeiten mit den tatsächlichen Verhältnissen in den uns bekannten Staaten zu Platons Zeit aufweisen." A factor sustaining the common misreading is the view that Plato is here giving a hostile picture of contemporary Athenian democracy (though it is clear that

lation to their current political use, and can be understood only in terms of his theory of the soul. Thus oligarchy and democracy come about with progressive loosening of rational overall control of the soul; they are the conditions where desires function in inappropriate ways. Later, in the *Statesman* and *Laws,* Plato does discuss these types of state in ways that are related to actual politics; he uses the terms for what other people use them for, namely the rule of the many and the rule of the few.[18] Although we cannot contextualize the *Statesman* or the *Laws* in historical facts about Plato or his attitudes any more than we can for the *Republic,* we can at least relate them to current understanding of political terms, as we cannot in its case.

It is likely (though I would not want to be reductive about this) that the wide-spread modern habit (at least in anglophone countries) of reading the *Republic* as a political work, and in particular as Plato's "answer to democracy," may spring from concerns that date particularly from the nineteenth century. For it was only from roughly the middle of the nineteenth century that Greek political institu-tions, especially Athenian democracy, came to the fore as subjects for discussion in a way relevant to contemporary concerns, and Athenian democracy replaced the Roman republic as the ancient model that political theorists found most salient. It was also in the middle of the nineteenth century that study of Plato had a resurgence, especially in the universities,[19] and the confluence of the two

---

neither "democracy" here nor any of the other types of state bear much relation, if any, to contemporary institutions).

[18] For example, the discussion at *Statesman* 291D–303B.

[19] On the study of Plato, see the excellent contributions by Glucker (1987 and 1996). Glucker is sensitive, as many historians of nineteenth-century ideas have not been, to the fact that there are different Platos. After neglect in the eighteenth century Plato was revived in the translations of Thomas Taylor, which greatly influenced many of the Romantic poets—but this was a mystical and Neoplatonist version of Plato. Plato as a philosopher who argues and regards the practice of dialectic as crucial was not rediscov-ered until the efforts of James Mill, John Stuart Mill, and George Grote, which by mid-century had revived philosophical interest in Plato (as well as influencing a creative writer like Peacock). On the role of the Utilitarians in reviving interest in Plato as a philosopher, see Demetriou 1996. However, it was Jowett's translation of Plato's dialogues which made Plato into a popular English-language classic book, and his getting the *Republic* onto the Oxford Greats syllabus as a set book in 1853 started the dominance of that work in clas-sical teaching which has persisted ever since. (See Demetriou for some anti-Utilitarian predecessors of Jowett.) Jowett's idealist, edifying interpretation of Plato has been the dominant one in late-nineteenth- and twentieth-century Plato studies, as have the as-sumptions that the *Republic* can be understood in political terms, and as the centerpiece of "Platonism," understood as a body of doctrine. Attacks on Plato like Crossman's and Popper's have revised Jowett's evaluation of Plato, but have not criticized, indeed have strengthened, much of his methodological approach.

tendencies can certainly be seen as at least part of the reason for our twentieth-century tradition, in the English-speaking West, of seeing the *Republic* in a mainly political context.[20] From the mid-nineteenth century on, we have got accustomed to reading the *Republic* in comparative isolation, in its content, from Plato's other dialogues, and also as a crucially political dialogue. Although in principle these two tendencies are quite distinct, in practice the former has encouraged the latter, since separating the ethical theory of the *Republic* from that of the *Apology, Crito,* and *Gorgias* encourages us to read it in a distinct context, as though Plato were now developing it only in the context of the ideal state.

I do not have the scope here to trace the fascinating vicissitudes of the nineteenth- and twentieth-century tradition of political interpretation of the *Republic,* but one point is worth at least indicating. For some time the work has had a prominent place in university teaching and research; it has engaged the attention of a huge number of scholars and philosophers. The result is not merely disagreement but total opposition; from Victorian meritocratic liberalism to Popper's fascism, Plato's political thought has been planted all over the conceptual map. The degree of violent controversy as to what Plato's political ideas actually are suggests, in a kind of indirect argument, that what we find in the text must strongly underdetermine the different interpretations. And this might give us another reason to wonder if the political interpretation is giving us the right focus.

What if we detach ourselves from this recent tradition, and also from the historicized political interpretation? It may seem that if my arguments have worked, they have worked too well; once we appreciate the phantom nature of much of what has traditionally been accepted about Plato's intentions, are we not left with the work itself, and an apparently free choice of standpoints to take up, uncontrolled by any firm historical context?

We can, however, make progress here. For we do have evidence of the tradition in which the *Republic* was read in the ancient world. We have works by later philosophers, including Platonists, which treat the *Republic,* along with other Platonic dialogues, as a contribution to moral theory. If we read the work in the

---

[20] See Turner 1981; for a review of Turner and of Jenkyns 1980, see Stopper 1981. Roberts (1994) gives a valuable account of the "turning of the tide" in discussions of democracy in the nineteenth century. (Her earlier discussion of Plato and Aristotle, however, is vitiated by her uncritical acceptance of the idea that we have a firm historical background for them, in terms of which we can see them as having a "project of lending the sanctity [*sic*] of weighty philosophical argument to the anti-Athenian position" [p. 71].) Richard (1994) provides interesting material on early American attitudes to the classical past, but in an unanalytic way which casts little light on the question of rejection of Athenian democracy as an "antimodel."

tradition of ancient moral philosophy, we have real support from the ancients, and are not just expressing our own prejudices as to what is philosophically interesting about it.

Here, however, we meet the second argument I mentioned earlier. Even if the *Republic* should be read primarily as a moral theory rather than as a contribution to politics, still the moral theory itself seems to contain a political component. Plato poses the question why I, an individual, should be moral, but surely the sketch of the ideal state is essential to his answer? Thus, even if we reject the historicized approach, we might still think that the *Republic* is essentially about politics in that its political aspect is crucial to its moral argument.

We might think that this is the case because of the importance to Plato of the soul-state analogy. It is sometimes thought that the structural analogy between the soul of the individual and the organization of the state implies that neither can be properly studied in independence, and thus that neither can have interpretative primacy; it is taken to imply a politicized ethics and an ethicized politics. Nothing overtly in the dialogue justifies so strong an interpretation, however. What is actually said is that the state is brought in to illuminate the soul, because justice in the state is supposedly easier to discern (368D–369A); once we have read the answer there, we can go on to apply it to the individual.

Of course, illumination and explanation can go both ways, and sometimes Plato says that individual and state are mutually illuminating (434D–435A). But there are passages which make it clear that it is of no importance whether the ideal state can exist or not, since its function is to enable the individual to get an idea of morality which he or she can internalize and live by (472B–D, 592A–B). There are passages (473C–E, 499B) which have sometimes been used to support the view that the political proposals cannot be read merely as illustrative of individual morality; for there Socrates insists that no society or individual can become just until philosophers become kings.[21] Other passages, however, indicate that Plato means that it is normally very difficult, or even impossible, for an individual to get the good upbringing and education that would produce a moral person; hence we should not be surprised that in the world as it is, few or none of those with the native gift to do so do become moral (cf. especially 490E–492A). Plato is indicating that for an individual to become moral, he must do more than tinker with his beliefs and attitudes—he must grasp the *ideal* of virtue, which is

---

[21] 473E is complicated by the fact that in E5 many editors, including Burnet, read *allēi* for the manuscripts' *allē*, thus changing the subject of the sentence. Either way the sentence is awkward, since either the state or the individual is said not to be happy "either privately or publicly," creating a puzzle as to how the state can be happy privately or an individual happy publicly.

presented via the picture of the ideal state. The message, however, is not the simpleminded one that he should wait for some philosopher-kings to come along, or try to become one himself. Rather, he should internalize the ideal of virtue as a "city of himself" (592A7)—that is, he should internalize in his soul the structure pictured in the ideal city. He may achieve this, however, and still fail to do more than improve his own lot; only where other people do the same is there hope for an individual to improve matters communally as well as in his own case (496C–497A). None of these passages demands the interpretation that an individual can be virtuous only in a state of the kind that Plato sketches, and some of them, particularly the famous ending of book 9, say the very opposite; there political language is clearly applied to the individual's internal state, and the ideal state is a model for the structure of the moral individual's soul.[22]

It might be objected at this point that the ideal state may not be required as a context for the virtuous person to be virtuous in, but surely the emphasis on education in the early books suggests that Plato thinks that it is required as a context for the person to *become* virtuous. How can any of us become virtuous unless we are the products of the kind of radically new education and habituation that Plato sketches there? It would, however, run contrary to the kind of epistemological account that we find in the dialogue for Plato to insist that virtue can be the product only of a particular set of institutions. The ideal state is, after all, in the imaginative scheme of the dialogue, the product of people with knowledge and virtue, and Plato does not set the *Republic* itself forward as being any such thing. The most he commits himself to is the position that the structure of the ideal state, as a model of rational control, is the structure that the would-be virtuous person must internalize. That is, after all, the point of the soul-state analogy. And it is consistent with this that the development of the ideal state is so skimpy, since Plato develops it only as far as he needs to make this point.

Of course, if it is to be a model for morality in the individual, the ideal state

---

[22] At 592A–B there is abundance of such language. Socrates says that the virtuous person will be willing to "practice politics" (*ta politika prattein*) only in "the city of himself" (*en ge tēi heautou polei,* a very striking phrase), but not in his native city. The city "we have been founding" is "established in words" (or "arguments," *logoi*), since it exists nowhere on earth. It is then suggested that perhaps (or "of course") it exists as a pattern "in the heavens" for the person willing to look at it and thence "refound himself" (*heauton katoikizein*—a word used of cities here applied to what the individual does to himself). Finally, it is said that it makes no difference whether the ideal city does or will exist, since it will be the concerns only of it, not of any other, that the virtuous person will practice. (The Greek says that he will, literally, "do the things of it"; translations such as "practice the politics" and the like go too far). I am grateful to Chris Bobonich for stressing the importance of the passages discussed in the paragraph above.

must be clearly acceptable to the reader as an example of morality in its own right; and this has always proved to be the weakness of the analogy, since Plato ignores contemporary political thought so utterly in insisting that the authoritarian and elitist structure of his ideal state embodies morality or justice. Nonetheless, we have to accept that Plato does think, though without good argument against contemporary political ideas, that his ideal state will be accepted as embodying a structure which is, in a state, moral; otherwise, the argument that the would-be moral person must internalize and live by this structure would have no force.[23]

Robin Waterfield, a recent translator of the *Republic*,[24] suggests that the politics of the *Republic* are best seen as metaphorical. "It is possible to read the book as a predominantly individualist approach to the issues, with the traditional political terminology of the debate suborned and largely turned over to metaphorical purposes, to describe the inner state of the individual" (p. xvi). Waterfield's suggestion has the advantage of avoiding two problems with the traditional political interpretation which have not been raised so far. One is that the political suggestions themselves are absurd if the details are taken literally.[25] If we are supposed to be taking the Nuptial Number seriously, we are in the realm of fantasy rather than political philosophy. And in fact most interpretations do not focus on details like this, but proceed to what have become, by convention, the serious political principles that we find to arise from the *Republic* (the claim of expertise to rule, inegalitarianism, and so on). Few, however, have a rationale for avoiding the absurdities of literalism.

The other problem is that the political parts of the book are brief and underdeveloped. To treat the book as a contribution to political theory is to privilege just those parts of it that need most interpretation and hermeneutic infill to make them even coherent.[26] We may not notice the brevity and offhand nature

---

[23] But it is surprising how relatively little attention this point has got from scholars commenting on the *Republic* (with the honorable exception of Gregory Vlastos, who stresses it).

[24] Plato, *Republic,* trans. Robin Waterfield, World's Classics Series (Oxford: Oxford University Press, 1993).

[25] "A great deal of the book is simply absurd if read as serious political philosophy" (p. xviii). I think that this point is quite important. One reason that the *Republic* has stayed in so many versions of the "canon" of Western thought may well be that if read literally as a political work, it provides an easy target; even the dullest student in the class can see what is wrong with the idea that philosophers should be kings.

[26] "As a manifesto [the politics of the *Republic*] is naive and fragmentary. Anyone reading the book with a view to finding a political philosophy to follow or to criticize is going to be disappointed and will be forced to supply a lot of the evidence" (Waterfield, p. xiv).

of these parts if we read them in a modern tradition which has already supplied us, through textbooks, with the main lines of "Plato's political thought." But if we stand back and ask how we are supposed to get from the actual text to the substantial political theory, we find that the standard accounts contain a lot of bricks with vanishingly little straw.

There are difficulties with the view that what Plato says about the state is meant merely as metaphor, however. If each political proposal is a metaphor for something to do with the individual (Waterfield suggests, for example, in his note on 460C, that the abortion and infanticide proposals are really about "the rejection of unwanted ideas"), then we have to look for a thoroughgoing set of detailed correspondences, and this rapidly becomes unconvincing. If we reject detailed correspondences, then we are left uncertain what is meant here by "metaphor"; on any view, the proposals about the state are in some way illustrative.

We cannot judge how important the political aspect of the work is without looking at the structure of the main ethical argument. Here is it useful for us to look at evidence which has not usually been invoked in this connection, namely that of the later Platonists. Where ethics is concerned, as has already been stressed, later Platonists have the advantage for us that, when they read the dialogues, their questions and answers belong in an already developed eudaimonist tradition of ancient ethical debate; their understanding of Plato's ethics deserves to be taken seriously.

Alcinous, as we have seen, takes Plato to hold views which fall squarely within the eudaimonist tradition. When it comes to the relation of virtue and happiness, he stresses passages in Plato which distinguish between kinds of goods—the merely human goods, such as health, strength, success, and such conventional goods, and the divine good of wisdom, identified with virtue. Happiness for us consists in a life of wisdom and virtue, since only virtue is good, other things being good only insofar as they are put to good use by virtue. Virtue, then, being the only good, is sufficient for happiness; we have seen Alcinous using Stoic terminology to show that in his view Plato lines up with the Stoics against the Aristotelians in the great ethical debate of antiquity, whether virtue is sufficient for happiness or not. And ancient writers such as Cicero agree; not just the Stoics, they think, but Plato argues that virtue is sufficient for happiness.[27]

So far modern interpreters might agree that this describes the theory of what we call the Socratic dialogues, the group of dialogues already discussed in Chapter 2 as putting forward the radical thesis of the sufficiency of virtue. However, the *Republic* is generally thought to represent a different, and later, view. But the developmental view of Plato, as we have seen in Chapter 1, was un-

---

[27] Cicero, *Tusculan Disputations* 5.34–36.

heard-of in the ancient world, and Alcinous boldly says that the sufficiency of virtue is to be found in very many of Plato's works, "but particularly in the whole of the *Republic*."[28]

Modern scholars do not, by and large, share the ancient Platonists' view that Plato sustains the sufficiency of virtue for happiness in the *Republic;* the usual view is the developmental one, namely that Plato holds the sufficiency view at an early period, but in the *Republic* retreats from this to a weaker view, namely that the virtuous person is happier than the not-virtuous, but may fail to be happy, if external circumstances are bad. This view is defended as "the comparative view" by Terence Irwin.[29] Further, since the *Republic* presents the ideally virtuous person in the ideally virtuous society, this seems to support the idea that the good conditions of the ideal society are necessary for the virtuous person to be happy. If this is so, then the *Republic*'s main argument will not show that the virtuous person is happy, only that he is happy in the conditions of the ideal state, though in any state he is happier than the non-virtuous person.

Some aspects of the *Republic* may suggest this,[30] but wrongly; there is strong evidence that the ancient Platonists are correct. We can see this clearly if we look at the passages which are structural for the main moral argument. In book 1 Socrates in his dispute with Thrasymachus is clearly defending the sufficiency thesis.[31] When, however, at the beginning of book 2 Glaucon and Adeimantus say that they will restate Thrasymachus's challenge, they do so in a long passage which is couched in comparative language; Socrates is asked to show that the moral person is happier than the immoral, or has a better life, or that immorality is the greatest evil and morality the greatest good.[32] The prominence of comparative language here has encouraged many to hold that Plato is now under-

---

[28] Alcinous *Handbook of Platonism,* chap. 27, 5.

[29] Irwin (1995) argues, "The difference between *Republic* 1 and *Republic* 2 foreshadows a division between, on the one side, Socrates and the Hellenistic schools and, on the other side, Plato and Aristotle" (p. 200). On this view, Plato shares with Aristotle the view that happiness requires external goods as well as virtue. In the *Republic* external goods are provided by the favorable conditions of the ideal state. "The philosopher-rulers plainly have favourable external conditions added to justice. . . . The comparative claim allows us to say that these favourable external conditions (living in a just society, being reliably supplied with basic resources, receiving honour, etc.) contribute to the happiness of the philosophers" (p. 192).

[30] The work's moral psychology appears to be strikingly different from that of the Socratic dialogues. I argue in Chapter 6, however, that it is best so interpreted as to be compatible with that view, so there is no argument for development here. Further, the more developed moral psychology of the *Republic* does not affect the question whether Plato is defending the sufficiency thesis.

[31] Cf. 353E–354A.

[32] Cf., for example, 367B, 362C, 366E.

taking to show not that the moral person is happy, but merely that he is happier than the immoral.[33]

Two points are relevant here, however. We cannot infer the presence of the comparative thesis from comparative language; for it is possible for A to be happier than B where B is not happy at all (and Plato not infrequently uses comparative language in this way). So Plato can perfectly well answer a challenge to show that the moral are happier than the immoral by showing that virtue is necessary and sufficient for happiness, so that the immoral are always unhappy; and this in fact turns out to be his answer.

Further, we should bear in mind the dramatic form of the challenge as it is set up in book 2. When Socrates sets up the challenge, he commits himself to showing that virtue is really in the agent's interests, even when all the appearances are to the contrary. Glaucon portrays two figures, of the vicious person who appears virtuous, and the virtuous person who not only is deprived of all conventional goods like success, health, and so on, but even lacks the reputation for virtue. Socrates undertakes to show that, even in these conditions, virtue is in the person's interests and will lead to happiness. The passage is reminiscent of the challenge, standard in Hellenistic ethics, to show that the virtuous person is happy on the rack (or the wheel, or in the bull of Phalaris). This certainly looks like a challenge that could be successfully met only by demonstrating the sufficiency thesis.

We should also ask ourselves whether the comparative thesis is in fact notably weaker as an answer to the challenge. If so, Plato will now (as opposed to the Socratic dialogues) hold that it is too extreme and counterintuitive to claim that the tortured virtuous person is really happy—but more reasonable to claim that he is not actually happy, but would be in ideal conditions, and is still happier than the flourishing wicked person. This is still a very strong claim, and does not look much like a retreat to common sense. Further, the comparative thesis has, from the start, a striking oddity which this passage reveals: virtue has the power to make the tortured and reviled virtuous person happier than the flourishing wicked person—but not quite enough power to make him happy. Perhaps this is due to the thought that wickedness makes you not just unhappy but *so* unhappy that even if you have all conventional goods, you will still be less happy than the virtuous person in the worst possible circumstances. But then wickedness seems more powerful than virtue, in an unexplained and unintuitive way. The comparative thesis, then, lacks what might have seemed to be an advantage.

---

[33] This has been encouraged by the long arguments in book 9 to show that the lives of the moral and immoral can be ranked for happiness in the way they are ranked for morality, and that the moral person has more (729 times more, in fact) pleasure than the immoral. These passages, however, do not form the final answer to the challenge of book 2, which has quite a different form (see p. 86).

In book 9 we find a point[34] where there is a reference back to the book 2 challenge, and we get the final answer to it. And that answer is given in non-comparative language. The discussion reverts to the language of book 1, whether it "is in your interest" to be moral. The conclusion that it is, is answered entirely by reference to the agent's internal state—the rational ordering of the soul. And Plato insists robustly on two points. First, to lose the internal harmony of virtue for a conventional good like money is to make a radical mistake about what benefits you, one as grave as that of a person who sells his child to cruel men just to make money, or Eriphyle, who took a necklace as the price of her husband's life.[35] However much money you make, this is not in your interest and will not bring you happiness. Conventional goods, it is clear, have no weight as against virtue where happiness is concerned.

Second, the long passage which follows claims repetitively that the virtuous person will be interested in health, money, and honors only insofar as they sustain his inner condition of virtue; he will look to virtue, and not to these goods themselves, in his dealings with them.[36] Conventional goods, that is, do not add anything extra to the person who is virtuous, whose only concern with them is to use them wisely. This seems not to leave room for the virtuous person to need conventional goods to add on to virtue in order to be happy; for conventional goods have already made all the contribution they can make as the context and materials of the virtuous life.

Similarly, in book 10 Socrates says[37] that he will now restore to the virtuous person the external rewards that were subtracted earlier, as part of the initial challenge.[38] But before he restores human rewards such as success, he makes the point that the person with virtue already possesses, in virtue, something that brings good things just from being what it is; virtue can be seen as the gods' gift, since the gods, being virtuous, love those like themselves. The gods' love does not, however, display itself in giving the virtuous person worldly advantages. Rather, the person the gods love will make the best of worldly *dis*advantages and external evils. If he meets with poverty or disease "or some other apparent evil," still this will turn out well for him. For the virtuous person will put external evils

---

[34] 588B.

[35] 589A–590A.

[36] 591C–592A.

[37] 612C–614E. This passage has been discussed in Chapter 3, since in it is introduced the idea of virtue as becoming like God.

[38] This is not, and is not presented as, part of the original challenge, which has been met by the end of book 9; it is presented as a supplementary point. It thus does not show that the original challenge requires conventional goods to be added to virtue before the challenge is met.

to virtuous use, and thus they will not really be evils for him, things which could spoil his happiness.

Here again we find a ringing endorsement of the thesis that virtue is sufficient for happiness. Anything other than virtue—conventional goods like health and wealth or evils like poverty and disease which are conventionally held to detract from happiness—is seen merely as material for the virtuous person to put to use. The person who lives virtuously achieves happiness, since what others consider to be goods and evils are not good or evil in themselves, only as put to virtuous use. Poverty and disease are not, for the virtuous person, evils detracting from happiness. The main moral argument of the *Republic,* then, seems to be an argument for the sufficiency thesis.

Moreover, there are passages throughout the body of the dialogue which fit better with the sufficiency thesis than with the comparative thesis. We find the analogy of virtue and health, and the claim that the virtuous person has real happiness whereas Olympic victors have only the appearance; these are claims which have elsewhere been associated with the sufficiency thesis.[39] We find that the good person is the least attached to conventional goods, including the good, even the lives, of his friends and family.[40] We also find repeated use of the idea that we should find morality and immorality, and see which you need to be happy, "whether or not you escape the notice of all gods and men."[41]

Two ideas are particularly striking here. One[42] is that we are told that we are looking for examples of complete morality and immorality, not so as to put them into practice, but so that we can consider our own case and realize that, as these examples stand to happiness and unhappiness, so do we ourselves to the extent that we are moral or the opposite. That is, there is a direct relation between morality and happiness, one which can be transferred to whoever considers the matter, and one to which that person's external goods, or lack of them, are clearly irrelevant.

Further, we find passages where the value of conventional goods is said to be utterly different from what most people think; far from making any life better, they have a value which depends on the kind of life within which they have a role. As well as the passage above, at the end of book 9 we find[43] that the philo-

---

[39] The virtue and health analogy appears at *Republic* 445A–B; it has previously occurred at *Crito* 47D–48A and *Gorgias* 504B–505B. The analogy with Olympic victors at *Republic* 465D–466D appeared at *Apology* 36D–E.

[40] 387D–E.

[41] 427D, 444E–445A, 580C; the last is emphatically placed after the comparison of lives.

[42] 472B–E.

[43] 491A–C and 495A.

sophical nature can be ruined by so-called goods; conventional advantages when put to use by an ignorant soul are bad, not good, for it. Most notably,[44] we find that the unhappiest person is not the tyrant type (the *turannikos*) but this kind of person when he has lots of conventional advantages and is thus able to become an actual tyrant (a *turannos*). Again, conventional advantages like money, health, and wealth are bad for the person who is wicked. This is another view familiar from the Socratic dialogues; there are in the *Republic* many points of continuity with the ethical theory of those dialogues.

The sufficiency thesis thus appears to be the best interpretation of the main argument of the *Republic*. If this is true, however—if the virtuous person is happy just because of being virtuous, and external evils do not detract from this, since external goods are not a part of happiness in their own right—then Socrates has certainly met the challenge to show that the virtuous person stripped of worldly goods, tortured and suffering from undeserved disgrace, is nonetheless happy. However, it is now a moot point what role is played in this demonstration by the ideal state. Since in both the book 2 and book 10 passages we have it stressed in the most dramatic possible way that the virtuous person is happy in the worst possible circumstances of the actual world, it is clear that the virtuous person doesn't need the conditions of the ideal state to be happy. In the ideal state, of course, virtuous people are rewarded by the appropriate position in society, the way of life which enables them to flourish and the creation of an environment in which even the non-virtuous will recognize and appreciate their virtue. None of this, however, is required for the virtuous to be happy, since they can be happy, as long as they are virtuous, not only in the actual world but in the worst possible circumstances of the actual world. So, if the main moral argument shows that virtue is indeed sufficient for happiness—this being the ancient Platonist interpretation, which I have argued is strongly supported—the account of the ideal state does not form part of the main argument; indeed, it cannot. The ideal state is introduced to illustrate and clarify the nature of virtue in the virtuous person, but the conclusion of the moral argument is independent of the political aspects of the work; moreover, it has to be, since the conditions of the ideal state do not form part of what the virtuous person needs to be happy.

This separation has important implications. As an ethical theory, distinct from the politics, the theory of the *Republic* is most naturally read as a contribution to the debate over our final end which develops most clearly between the Stoics and the Aristotelians. There is no reason to see it as linked to the anti-egalitarianism of the political proposals; for it offers an answer to the question

---

[44] 578B.

raised in the first book, namely, how ought one to live?—a question addressed to anyone. It is this answer which the Stoics correctly think is similar to their own. The political parts of the book which divide people into three classes and three ways of life designed to achieve happiness in radically different ways are not an essential part of this answer, and this must have been a factor in the Stoics' willingness to allow that there was convergence with their own moral ideas, since they reject Plato's political anti-egalitarianism without holding that they are thereby committed to rejecting the *Republic*'s main argument. Also, when the Platonists give an account of Plato's ethical views, they regard his ideas as a straightforward contribution to moral theory; it does not occur to them that they should be read in a way limited by the political proposals, and thus confined to a small elite.[45]

Further, nothing ties Plato's position on virtue and happiness to any particular stance on either the desirability or the feasibility of the proposals about the ideal state. Since these have the role of illuminating the main moral argument, the question whether any of them is realistic and viable becomes an entirely separate matter, something that you might or might not be interested in.

It may be objected that it is misleading to use the later Platonists as I have done; why should we conclude anything about the *Republic* itself from the interpretations of people who are so much later? Where ethical theory is concerned, this is not a good objection; indeed, investigating it provides support for the position I am suggesting. For it is remarkable that once eudaimonistic theory gets established, it carries on quite indifferently to changes in historical and political context. The differences in political context which separate Plato from Cicero are not much less than those that separate Plato from us; and yet Cicero's works show us that ethics was debated and discussed in just the same terms that we find in Plato. The extreme divergences in political context are, of course, bound to affect Cicero's, and our, attitudes to Plato's political ideas; but clearly, once the basic questions and assumptions of eudaimonism were established (whether by Socrates or by Democritus), they appeared equally compelling to Greeks, Romans, and others whether in fourth-century city-states or under the Roman republic and empire. The posing and answering of ethical questions does not alter in any important way as a result of the massive political changes in the Greco-Roman world; once established, the basic eudaimonistic framework proved remarkably robust and solid. The lateness of our evidence from the Middle Plato-

---

[45] I have talked only about Middle Platonist handbooks, focusing on Alcinous. It is also of interest, however, that Albinus thinks that the pedagogical reason for reading the *Republic* is that it gives a sketch of the education (*paideia*) that is needed for the acquisition of virtue; it is a dialogue read for the edification of the individual, and there is no suggestion of political implications (Albinus, *Introduction* 5).

nists reflects the length of time before Plato was interpreted as holding systematic doctrines; it does not cast doubt on the durability of the ethical framework.[46]

It may also be objected to my account that later ancient philosophers also maintain a concern with the political aspects of the *Republic,* and not just with the main argument about virtue and happiness. After all, Plato himself refers back to the political part of the *Republic* in the *Timaeus-Critias,* and one of the most famous passages in Aristotle is his criticism of some of the work's political proposals.

Plato's own reference, however, does not support a political interpretation of the *Republic.*[47] Nonetheless, the reference to the *Republic's* ideal state in the *Timaeus-Critias* is extremely interesting, and clarifies, more than has been done hitherto, the role of the work's political content for Plato. In the *Republic* discussion some general political principles do emerge, although they are not argued for or supported—for example, the principle that possession of expertise gives the expert the right to rule, and to force the results of his expertise on others. In the *Statesman* and *Laws* Plato subjects this and other principles to argument and examination, and we find serious political philosophy. To the extent that the *Republic* contains the beginning of these discussions, it contains political philos-

---

[46] The fact that later writers discuss ethics in just the same terms as Plato and Aristotle shows decisively how wrong is the view, which sometimes is still to be found, that Greek ethical thought has an essential connection with the *polis.* Cf. Barker 1906, 82: "The question which Plato sets himself to answer [in the *Republic*] is simply this: What is a good man, and how is a good man made? Such a question might seem to belong to moral philosophy, and to moral philosophy alone. But to the Greek it was obvious that a good man must be a member of a State, and could only be made good through membership of a State." Where is this "Greek" view supposed to be found? There are two candidates for the founders of ancient moral philosophy, Socrates and Democritus, and both of them discuss the individual's virtue and happiness in ways that utterly falsify Barker's remark. Nor does Barker think of the implications of his remark for the moral philosophy of the Socratic dialogues. We are supposed to be assuming the existence of a "Greek" attitude to help us interpret the *Republic;* but the supposed attitude is a fiction generated by reading the *Republic* in isolation from the Socratic dialogues and assuming that it must be read in a political context.

[47] At *Timaeus* 17C Socrates appears to say that the main part of "yesterday's discussion" (clearly the *Republic*) was the political part about the state. This is not so, however. The sentence runs: *chthēs pou tōn hu'emou rhēthenton logōn peri politeias ēn to kephalaion, hoia te kai ex hoiōn andrōn aristē katephainet'an moi genesthai.* As Proclus notes in his commentary on the passage, we can understand a pause either after *logōn* or after *politeias.* On the second view (for some reason dominant in English translations and also found in some German ones), the *kephalaion* of the *Republic* is the part about the state. But on the former reading, Socrates is simply saying that in yesterday's discussion about the state, the *kephalaion* was the point about making it the best. This implies nothing about the relative importance, within the *Republic,* of the political and other parts. (This reading seems to be favored in recent French, Italian, and Spanish translations.)

ophy of a traditional kind, though not developed very far. But the *Timaeus-Critias* is the only other place where we find reference to the specific details of the ideal state—no family life, women trained to fight, and so on. What Plato proposes to do there is to put the "static" picture of the ideal state "into motion"; what we find, in fact, is the unfinished project of a historical fiction, the "history of Atlantis."[48] This strongly suggests that in the *Republic* Plato thinks of these details in the same way, as imaginative constructions rather than as serious matter for political discussion, never mind practical proposals. And this is what we would anyway expect from the *Republic's* own epistemology: the sketches of marriage festivals, taking the children on ponies to the battlefield, and the like are just the sort of imaginative construction suitable for a fiction of the *Timaeus-Critias* sort, beneath the level of serious intellectual discussion.

As far as Aristotle is concerned, there are two important points to be borne in mind. One is that Aristotle, along with other ancient writers, takes it for granted that the political aspects of the book should be discussed quite separately from the main argument. His objections to the political aspects of the *Republic* are, after all, found in his *Politics,* not in his ethical works. Similarly, Alcinous, along with other Middle Platonists, assumes that the main argument will be discussed in the account of Plato's ethical thought, whereas the political aspects are discussed later and quite separately, in his chapters on politics. Ancient philosophers do not have the modern habit of discussing the *Republic's* moral argument along with politics, as though it could not be extracted from the sketch of the ideal state. Many people in antiquity were familiar with the stranger political ideas of the work (especially, of course, the "women and children in common" idea), but they did not take the argument about virtue and happiness to depend on them or to be discussed together with them (and, I have argued, they were right not to do so).

Second, even Aristotle's *Politics* does not stand to the political parts of the *Republic* in anything like the relation that his ethical works stand to its main ethical argument, namely as a work which presents an explicit version of something that can be discerned implicitly in the earlier work. For Aristotle, the *Republic* emphatically does not set the agenda for political philosophy. He criticizes it along with other examples of unrealistic and utopian proposals, but it does not figure in the development of the two themes most dominant in his own political philosophy: the nature of political rule and the issue as to the best form of government (*politeia,* or "constitution"). Aristotle adverts right at the start of the *Politics* to what he regards as Plato's biggest mistake, namely his failure to distinguish political rule from the mere exercise of power; but, although we might

---

[48] The status of the Atlantis story as conscious fiction is discussed by Gill (1977, 1979).

think that the *Republic* offers the most vivid example of this, it is an issue which gets more explicit discussion and development in the later dialogues *Statesman* and *Laws*.[49] And when Aristotle discusses what is for him probably the most important issue of political theory, namely, what is the best *politeia*, he criticizes and tries to improve on Plato's suggestions in the *Statesman* and *Laws*, but unsurprisingly ignores the *Republic*, where this question is not considered, since Plato there rejects the idea of modifying or improving existing political institutions.[50]

Thus the *Republic* stands aside from Plato's own later political dialogues, Aristotle, and such later writers as Polybius and Cicero: it contributes nothing to what became the basic question of political theory. We can see this vividly from Cicero's own work *De re publica*. Cicero uses Plato's work as a literary model, but its content is entirely different in kind. He does not criticize Plato's work, but carries on the now standard debate as to which is the best form of constitution; his own ideal state is far more like a sentimentalized version of the Roman republic than anything in Plato. Moreover, Cicero does not undertake to emulate the *Republic*'s main ethical argument. His work contained a defense of justice of some kind, but it seems to have been purely political; whatever the exact role in it of Carneades' famous speeches for and against justice, it is concerned with the justice of Roman imperial rule, not with virtue in the souls of individual Romans.

Zeno of Citium, by contrast, does criticize the ethical ideas of Plato's work. Zeno's short and provocative *Republic* seems clearly intended as a riposte to Plato's dialogue. Zeno regarded the ideal state as an ideal construction to illuminate the nature of the virtuous person; his ideal city is a city of the wise and virtuous only, and in no way intended as a practical proposal. He takes over the kind of device Plato mentions for increasing true community: thus in the ideal state there would be no nuclear families, no artificial modesty about the body, and so on.[51] But for Zeno, the ideal community is formed of all citizens; Plato's

---

[49] Books 3 and 4 of the *Politics* are largely devoted to the attempt to establish the sense in which political rule involves recognizing the equality of ruler and ruled, and thus provides a basis for a political community of equals. For Aristotle, this marks off political rule as different in kind from exercising power over unequals of various kinds, particularly the relationships discussed in book 1. Aristotle is right that the basic weakness of Plato's views on political rule is his refusal to allow that it is different in kind from other kinds of exercise of power, a point he makes explicitly at *Statesman* 259A–C.

[50] The discussion at *Statesman* 291D–303B is obviously in Aristotle's sights at *Politics* 1279a22–1280a6 and 1289a26–b26. Aristotle ignores the *Republic*'s very loaded account of "democracy," "oligarchy," etc., in favor of the *Statesman*'s far more politically relevant accounts.

[51] See Schofield 1991, chap. 2, for discussion of the ways in which the fragments of Zeno's work seem to reflect or engage with Plato's work. Schofield thinks that Zeno's ideal city had a political ideal, but this is one which is hardly political in the conventional sense,

inegalitarianism about the ideal community of the *Republic* is rejected. The Stoics, who were inspired by the figure of Socrates and seem to have approved of some at least of Plato's Socratic dialogues, in which Socrates exhorts all and sundry to virtue, correct those aspects of the *Republic* which fit badly with the thesis that any rational being who reflects in the right way can become virtuous. Moreover, they regarded the ideal state as an ethical pattern; their interest in political philosophy more narrowly construed is minimal.[52]

What of the Platonists themselves? Alcinous in his account of Plato's doctrines deals with politics separately, after ethics, the emotions, and friendship. He draws on Plato's later dialogues as well as the *Republic,* and, although he mentions a few of the most striking political features of that dialogue, such as the class system, he sees Plato in terms of the conventional issue of constitutions. He indicates the dependence or not of forms of government on given conditions; thus the *politeia* of the *Republic* comes in as a form of government which is "non-hypothetical." He is also concerned with the ranking of forms of government from best to worst; here he corrects the ranking given in the *Republic,* in which democracy is worse than oligarchy, to bring it into line with the ranking in the *Statesman,* where the terms are used in their normal senses, and where oligarchy is ranked as worse than democracy. The only unexpected feature of Alcinous's interest in the *Republic* is his focus on its concern with war. He stresses the point that only the primitive state of book 2 is free from war, warfare dominates his selection of topics from both the *Republic* and the *Laws,* and he concludes with the pessimistic comment, "Politics concerns itself with a vast array of subjects, but above all the question whether or not one should make war." Alcinous, that is, is left with nothing to say about the politics of the *Republic* except a string of desultory and unconnected remarks.

In the ancient world, then, the political aspects of the *Republic* were treated separately from the main moral argument, and, although the book was of course memorable for its striking ideas, its political aspects did not fit into, or set the agenda for, what were to become the main lines of political philosophy.[53] The

namely unification through love, specifically a sublimated form of personal love. Zeno takes over Plato's idea of unifying a community through sublimated affection, but rejects the idea of an inegalitarian division into classes, and the complex educational system.

[52] For this last claim, see Annas 1993, chap.13, 3. Schofield (1991) argues, "Zeno and Chrysippus created the intellectual conditions for the demise of political philosophy in the classical republican or communitarian style of Plato and Aristotle, and for the beginnings of the natural law tradition of political thought" (p. 2). In Annas 1993 I argue that the Stoics' deployment of natural law is not a specifically political one.

[53] Middle and Neoplatonist commentators frequently wrote on the *Republic;* in popularity among commentators it was second only to the *Timaeus.* However, as we can see from Dörrie and Baltes 1990–96, 3:44–46 and 210–19, interest focused on the mathe-

main moral argument fitted into the mainstream of ethical debate and theory, however, and, once this was explicitly set out by Aristotle, and developed in debate with other schools, it was natural for Plato's position to be seen in terms of the Stoic-Aristotelian debate as to whether virtue is sufficient for happiness, or needs external goods as well. We have already[54] seen the aggressive Platonist claim that Plato is on the side of virtue and its sufficiency for happiness. In the ancient world the main argument of the *Republic* was seen as being essentially the same as that of the Socratic dialogues, not as marking a major change, and not as being boxed into the sketch of the ideal state, and thus applicable only to a small elite. This separation of the moral from the political strands can be seen plainly in the way that Marcus Aurelius regards "Plato's state" as a useless diversion from serious moral concern with what one is doing.[55]

If we take the ancient Platonist interpretation of Plato at all seriously, two points emerge here as salient. One is that it is better policy to look at the ancient intellectual traditions of reading the *Republic* than to go along with the modern habit of looking for background on "Plato's life and times," as though Plato were a writer like Locke or Hobbes; for in Plato's case, this background is nonexistent. Besides, the ancient reading of the *Republic* has, as I have argued, at least one major advantage: we can give a coherent account of its ethical theory as continuous with that of the Socratic dialogues, rather than as an artificially isolated and peculiar attempt at ethical theory within the confines of a sketch of an ideal state.

Second, we may be encouraged to rethink our view of the *Republic* and how to read it. It is easy to remain unaware of the extent to which our attitude to it,

---

matical passages and the Myth of Er. Proclus, who wrote several essays on aspects of the *Republic,* deals only with the equality of men and women among political topics. As Dörrie and Baltes say, we can see from this, "Welche Themen in Platons Staat besonders interessierten: nicht die eigentliche politischen, sondern die wissenschaftlichen und philosophischen" (3:208). Almost no interest was shown in commenting on other more political dialogues. Tarrant (forthcoming) points out that, although Proclus at least mentions the possibility of the *Republic*'s having a politically oriented goal, for later commentators such as Olympiodorus this idea has receded to the point that the phrase *politikē eudaimonia* no longer means "political" or "social" happiness, but refers entirely to the individual conceived of as structured like the state.

[54] In Chapter 2.

[55] Marcus Aurelius *Meditations* 9.29. He urges himself not to hope for "Plato's state" but to pay attention to what he is doing, even if it is trivial. (Or, on an alternative reading, not to regard it as trivial; either way, realistic attention to one's situation is contrasted with concern for utopian schemes.) "For who can change people's beliefs? And without change of beliefs what is there other than the slavery of people who groan and pretend to be convinced?" Unfairly or not, Marcus contrasts the real work of philosophy, which is "simple and modest," with the "arrogant pomposity" (*semnotuphia*) of constructing an ideal state.

as a political work, and as the obvious centerpiece of Plato's thought, derives from Victorian traditions, particularly that of Jowett.[56] Yet we no longer share the Victorians' concern with the book as Plato's "answer" to the "problem" of democracy; the "problem" itself is no longer a live political problem for us. The accepted way of reading the *Republic* as a political work is a good example of how traditions of reading and teaching a work can outlast the assumptions on which they were originally based; the infrastructure decays without its being noticed. In the case of the *Republic,* a return to taking the ancient interpretation of the work seriously results in a striking improvement in our view of Platonism. If we try to jettison the assumptions that the *Republic* is a contribution to political theory, and that it is obviously the most important and central of the dialogues, the natural culmination of a development from the Socratic dialogues, and if we try to restore it to its ancient place—one dialogue among many in which Plato develops an argument about the sufficiency of virtue for happiness—we shall have done a great deal to restore balance and proportion to our study of Plato's thought.[57]

[56] Jowett's idealistic reading of the *Republic* has been by far the most dominant. The crude reaction against the *Republic* on the part of writers such as Crossman and Popper accepts Jowett's picture and simplistically reverses the value given to it; it does not challenge the Victorian reading in any profound way.

[57] The material for this chapter has developed through many versions. I am grateful to audiences at the University of Arizona, the University of Notre Dame, the Center for Hellenic Studies, University College Dublin, Oxford University, Boston University, the University of Michigan, Kenyon College, the University of California at San Diego, and the University of California at Los Angeles. I am particularly grateful for comments from Richard Kraut, Martha Nussbaum, David O'Connor, Christopher Bobonich, Emidio Spinelli, Terence Irwin, and Gail Fine as well as the lecture audience and seminar members at Cornell.

[V]

WHAT USE IS THE FORM OF THE GOOD? ETHICS AND METAPHYSICS IN PLATO

What use is the Form of the Good? This is, of course, a question which Aristotle memorably poses in a passage of the *Nicomachean Ethics*. "It is hard, too, to see how a weaver or a carpenter will be benefitted in regard to his own craft by knowing this 'good itself', or how the man who has viewed the Idea itself will be a better doctor or general thereby."[1]

The natural first response to this is that it is somewhat crass. The Form of the Good, whatever it may be, is not meant to be a practical guide to shoemaking. Rather, what Plato means is that extensive theoretical and abstract study is needed to ensure that practice is done well. In the ideal state, reason, in the form of the virtuous philosophers, rules, and the long passages in which they are described as achieving understanding of the intellectual realm, dominated by the Form of the Good, express Plato's view that virtue is in some way deepened by a true view of the whole of reality. "Plato's Good" was from the start ridiculed for its obscurity, but many have sympathized with what they take to be an idea behind it which is correct in a perhaps less extravagant version: that a correct grasp of morality must be based on a correct grasp of metaphysics. Even if we share Aristotle's feelings about the Form of the Good, we are probably inclined to find it natural that Plato should do something that we see as trying to base ethics on metaphysics. Indeed, this is surely one of the reasons the *Republic* is so often seen as a kind of culmination of Plato's thought, one which provides desired support for claims

---

[1] Aristotle *Nicomachean Ethics* 1097a8−11 (Ross translation, revised by J. L. Ackrill and J. O. Urmson). It is the only part of the criticism in this chapter that seems to be directed at the *Republic* at all closely, since the Form is here taken to be a "paradeigm" for us to look at and so improve our practical skill.

made earlier in the Socratic dialogues. We find, as we have seen, Socrates hold-ing that a good person cannot suffer any harm,[2] that one should never retaliate, even to unjust provocation,[3] and that it is better to suffer wrong than to do it and better, if one does wrong, to be punished than to escape punishment.[4] These are very bold claims; they are likely to strike us as outrageous, even if we find our-selves in sympathy with them. Plato is often read as though there were something incomplete about claims like this, as though his ethical ambitions had outrun his justifications for them, and the *Republic* is seen as Plato's attempt to provide the kind of support such claims require. A bold metaphysical theory like the theory of Forms is what is needed, it is often assumed, to support such a challenge to accepted values.

Perhaps, however, this is a modern way of looking at the matter, one that does not produce the best way of approaching Plato. Once again, ancient ways of look-ing at Plato may help to suggest to us a new perspective that has, at least, a good chance of reflecting the balance of Plato's concerns. Ancient Platonists stress the radical nature of Plato's ethical claims, and they also stress his metaphysics and the theory of Forms. Yet they do not present the former as dependent on the latter, and they do not tell a story of Plato's development according to which Socrates, or early Plato, had exciting ethical ideas which were left hanging but which later Plato then propped up by a metaphysical theory.[5] Before returning to the ancient Platonists, however, it is worth looking at some ways in which the idea that the *Republic*'s metaphysics support its ethical theory turn out to be unsatisfactory.

In the Socratic dialogues Socrates is searching for a special kind of wisdom which will give the person who has it overall knowledge of how best to live her life; this wisdom is identified with virtue, and it is thought of on the model of a skill or expertise, a practical ability to get things right which presupposes an overall understanding of the area and the way it is best handled. He represents

---

[2] *Apology* 41C8–D2.

[3] *Crito* 49C10–11.

[4] *Gorgias* 472D1–E7.

[5] Aristotle tells us that Socrates did not "separate" Forms whereas Plato did (*Meta-physics* 987a32–b10, 1078b12–1079a4, 1086a37–b11), but this is a claim about the meta-physics of Forms, not about Platonic ethics. Aristotle sees two contrasts. One is between Socrates, who was mainly interested in ethics, and Plato, whose interests were broader; the other is between Socrates' tentative attempts at definition and Plato's provision of "separated" Forms as objects for definition. He does not see Plato as propping up a Socratic theory of ethics. There is much one might reasonably query in Aristotle's story of Socrates' relation to Plato. The Socratic dialogues are not best construed as attempts in Socrates' own person to produce definitions of concepts. Aristotle neglects the gener-ally negative nature of Socrates' arguments, which are directed at showing that someone else lacks knowledge of what they are supposed to be expert in.

himself as certain that possession of this skill in living one's life is required for happiness, and thus is the most important thing in one's life; achieving it is the task that all should devote their efforts toward.

The search for virtue as a skill has many aspects; here I mention only two, which are relevant to the issue of ethics and metaphysics. One is, I think, a false trail. The Socratic dialogues are sometimes read as though their main features were the search for so-called Socratic definitions, that is, as answers to the question, "What is . . . courage, a friend, virtue?" and so on. There has been considerable controversy over the question of exactly what form these definitions take, and how the search for definitions relates to the rest of Socrates' methodology. It does appear, however, that there is a link between the search for such accounts of piety, courage, and so on, and Socrates' search for the generalized skill which is virtue. Socrates demands that, just as the expert must have understanding of what his expertise or skill is about, so the courageous person must have understanding of what courage is, and be able to give an account of it; failure in this indicates that the person lacks the relevant virtue, just as it casts doubt on the claims of a craftsperson to have mastery of a craft.[6] Hence we find a demand for a certain kind of theoretical knowledge to give this kind of account, namely accounts of what courage, virtue, and so on are. If, as many have, we see Forms as emerging from this demand, and a new approach to it, we get a fairly direct link between "Socratic" ethics and "Platonic" metaphysics.

But there is an important point here. Even if Forms are seen as emerging as answers to the Socratic "What is X?" question, there is no particular link to the demand in the *ethical* case; the development and "separation" of Forms, whatever it amounts to, applies to the cases of the double and the half just as much as to the good and the bad. Aristotle tells us that Socrates was mainly interested in ethics, and that Plato had broader interests, and he also tells us that Socrates did not "separate" forms and that Plato did; but he conspicuously does *not* tell us that Socrates produced an ethical theory which Plato subsequently backed up by "separated" Forms. A broader theory of Forms might serve to support Socrates' claims about ethics, but it would not support it in any way relevant to ethics.

Second: the *Republic* is certainly a work in which those who use their reasons correctly arrive at certain moral truths, and within his sketch of an ideal state Plato draws one very authoritarian and elitist corollary of this: those who do have moral knowledge are entitled to impose it on the lives of those who do not.[7] This seems to be something new with the *Republic,* and it can easily be as-

---

[6] This intellectual demand on the practitioner of a skill can be found at *Gorgias* 465A, 501A.

[7] If the ideal state is read, as I have suggested, as having the function of a model for the aspirant to virtue to internalize, then the elitist nature of proposals such as these need not trouble us too much, since they need not be read as political proposals which are both

sumed that the philosopher-rulers' authority to do this derives in some way from the work's metaphysical theory: it is because they have struggled out of the depths of the Cave and succeeded in completing the long road to enlightenment and illumination in terms of the Form of the Good that they are entitled to direct the lives of those who cannot do this.

If we look carefully, however, we see that even in the central books what makes the philosophers' pronouncements about value authoritative, and directive for other people, is simply appeal to examples of directive skills, where the expert in a practical matter has a right to be obeyed based precisely on the fact of his expertise. We find the examples of the ship's captain, who has the expertise to sail in the interests of the whole crew, whether they appreciate this or not, and of the doctor, who knows what is best for the patient—again, whether the patient recognizes this or not.[8] It is expertise which grounds the thought that others ought to do as the captain and doctor say, even if they disagree with the particular judgments that the experts make. But this appeal to expertise, especially to the examples of the navigator and doctor, is hardly new; it is an old familiar story from the Socratic dialogues.[9] The authoritarianism of the *Republic's* claim about philosophers' moral knowledge springs not from their intellectual training, nor from grasp of the Form of the Good, but from Socrates' idea that you should do what the expert says.

We can in fact find this authoritarianism in dialogues that otherwise seem far indeed from the elitism of the *Republic's* sketch of the ideal state. In the *Lysis,* for example, there is a short passage in which Socrates elicits from the boy Lysis the position that it is knowledge, construed as understanding or wisdom, which gives one the right to be trusted by others in telling them what to do.[10] Only the person who knows what he is doing, Socrates insists, can produce what benefits or is good for himself and others. And from this fairly commonplace point Socrates develops a powerful thesis about expertise: "As regards matters of which we possess knowledge, everyone . . . will trust them to us and we shall do what we want with them . . . [and] we for our part shall be free in these matters and masters of other people, and those things will be our business, since we shall profit from them. Whereas, as regards matters of which we have no understanding, not only will no-one trust us to do what we please in them, but everyone . . . will do

---

obnoxious and simpleminded. As pointed out in Chapter 4, however, there remains a problem in that the ideal state, structured as it is, does not, as it should for the overall argument, give us a readily acceptable model for morality in society which can then be easily applied to the individual.

[8] *Republic* 389B–C, 488A–489A, 489B–C, 564B.

[9] We find the same examples of experts throughout the Platonic dialogues, chiefly doctors and navigators.

[10] *Lysis* 207D–210E.

their best to thwart us, and we for our part shall be subject to others in those matters, and they will not be our business, since we shall not profit from them."[11]

The idea of exercising expertise on a subject matter with success plays a large role in Plato's conception of the virtuous person's understanding; but one of the points about it which is less stressed, though certainly present, in the Socratic dialogues is that it is not, in itself, sensitive to the distinction between one's own affairs and those of others. If you are successful in running your affairs, why should you not be as successful in running mine? What could the difference be, if what is at stake is expertise? If there are grounds, as we surely think there are, for holding that your success in exercising expertise in your own affairs does not entitle you to run mine, they come from considerations of individual autonomy and choice to which Plato is notoriously indifferent; they are not latent in the idea of exercising skill itself. And so we find it assumed that the expertise which will give you understanding of your own life and the best way to order it will also give you understanding of the best way to order the lives of others. In the *Lovers* we find that the expertise of the just and temperate person is the very same as that of all types of ruler—king, tyrant, statesman, household manager, and master.[12] In the *Theages* and *Alcibiades* Socrates tries to persuade young men to care for the state of their own souls before embarking on politics; he assumes that the virtue he wants them to practice will be exercised in ruling others as well as in their own lives. And in the *Euthydemus* Socrates exhorts a young boy to practice virtue as an expertise which will enable him to appreciate the true value of other things in his life; when the idea reappears later in the dialogue, this expertise has, with no comment, become "the kingly expertise," the skill of a person who rules over others.[13]

Some of this conflation doubtless comes from ordinary conventional beliefs; Plato's Protagoras, for example, says that he teaches excellence in deliberating in the management of one's affairs and those of the city, and other Sophists

---

[11] *Lysis* 210B–C, trans. Donald Watt, in *Plato, Early Socratic Dialogues*, ed. T. J. Saunders (London: Penguin, 1987).

[12] *Lovers* 137A–139A, esp. 138C. The conflation of different kinds of power, that of the lawful statesman and the tyrant, and that of the head of the household and the master of slaves, is less surprising in light of Aristotle's repeated criticism of just this point in the *Politics;* Aristotle insists that political authority is not in fact the same thing as the exercise of power. The conflation of the virtues of temperance and justice is also surprising, but less so if what is in mind is the understanding which is thought of as being what all the virtues essentially are.

[13] *Euthydemus* 278E–282E, 288B–292E. There are interesting passages in Xenophon *Memorabilia* 2.1.17 and 4. 2.11, where Socrates is said to call "the kingly expertise" happiness and to require virtue for it. It is uncertain whether this corresponds to a non-Platonic tradition about Socrates or echoes the passages discussed here.

agree in this characterization.[14] However, it is hardly common sense, and requires Plato's particular stress on expertise as the model for the wisdom that constitutes virtue, to produce the following as an agreed description of Socrates' position:

> Anyone who doesn't know how to use his own lyre obviously doesn't know how to use his neighbour's lyre either, and anyone who doesn't know how to use others' lyres doesn't know how to use his own either. . . . Anyone who doesn't know how to use his mind is better off leaving the mind alone and not living . . . if he really has to live, then it's better for him actually to spend his life as a slave rather than as a free man—to behave like someone handing over the rudder of the ship of his mind to someone else, someone who has learnt to steer human affairs, which is how you often describe political expertise, Socrates, which you also say is the same as expertise in law and morality.[15]

The claim here is one which we find striking when we meet it in the *Republic*, where the most analogous passage comes near the end of the dialogue,[16] after we have been exposed to the philosophers' lengthy abstract training. Here too we find the thought that the person weak in reason should be the slave of the reason of another, since this is best for him. We can now see that the extreme nature of this claim is not new in the *Republic*, and does not derive from that work's specific features. It has been sometimes noticed that the authoritarianism of the *Republic* depends on intuitive appeal to the directive nature of skills; it has been less noticed that we find just the same feature of expertise in other dialogues.

The authority in question thus turns out to be an epistemological authority; it is throughout the authority of the expert, though in the *Republic* this requires a great deal more training and reflection than in the other dialogues, and is also based on grasp of a metaphysical theory which involves extensive claims about the nature of reality. But this claim of authority, and the changing grounds for it, come from Plato's concern with how we can have knowledge of ethical matters, and his changing position on this; it does not come directly from his concern with ethical matters (and thus need indicate no change in this). A concern with epistemological authority is different from a concern with content; the striking enough differences between the *Republic* and the Socratic dialogues are, I have argued, not differences in ethical content, and the elaborate epistemolog-

---

[14] *Protagoras* 318E.

[15] *Cleitophon* 407E–408B, trans. Robin Waterfield, in *Plato, Republic,* World's Classics Series (Oxford: Oxford University Press, 1993), p. 464.

[16] *Republic* 588B–592B, esp. 590C–D.

ical and metaphysical developments of the *Republic* merely give us a different version of the authority of the expert.

Even if we accept this point, however, we might think that it does not exclude the possibility that the *Republic's* elaborate epistemology and metaphysics might also make a difference to the content of the ethical theory in the dialogue. Surely, in view of its prominence in the dialogue, it must make some impact on the content of what the philosophers hold to be true about value?

How, though, could it make a difference? On this issue the *Republic* is extremely sketchy. In the central books of the *Republic* we famously find emphasis on turning away from one approach to finding out the truth toward another way, one which is unfamiliar to most people and involves practice in certain kinds of highly abstract and mathematical thinking. As a result, the philosophers described in the central books have a radically different perspective from that of ordinary people. Plato now demands that virtuous people, to be fully virtuous, need to be philosophers, where this means: to have achieved, by a long and demanding route, knowledge, the conditions for which are now far higher than he elsewhere demands. But does this alter the content of the moral theory that the virtuous person exemplifies and understands? It might seem as though it does, since it is in the central books that we find an important aspect of the virtuous person's understanding: he or she comes to comprehend that virtue is not simply in their own interest, but makes a demand on them, to which they respond, whatever their interests. And in the *Republic* this is presented in the context of the philosophers' education in abstract thinking. But it is nowhere indicated exactly how the account of Forms is to be taken to produce this understanding. And, as we can see from the Stoics, the understanding of virtue that the philosophers achieve could just as well have been achieved given some quite different metaphysical account; for they agree that virtue makes this kind of impersonal demand, but utterly reject Platonic metaphysics and epistemology. This is not to deny all relevance to the theory of Forms, but to suggest that it is unpromising to look in the *Republic* for a direct way in which it has impact on the content of the dialogue's moral theory.

If we look at the ancient Platonists who tell us what Plato's "doctrines" are, we find three points which are interesting here. One is that, seeing Plato's thought as constant overall, not in terms of overall development, they see continuity between the ethical theory of the *Republic* and that of other dialogues which we are more accustomed to see as "earlier." Alcinous, as we have seen, says that Plato holds that virtue is sufficient for happiness throughout the dialogues and especially in the whole *Republic*.[17] Second, he discusses the theory of Forms and sees

---

[17] Alcinous *Handbook,* chap. 27.

it as a prominent part of Plato's metaphysics; but he discusses it in a separate part of the work. Third, he and other Platonists who describe Plato's ideas in Stoic terminology find themselves in agreement with Stoics who, like Antipater, one of the heads of the Stoa, claimed that Plato agreed with them in much of ethics, particularly on the crucial issue of the sufficiency of virtue for happiness. Since the Stoics can hardly have expressed agreement with an ethical theory which they took essentially to depend on a metaphysical view they rejected, we find that we cannot make sense of the ancient reception of the *Republic* unless we also distinguish the content of its ethical theory from its metaphysical claims, and take the former to be independent of the latter.

There might, however, be a further way, consistent with the ancient perspectives, in which the Form of the Good could be relevant to ethics, and one springing from the point stressed earlier, that the epistemological authority is that of the expert: the metaphysics might ground the ethics in the way that theory grounds a skill or expertise. After all, Plato thinks of virtue as being itself a kind of skill, and he also insists that the person with the skill must have understanding of what the skill is about and what she is doing.[18] In the *Republic* acquiring this understanding has become demanding and theoretical. Plato now insists that truly to have the expertise of the virtuous, one must spend years on abstract study, finally achieving insight into an ambitious metaphysical scheme. This can readily be seen as an extension of the original claim that somebody with a skill must have rational insight into how her skill works and what its basis is; in the *Republic* Plato has merely raised the level for what is required for the theoretical component of a skill.

One problem here is that in the *Republic* we find not an actual theory, but rather a sketch of the kind of form a theory would have. Socrates stresses at great length the point that he is not in a position to produce anything amounting to an expert account; he merely has feeble and inadequate beliefs about it.[19] So there is something at least misleading about the idea that in the *Republic* we find a metaphysical theory which grounds ethical practice in the way that a skill may have theoretical grounding; for the ethical theory is presented in a perfectly confident way, a way moreover which structures the entire work, whereas the metaphysical theory is hinted at in the broadest and most tentative terms. It might be responded that the theory does not have to be filled out if Plato intends it only to suggest certain connections between moral and metaphysical theory. But the skimpiness of the presentation undermines any confidence in the connections, as well as in the metaphysical theory itself.

[18] We find this also in the *Gorgias* (465A, 501A).
[19] *Republic* 506B–507A.

Furthermore, although the idea that Forms provide a theoretical grounding for the practical abilities of the virtuous person seems like a reasonable extension of the idea that someone with a skill must be able to give a rational account of the basis of that skill, we find a major complication in the fact that, in the central books, the perspective of the truly virtuous person is not just different from that of ordinary people, but fiercely at odds with it. This is the idea that emerges in the repeated insistence that the journey out of the Cave involves tearing oneself away from what attaches one to the empirical world, and the reiterated stress on the idea that the world of everyday experience is trashy and unworthy of serious attention. The *Republic* is where we find some of Plato's most strongly worded dismissals of the ordinary person's viewpoint. As a perspective, it is no more worth taking seriously as a guide to truth than the reports of prisoners on the shadow-puppet show in the Cave. The person who has escaped this and achieved enlightenment condemns his former perspective in every way; when he has to communicate with the unenlightened, he provokes hostility from them.[20] There could hardly be a more vivid way of making Plato's point that a true view of value, and of the importance of morality, is completely at variance with what most people think.

Familiar as this point is, we find a problem in the fact that Plato continues to think of the virtuous person as an expert with a skill, and to represent his claim to the deference of others as just the general claim of the expert to know better than the amateur what is in everyone's interest. For we would not expect the expert who achieves theoretical grounding of her skill to turn around and dismiss all intuitive practice of the skill as trash and rubbish.

There is an obvious response, however: Why not? The expert's view, when he has understood the grounding theory, may well conflict with and devalue that of the ordinary person. The captain of the ship, for example, has knowledge of the seasons, winds, stars, and so on, although his directives are rejected by the mutinous crew, who refuse to believe that there is such an expertise.[21] This point does not depend on Forms, or on any particular metaphysical theory. The amateurs who reject the claims of the expert, and refuse to believe in his expertise, can be found already in the *Gorgias,* where the doctor's skill is rejected by those who do not want to follow his prescriptions.[22] What happens in the central books of the *Republic* is just another case of this: those who get out of the Cave and make the ascent to intellectual understanding of the Forms find that this

---

[20] *Republic* 515C–517A.

[21] *Republic* 488A–489A.

[22] *Gorgias* 521D–522C; the comparison with Socrates' practice of philosophy is explicit.

study is so much more worthwhile than attention to practical matters that they would, left to themselves, prefer to continue in it, and notoriously do not want to leave the study of Forms to take part in the actual running of their own and others' lives; this is just what happens when the theoretical grounding of a skill pulls away from what is intuitively supposed about the practice of that skill.

But the philosophers find that they have become alienated not just from the practice of others but from their own. Surely there is in fact something odd if the studies enabling you to understand the grounds of a skill are guaranteed to inhibit you from exercising that skill. On this view, virtue turns out to be self-undermining: understanding its basis turns you against practicing it. The analogue would be the captain who finds the study of the stars so gripping that he regards steering the ship by them as a tedious necessity, or the doctor who gets so attracted to the abstract study of pharmacology that he hates having to spend time actually writing prescriptions for patients.

Still, we may say, this happens; perhaps it is surprising, but there is nothing paradoxical, or fundamentally objectionable, in the idea that a skill might be self-undermining in this way, interest in its theoretical base pulling against devotion to its practice. But here we come up against a problem that is acute for the *Republic*. If we read the central books in a way that takes the political aspects literally, we get a picture of one set of people who would rather theorize than run the lives of another set of people. But the ideal state is meant to be a model of virtue in the individual; whether it is only that or not, we have to make some sense of construing the philosophers' alienation from practice in terms of what goes on within one individual. And here we surely do find something odd and problematic: reflecting on the theoretical basis of your own virtue turns out to inhibit you from practicing it. The more successfully I reflect on why I am virtuous, the less inclined I am actually to act virtuously. This conception of virtue seems to make it into a necessarily self-undermining skill, and the problem clearly lies in the account of the theoretical grounding which identifies it as one which, when understood, draws you away from the practice it grounds. If, then, the theory of Forms is taken to be a theoretical grounding for virtue as a skill, then it seems to be the wrong kind of grounding, and Plato seems to have made a mistake. (At least, he seems to have made a mistake in thinking that Forms, and the kind of desire for studying them which they call forth, could form a suitable basis for virtue as a practical skill; the philosopher as practically virtuous and the philosopher as passionate student of the abstract and transcendent are conceptions which pull apart, and do not pull together.)

This is, we should note, not the same problem as the problem which is traditionally called "the return to the Cave." That is a problem of why I should be moral when this involves benefiting others at what appears to be my expense, when morality was supposed to be shown to benefit me. The brief answer to this is that in the central books the virtuous come to understand that the demands of virtue go beyond their own self-interest narrowly conceived, and thus they do what morality requires straightforwardly because they are moral people, without reference to whose interest is served.[23] The present problem concerns not Plato's ethical claims but rather his emphasis on the worth and joys of abstract thinking, which makes *any* return to actual practice seem worthless by comparison, something that the would-be contemplator would have to be forced to do.

So far, the theory of Forms provides neither authority nor content for the ethical theory of the *Republic,* and, if it is treated as the theoretical grounding for virtue as a skill, it has the famous undesirable result of undermining the practice of the skill. Our lack of success so far may, however, not be a good reason for joining Aristotle's view that the Form of the Good is useless. After all, at some points Plato developed a quite different model from the *Republic's* of a metaphysical background to ethics, one which, unlike it, was taken up in the mainstream of ancient ethical thought. Looking at this alternative model may help us to a more sympathetic and realistic understanding, in ancient terms, of the role of the Form of the Good.

In the *Gorgias* one theme that Socrates develops is the need for an overall ordering of the desires in one's life, if one is to lead a life that can be happy. Against Callicles, who defends the view that what matters is intense gratification of desires regardless of their nature or source, Socrates argues that a good life requires rational planning overall, and that this implies organizing and ordering desires and the pleasure that comes from fulfilling them. This fits in with the idea that virtue, as a directive kind of wisdom, is a skill, since skill, he emphasizes, imposes form on materials and thus produces an ordered, rationally comprehensible object.[24] Thus virtue will be the skill which organizes a human life in a rational way. Then he goes beyond the practical human realm to situate the ordered, happy human life in a larger context. It is order and organization that hold together the whole universe, heaven and earth, gods and men—an opinion ascribed to "wise men," presumably previous philosophers. This is what makes the universe a *kosmos* or ordered whole, rather than a mess. Socrates adds, in a not very serious tone, the point that Callicles defends unrestrained desire-satisfaction because he has neglected geometry, the expertise of human and cosmic proportion.[25]

Here we find the analogy of microcosm and macrocosm, of individual mind

---

[23] *Republic* 520D–E.
[24] *Gorgias* 503D–504E.
[25] *Gorgias* 507D–508A.

and cosmic order. Reason here does not put us in touch with a separate intellectual realm like Forms; rather, by the workings of our own reason, we can see reason at work on a bigger scale in the world, ordering the universe as a whole. And this provides a model for us; we are to be impressed by the large-scale workings of reason and to be encouraged by this to develop further our own reason and its effect in organizing our individual lives. Socrates puts the view forward here as that held by other philosophers, as he does also when it recurs in the *Philebus*,[26] though he does not represent tradition alone as a good reason for accepting it, and appears to find it intuitively appealing.

The *Philebus* develops the idea that the reason in us is derivative from cosmic reason, just as the element fire in us is produced and directed by the element fire in the cosmos. Again, this is not argued for but accepted as part of shared ideas, and it gives a basis for the idea that cosmic reason gives us an ideal or pattern. The workings of reason in the universe, that is, give us a better idea of what reason is capable of than the comparatively puny workings of our own individual reasons. By appreciating and admiring rationality on a large scale, we are to be moved to make ourselves ever more rational, since this is the way in which individuals can best fit into, and further, cosmic rationality. Plato leaves it vague and undetermined just how exactly we are to be moved by the spectacle of reason in the universe to order our own lives. Presumably, he takes the whole set of ideas here to be intuitive, and not to need much further spelling out.[27]

The Stoics were the philosophers of antiquity who developed furthest the idea that cosmic reason orders the world in ways analogous to the way our reason orders our lives, and also the idea that we should see ourselves, insofar as we are rational, as parts of a rational whole. But the idea had some appeal to all philosophers other than the Epicureans; Plato's appeal to cosmic reason as a background to the virtuous ordering of our lives was far more in the ancient mainstream than his appeal to the Form of the Good.[28]

In neither the *Gorgias* nor the *Philebus* does Plato say *how* cosmic reason could possibly ground or justify conclusions about our own reason (except for the

[26] *Philebus* 22C, 28D–31B, esp. 28D–29A. It is generally thought that the Pythagoreans are the thinkers that Plato mainly has in mind, but evidence is lacking. Cf. 63C–64A.

[27] At *Timaeus* 90B–D we find the picture of improving the motions of our thought by literally bringing them into conformity with the cosmic revolutions, which we replicate in our heads. It is hard to know how seriously Plato takes the detail of this.

[28] See DeFilippo and Mitsis 1994, which stresses the continuity perceived in the ancient tradition between Socrates (especially in the Xenophontic tradition; cf. *Memorabilia* 1.4) and the Stoics on the role of cosmic rationality seen as a producer of divine commands. They emphasize Cicero *De natura deorum* 2.5.13–8.22 and Sextus Empiricus *Adversus mathematicos* 9.92 ff., where this connection is made.

thought that in both macro- and microcosm reason should be dominant, rather than just another ingredient). Nor do we get any indication how we could be supposed to get to our conceptions of virtue and happiness; it is hard to see how we are supposed even to begin to do this. Clearly, one thing we are not supposed to do is to fill in the gap with a specific set of principles supposedly guaranteeing a reflection on earth of the cosmic harmony of the heavens. This is an idea to which many have been tempted, but if cosmic rationality is supposed to guarantee victory for the good among us, the results can hardly be called encouraging. We find Sextus Empiricus later presenting as a standard opposition of arguments, "Against those who seek to establish that there is Providence from the orderliness of the heavenly bodies, we oppose the view that often the good do badly while the bad do well, and conclude from this that there is no Providence." [29] Plato clearly does not have such a crude direct relationship in mind. Rather, he gives us the sketch of a background of cosmic reason and order and the general idea that our reason functions in some way like it. In fact, this may direct us to a passage in the *Republic*[30] where the philosopher is said to be attracted to, and to make himself as like as possible to, the divine and orderly realm revealed by philosophical thought. If one accepts the idea that the Form of the Good, which is mysteriously "beyond being," is not itself a Form, or a mega-Form, but is better conceived of as the ordered structure of the realm of Forms,[31] then the *Republic* contains a parallel to the idea of the *Gorgias* and *Philebus* that we should by exercise of rational thought in some way emulate the larger-scale rationality in the cosmos which philosophical thinking reveals. This is, I think, the best way to understand the role of the Form of the Good—as rational structure on a cosmic scale which our own reason is to be moved to emulate.

So far we have found vagueness and lack of specificity in Plato as to the connection of metaphysical background to ethical theory. Cosmic reason forms a background to virtue, but there is no way that we can derive eudaimonistic concepts from cosmic reason, so that the metaphysics does not directly support the ethics. Plato clearly does not see this as a worry, nor do the ancient Platonists, and if we look at their handling of the matter, we can perhaps see how much of our own dissatisfaction, if we feel any, is spurious, the product of modern preoccupations which lack resonance in the ancient world.

We find the ancient Platonists assuming, as a matter of course, that Plato's philosophy should be approached in terms of the three parts of philosophy: physics,

---

[29] Sextus Empiricus *Outlines of Scepticism* 1.32, trans. Julia Annas and Jonathan Barnes (Cambridge: Cambridge University Press, 1994).

[30] *Republic* 500B–D.

[31] Cf. the suggestions of Irwin 1995, pp. 272–73.

ethics, and logic. Indeed, there is a tradition that this goes back explicitly to Xenocrates, Plato's second successor in the Academy, and it is possible that Xenocrates interpreted Plato's work in these terms. Sextus Empiricus carefully tells us that Plato is "potentially the leader" of those who divide philosophy up this way, since he had plenty to say in all these areas, but explicit adherence to it is found in Xenocrates.[32] However this may be, it is the Stoics who are most prominently associated with the idea, and explicitly use it as a model for the structure of their philosophy. Different Stoics used different metaphors for the relationship of the three parts, and had diverse views about the best pedagogical order for teaching,[33] but there was no dispute about philosophy's being tripartite, a whole made up of distinct but interrelated parts.[34]

It is interesting, however, that later Platonists, who started to interpret Plato as holding doctrines, take up enthusiastically the idea that Plato's philosophy is tripartite, and should be approached via the division of physics, ethics, and logic— usually called just that, though at least one author find names for them that sound more Platonic.[35] We find this claim about Plato's philosophy in a number of authors, Platonists and others, who agree that Plato should be interpreted doctrinally.[36] Nor is this simply the unreflective following of philosophical fashion. It seems clear that ancient Platonists found it peculiarly appropriate to read Plato this way, since Plato is seen as being the first person to do philosophy in a way which covers a wide area but can be divided into three different areas of differing methodologies and subjects. Atticus, with characteristically violent language, says that Plato was the first to gather together the parts of philosophy, which had hitherto been torn apart and scattered like the limbs of Pentheus.

---

[32] Sextus Empiricus *Adversus mathematicos* 7.16. Plato holds the view *dunamei,* but Xenocrates *rhētotata,* i.e., in so many words. Sextus adds that the Peripatetics and Stoics also hold it explicitly.

[33] See Diogenes Laertius 7.139–41, Sextus Empiricus *Adversus mathematicos* 7.16–19.

[34] See Ierodiakonou 1993.

[35] Alcinous, in chap. 3 of his *Handbook,* calls them *theoretikē, praktikē,* and *dialektikē* (the understood noun in all cases being *gnōsis*).

[36] Atticus frag. 1 des Places; Apuleius *De Platone* 1.3; Diogenes Laertius 3.56; Aristocles ap. Eusebius *Preparation for the Gospel* 11.3; Augustine *City of God* 8.1–4; Alcinous *Handbook,* chap. 3; Sextus Empiricus *Adversus mathematicos* 7.16 ff.; Cicero *Varro* 19; Hippolytus *Refutation* 1.18 (p. 567 Diels); Eudorus ap. Arius Didymus in Stobaeus *Eclogae* 2.42.11–13 (he is a Platonist, but does not ascribe the division explicitly to Plato). For these and other passages, and discussion, see Dörrie and Baltes 1990–96, vol. 4. Boyancé (1971) argues that Platonists who list the parts in the order of physics, ethics, logic are following the order used by Philo of Larisa, whereas those who use the order of ethics, physics, logic are using that introduced by Antiochus of Ascalon; but the nature of our sources makes it difficult to come to such precise conclusions.

Plato, he says, made a complete living creature out of philosophy (something that did not, of course, happen in the Pentheus myth).[37] Atticus mentions some previous philosophers who had devoted themselves to the single parts of philosophy, but does not mention Socrates.[38] Augustine contrasts Socrates, who left a legacy which could be interpreted in radically different ways by the different "Socratic schools"—ascetic, hedonistic, skeptical, dogmatic—with Plato, who did what Augustine clearly finds preferable, namely uniting the different branches of philosophy into a system.[39]

One writer, Aristocles, not a Platonist but rather a Peripatetic writing a history of philosophy, makes a further interesting point. In contrast to the legacy of Socrates, he says, which split up, Plato both covered all the major areas of philosophy and divided them into three. Aristocles compares Plato to a doctor who cannot adequately treat a part of the body without treating the whole, telling an apocryphal story (which he doesn't believe, but seems to find *ben trovato*) of Socrates being rebuked by an Indian for trying to understand humans without also trying to understand the universe. However, Aristocles sees this as Plato's reason for *dividing* philosophy into physics, ethics, and logic: studying the part in the context of the whole also requires studying the part in its own right. Once you take on the job of studying the whole of philosophy, you need to divide it up into the appropriate parts. The idea seems to be that accepting an ambitious view of the scope of philosophy also requires taking the parts one at a time.[40]

What is interesting about the enthusiastic Platonist use of what may originally (pace Xenocrates) have been a Stoic way of looking at philosophy is that it brings with it a characteristic position about the structure of philosophy. The tripartite

---

[37] Atticus frag. 1 des Places.

[38] Socrates usually figures as the predecessor whose divided legacy contrasts with Plato's combination of philosophically wide scope and division of the subject into parts. One text (pseudo-Galen *Plac. Phil.* 1, *Doxographi Graeci* 597.2–598.2) claims that philosophy became tripartite "through Socrates" and his interests, but even this does not claim that this was Socrates' explicit view, and another passage (Galen *De Placitis Hippocratis et Platonis* 5.8.25–33 de Lacy) points out that all Socrates' followers took him to reject physics and logic (Plato, for example, in giving his physical exposition not to Socrates but to Timaeus, and dialectic to Parmenides and Zeno).

[39] Augustine *City of God* 8.1–4. Augustine claims that Plato also united theoretical and practical philosophy, consistently with adopting the threefold division. Dörrie and Baltes point out (1990–96, 4:225–31) that this matter is more complex. Calcidius in his Commentary on the *Timaeus* (269.20–270.25 Waszink) treats theoretical philosophy as identified with physics and practical with ethics, leaving out logic because of accepting the (Peripatetic) idea that it is not a part of philosophy in its own right but a tool for doing philosophy. Alcinous keeps the issue of theoretical and practical philosophy in a separate chapter from that on the three parts of philosophy.

[40] Aristocles ap. Eusebius *Preparation for the Gospel* 11.3.1–9.

view is non-foundationalist; no part has primacy in that it forms the basis for the others, and there is no set hierarchy of the parts. Just this is what makes the Stoic tripartite view distinctive.[41] The metaphors the Stoics use for philosophy bring out the idea that the parts are interdependent; the unity of the whole depends equally on the contribution of all the separate and very different parts. Philosophy is a living being, logic being the skeleton and muscles, ethics the flesh and blood, and physics the soul. (Or physics is the flesh and blood, and ethics the soul.) Or: Philosophy is an egg, logic being the shell, ethics the white, and physics the yolk. Or: Philosophy is an orchard, logic being the wall, physics the trees, and ethics the fruit.[42] Obviously, there is a certain amount of arbitrariness as to which part of philosophy is identified with which part of an egg, or an animal, or whatever. What is important is to get across the idea that, in their distinctively different ways, the different parts of philosophy are mutually interdependent. The yolk, white, and shell of an egg don't form a hierarchy, but they do need to hold together in a distinctive and mutually interdependent way, or you no longer have an egg. Similarly with a living thing, whose parts are *all* necessary in a mutually interdependent way to its continued function as a living thing.

Some Platonists explicitly welcomed this feature of the tripartite division of philosophy. Apuleius[43] says that Plato tried to bring the three parts of philosophy together so that the needed parts would not only not conflict, but even help one another with *mutual* aid, forming an organic whole as of what is brought to birth.[44] The latter point recalls Atticus's insistence that Plato made philosophy into a single living thing.

It is important that this model is non-hierarchical, as this excludes some views of the relation of metaphysics to ethics and allows and encourages others. On this view, ethics cannot depend on metaphysics for its content, or it would not be a distinct part. To attempt to derive ethical conclusions from metaphysical

[41] As is pointed out by Hadot 1979. Hadot himself has reservations about the adoption of this way of looking at philosophy by the imperial-period Platonists; he thinks that "Platonic dialectic" points toward a more hierarchical conception of philosophy.

[42] The metaphors can be found at Diogenes Laertius 7.40. The alternative view about the correspondence with a living thing is ascribed to Posidonius at Sextus Empiricus *Adversus mathematicos* 7.19.

[43] Apuleius *De Platone* 1.3.

[44] Plato, according to Apuleius, wrote "so as to be the first to link philosophy up as tripartite, and to show that its parts, which are reciprocally necessary, not merely do not conflict among themselves but even help one another with mutual aid. For although it was from different workshops that these parts of philosophy were taken by him (philosophy of nature from the Pythagoreans, logic from the Eleatics, and moral philosophy right from the source of Socrates), he produced a single thing from them all, like a living thing he had given birth to himself." The mixture of metaphors between workshop and birth is remarkable.

premises would be like trying to derive conclusions in logic from metaphysical premises; it would be to confuse two distinct philosophical tasks. Ethics has to be developed on its own, as logic does, and not confused with other things. Ultimately, however, ethics and logic have both to be seen in the context of metaphysics, in a way in which all parts hang together. Equally, of course, metaphysics, although it is developed on its own, has ultimately to be seen in the context of ethics.[45]

On this picture, ethics *as a whole* is better understood when we have also done metaphysics. We will grasp our own ethical nature better when we see it in the context of the nature of the world as a whole; an understanding of one area delivers to us a better understanding of the other. We will, for example, understand human rationality better if we see it not as an isolated ethical phenomenon comprehensible only in our own lives, but as an example of something visible on a bigger scale, in the regularities of the world and of the heavenly bodies. By having our understanding of rationality expanded in this way, we can come to be inspired to become more rational ourselves. We have not been given cosmic premises which mysteriously direct us to act in one way rather than another; rather, we have been given a picture of ourselves as rational beings in a universe where rationality is dominant, and this alters our conception of ourselves by deepening it and putting it in context. Cicero gives us a clear example of this in his exposition of Stoic ethics;[46] he concludes by pointing out that once you have grasped ethics, you then need logic, to make your grip on the truth secure by good argument, and also physics, to enable you to see ethics and human nature in the context of the nature of the cosmos. This leads him to appreciation of the unity of such a system.

Is such a picture ever explicit in Plato? It is certainly not explicit as a point of theory. But we have seen how it gives us the right picture for what would otherwise be a very puzzling relationship in the dialogues between ethics and metaphysics. And it is certainly supported by *Laws* book 10, a passage where the relation of ethics to metaphysical beliefs comes to the fore.

In this book of the *Laws* the Athenian worries that even the rightly educated citizens of Magnesia might find their ethical views destabilized by their losing confidence in traditional beliefs about the gods, based on religious practice.[47]

---

[45] For the Stoics, see Cooper 1995 and Annas 1995.

[46] *De finibus* 3; the important passage is at 72–74.

[47] Religious practice is stressed at 887C–888A. It is rather odd that Plato here seems confident that traditional religious practice will produce beliefs about the gods which will underpin morality; in the *Republic* he is notably hostile to popular beliefs about the gods. Even in the *Laws* he mentions theogonies (such as those of Hesiod, presumably) as dangerous, presumably because they contain stories such as that of the castration of Ouranos (cf. 888C–D); yet these seem to form a part of popular beliefs about religion.

The Athenian thinks that these should be enough for people to rely on to feel confident in their ethical beliefs; the picture of the world thus presented is one that should produce stable and co1. 2ct ethical beliefs, and he is angry and impatient with people for whom this does not suffice.[48] He allows, however, that once people are exposed to theories, such as those of the Sophists, which undermine traditional beliefs,[49] these are weakened or destroyed, and it is then no good merely to threaten people into conformity; once reflection destroys traditional belief, reflection has to be met on its own terms.[50] Traditional religious beliefs contain an implicit metaphysical view about the world; when this is destroyed, it has to be replaced by an explicit metaphysical view which adequately answers the questions that reflection has raised.

Thus, the Athenian produces complex arguments to prove to his satisfaction the truth of three claims: that the gods exist, that they care for humans, and that they cannot be bribed by humans. What is notable about the conclusions of these arguments is that what is established is nothing like traditional beliefs on the matter. The god whose existence is proved is cosmic reason governing the universe, not the Olympian deities. And the gods are proved to care for humans by an argument that shows that cosmic reason cares for the entire universe and thus for every part of it; the person who denies this is childishly insisting on their own point of view rather than allowing for the perspective of the whole. The traditional implicit metaphysics is not shored up, or restated; it is wholly replaced by a quite different way of looking at matters. This answers to the point that reflection has to be met in its own terms, but it means that the old questions are now given entirely different answers. The same role is fulfilled by very different kinds of belief.

There are several important implications of this replacement of traditional by rational beliefs about the gods. First, ethical beliefs clearly cannot be derived from the metaphysical background, since the person has to have the ethical beliefs already before needing the metaphysics. In fact, Plato stresses that such a

---

Presumably, Plato is relying on education in Magnesia to have purified popular religious beliefs. It is unclear whether Plato thinks that grounds for believing in the gods which Cleinias mentions at 886A–B, such as the regularity of the cosmos and the ubiquity of religious belief, are part of popular religion or not.

[48] 887C, 888A.

[49] Plato throws together a lot of ideas which do not in fact hang together particularly closely: materialist account of the universe, the position that morality exists "by convention," the position that morality is not worthy of respect by an intelligent and strong person. Perhaps Plato is too impatient to sort out all these very different ideas; at any rate, he holds that they all tend to destroy traditional beliefs in the gods, which is what he is interested in.

[50] 890B–C.

person may have nothing wrong with their ethical beliefs.[51] Nor can the rational metaphysical beliefs in any obvious sense justify or ground the ethical beliefs, since whatever it is they contribute was previously contributed by the implicit metaphysics of traditional religious beliefs. And, since Plato stresses that it would be preferable if people were willing to stick with these and not be led astray by Sophists in the first place, there is no necessity for people to move from traditional to rational beliefs in order to have a stabilizing background for their ethical beliefs.

What both the traditional and the rational beliefs do is clearly to provide a context which makes sense of ethics and thus renders the person's ethical beliefs more stable and reliable. This function is performed for the unintellectual by the implicit traditional metaphysics of religious belief, and for the more intellectual by the arguments establishing the existence of divine cosmic reason and its organization of the world.[52]

Plato values the stability that this background can give to ethical beliefs—so much so as to introduce, later in the book, his notorious penalties for "heretics" who would deny it. The important point here, though, is that he clearly regards it as being different from ethical education itself. You can have the right views on ethics and still go wrong if these are destabilized by argument about something else; and your views can be restabilized by argument which presents you with a new context for your ethical beliefs.

Admittedly, the Laws is special in that it envisages a division of intellectual labor. There are those who, like the Athenian, have access to the intellectual arguments needed to establish the new rational metaphysics; and there are those who, like the citizens of Magnesia and the Athenian's own interlocutors, are satisfied with traditional beliefs and so do not need to bother their heads with hard argument.[53] In other dialogues Plato is less ready to assume that for some people only part of what philosophy can do for them will be required. But the example of Laws 10 indicates clearly that for Plato ethics and metaphysics are what were later called distinct parts of philosophy, even where they do not turn up in different people.

The picture that we have got from the dialogues, then, is that metaphysics, in one or another form, provides a context for ethics, which makes overall sense of

[51] 899D–900C.

[52] The role envisaged here for metaphysics is recognizably like that envisaged by Cicero for Stoic ethics (above, p. 112); even the way the Stoics allegorized traditional religion suggests that they thought that, for the unintellectual, something like the same role could be played by a (suitably purified) version of traditional religion.

[53] Cf. the excessive caution the Athenian shows in presenting the rational argument to these unintellectual people (892D–893B).

it. Ethics is a distinct part developed with a cluster of eudaimonistic concepts which are independent of metaphysical concepts. Without metaphysics, though, a person's grasp of ethics is isolated, and may not be stable, just as it is also frailer without the help of logic, for the person is then exposed to the arguments of opponents without the training that would enable him to defend himself. Ethics, metaphysics, and logic relate as parts within philosophy as a whole; to think that ethical conclusions can be obtained from metaphysical premises is thus to be in a muddle about what ethics and metaphysics are.

Suppose you are a Platonist, holding that virtue is sufficient for happiness, and that a Platonic metaphysics of Forms is correct. You then begin to have metaphysical doubts about Forms, argue with Stoics, and eventually come to accept Stoic metaphysics: there are no such things as Platonic Forms, and the whole Platonic metaphysical dualism is deeply mistaken. What exist are physical bodies in causal interaction. (I leave aside problematic Stoic metaphysical items for the sake of simplicity.) What impact does this have on your ethical views? The Stoics also believed all along that virtue is sufficient for happiness, and for very similar kinds of reason to the Platonists: the value of virtue is different in kind from that of conventional goods, and eudaimonistic considerations press us to the conclusion that virtue is sufficient for happiness. No change in your ethical views therefore seems called for by a radical change in metaphysical views. Even if you take over Stoic ethical terminology, this will be for reasons deriving from ethics and not from thoughts about Forms or causal interaction. Hence, presumably, the willingness of some Stoics to allow that they agreed with Plato in ethics, while differing strongly in metaphysics.

It could be argued that although Platonists and Stoics differ as dualists and physicalists, there are still a lot of similarities between their metaphysical views: both believe in a teleologically ordered universe organized by cosmic reason. But, although this is true, this is also manifestly not the reason why they can agree so extensively in ethics. That comes from their convergence in discussions framed in eudaimonistic terms. Neither the agreements nor the disagreements in metaphysics affect their agreement that virtue has a value different in kind from that of the conventional goods.

To return to the Form of the Good, is Aristotle basically right, then, in thinking it of no practical use? As I have already indicated, we have got into the habit of reading the *Republic* in isolation, and it is easy to get into the habit of thinking that the large variety of topics discussed there must hang closely together, to a degree which can obscure for us the continuity of some concerns with those of other dialogues. If we think of the *Republic* as an indivisible synthesis of ethics, politics, and metaphysics, we may miss the continuity of its ethical theory with that of Socratic dialogues such as the *Apology, Crito,* and *Gorgias.* The ancient

Platonists did not do this, for they dealt with the different aspects of the dialogue separately, discussing Forms under metaphysics and the ethical theory under ethics. Doing this is just applying their standard philosophical method: to understand the whole, we first have to deal separately with the parts. They do not worry about Aristotle's question, because they read the dialogue differently. For them, defensible accounts of Plato's ethics and metaphysics will not muddle the two together, just because in the *Republic* the Form of the Good has a prominent role. A dialogue should be read as a whole, but we should not bring a confused methodology to its interpretation. If we reflect on our own practice, we can see that it is not very far from this; where we depart from it (for example, in the tendency to assume that ethics must depend essentially on metaphysics), this is because of projecting modern concerns on to ancient approaches.

Moreover, we can see why Plato was less worried than we might expect by the point that studying Forms can tempt you away from the practice of virtue. For virtue does not have to be self-undermining, as it would be if the ethics *depended* on the very metaphysics which draws away your interest. We are left with the much smaller problem that in the *Republic* metaphysics competes with ethics for our interest, in a way which is not true of the *Philebus,* say. And even this point can be exaggerated.

The ancient way of reading Plato in terms of the three parts of philosophy may seem uncongenial if we bear in mind the dialogue form and the skill with which Plato uses it. But such accounts of Plato need not be seen as in competition with the philosophical purpose of the dialogue form, that of detaching the author from the argument and directing our attention to the need for us to make the ideas our own by arguing for and against them. It is, or at least can be, a complementary activity. Philosophers from the ancient world on have both read the dialogues, appreciating the merits of the dialogue form, and produced their own philosophical accounts and arguments about the ideas which the dialogues contain. Further, this particular philosophical activity can guard us against some dangers, such as that of focusing too much on one dialogue, for example the *Republic,* and also of reading into it anachronistic and inappropriate demands, such as the demand that ethics be founded, in a hierarchical way, on something else.

[VI]

HUMANS AND BEASTS: MORAL
THEORY AND MORAL PSYCHOLOGY

The dialogues we group as "Socratic" and are nowadays generally considered to
be "early" have some striking features in common—unsurprisingly, since they
consider problems of the same general form. One of these is their moral psychology, the view they take on the inner nature of the virtuous person or, as Plato
more frequently puts it, the virtuous soul. From these dialogues we get the idea
that virtue is to be identified with a certain kind of knowledge. Ordinarily, we
think of a virtue as being identified by certain characteristics of behavior, and also
by the types of inclination that the virtuous person characteristically has to deal
with (positively or negatively) in order to become virtuous. Courage, for example, is typically thought of as paradigmatically displayed in war or combat,
and as requiring the agent to fight against fears and temptations to avoid danger.

In dialogues such as the *Laches* and the *Meno* we find Socrates rejecting the
idea that a virtue should be identified by a characteristic pattern of behavior; what
he is looking for is the inner state of the person, which explains why all these
different ways of acting are united as exemplifications of the virtue in question.
This inner state is identified with knowledge, the state ideally achieved by the
person's reasoning part. More surprisingly, the non-rational aspects of virtue appear to drop out. This second point is less intuitively understandable than the
first. It is clear on reflection that a description of the things that a brave person
does will not give us insight into bravery until we examine the ways these might
be unified. And we can see why virtue might require knowledge: the virtuous
person needs to understand what it is that she is doing. But why should the inner aspects of virtue that are not cognitive drop out? We do not find an argument for neglecting them, at least not one which addresses itself to the relevant
psychological matters. In the *Meno* Socrates argues for identifying virtue with

knowledge, but not on psychological grounds; he argues that virtue must always benefit us, and the virtues as ordinarily conceived do not always do that unless directed by knowledge; thus it is the knowledge element of them which really is the virtue.[1] The non-rational aspects of virtue here appear to be demoted to the role of health or wealth, something that virtue proper makes use of, rather than virtue itself. We probably feel that an important issue has been left unaddressed. The feelings of fear that the brave person has to overcome are not like health or wealth, things that the understanding has to cope with because circumstances happen to have put them in the way.

The resulting view is often called intellectualist, as are its corollaries. If a virtue is properly to be identified with the agent's knowledge, then we seem to have lost what distinguishes the different virtues, and to be left only with what they share; knowledge when displayed in circumstances of danger is courage, in circumstances of temptation is temperance, and so on, and the virtues simply are virtue, which is a kind of knowledge. Just what form this unification takes—whether of distinct virtues which are reciprocal, so that if you have one you have them all, or unity proper, there being no basis to distinguish different virtues—is explored, without decisive result, in the *Protagoras*.[2] Further, if virtue is constituted by knowledge, then wrongdoing and wickedness emerge as a kind of ignorance or misguidedness, and so as involuntary; they are like making a mistake rather than knowingly choosing the wrong course. And weakness of will, or *akrasia,* comes to look problematic. How can the agent on one occasion go against the knowledge that she has? The *Protagoras* again explores the idea that knowledge could be overcome and "dragged around" by things like desire, love, or pleasure, and concludes, though problematically, that this is not possible; knowledge, where present, must rule, and weakness of will has to be explained in some other way.[3]

In the *Republic,* however, we find a long and famous argument which starts from conflicts in the agent's soul, and concludes from the nature of these conflicts that the soul has three distinct "parts," rational, spirited, and desiring. This argument appears to endorse the thought that parts of the soul other than reason not only exist alongside it but can rebel against it. These parts are richly char-

---

[1] *Meno* 87c–89a.

[2] The *Protagoras* seems to have been influential with the Stoics in their consideration of virtue. See Schofield 1984.

[3] *Protagoras* 352A–357E. The argument is problematic because based on a form of hedonism which Socrates seems to be adopting for the sake of the argument, and which is not consistent with the views he puts forward on pleasure and reason elsewhere. See Appendix.

acterized and distinguished not just from reason but from each other. Moreover, the account of the virtues is worked out in terms of the soul's parts and their relations. First, the idea is expressed in terms of the model of the ideal state: wisdom in the state belongs to the Guardians, the ruling class; courage, to the Auxiliaries, who retain and put into practice the directives of the Guardians; and so on. Then the individual virtues are characterized. Wisdom is the virtue of the rational part of the soul when it is ruling; courage, the virtue of the spirited part when retaining the views of reason as to what should be feared and not. This idea is taken up in the long passage making up most of books 8 and 9, where the progressive degeneration of states follows the pattern of the degeneration of individuals the parts of whose souls get into inappropriate relationships. It thus appears that, far from an account of virtue's dropping any reference to parts of the soul other than reason, it now actually requires it. We no longer have the suggestion that wrongdoing is simply a form of misguidedness or mistake, and *akrasia* is no longer problematic—indeed, the story of Leontius which is used to distinguish the spirited part of the soul is generally taken to be a paradigm case of *akrasia*.[4] The account of the ideal state can also be taken to imply (though there has not been agreement on this) that some people at any rate can have virtues like courage and temperance while lacking knowledge, since their cognitive state falls short of the knowledge which is found only in philosophers.

These moves have generally been hailed as an advance, a progress to a better view of virtue. But, whether we think this or not, they certainly seem to display a view which is *different* from that of the Socratic dialogues. On the standard developmental view, of course, this difference in moral psychology is part of the wider difference between a "Socratic" and a "Platonic" stage in Plato's works (however this is to be related to the external Socratic problem). For one thing, the tripartite soul is found not just in the *Republic,* but also, and prominently, in the *Phaedrus* and *Timaeus.* Plato, on this view, having first put forward an intellectualist account of virtue, then comes to see that it won't do, and replaces it by an account of virtue built on the moral psychology of a tripartite soul.[5]

The above account is extremely familiar.[6] Once again, we find that in the an-

---

[4] *Republic* 439E–440D.

[5] The prevalence of this view is partly due to Aristotle, who accuses Socrates of reducing virtue to knowledge, while Plato more realistically recognized both rational and irrational parts of the soul. See *Magna Moralia* 1182a15–22.

[6] There have, however, been exceptions, such as Charles Kahn; see, for example, Kahn 1988, pp. 89–90, where he defends the view that "Socratic intellectualism" is a deliberate creation of Plato's.

cient world interpretation takes a rather different tack; and once again, we find convergence between Stoics and Platonists. The Stoics have a "monistic" psychology; they deny that there are parts to the soul, for the soul is uniform, and it is all rational. In their rejection of the idea of bringing into an account of virtue parts of the soul other than the rational, they seem clearly to line up with the "Socratic," intellectualist view of virtue to be found in the Socratic dialogues, and seem to stand in sharp contrast to the view of the *Republic*. Modern historians of philosophy often see them in these terms, as restating, against Plato and Aristotle, a more sophisticated Socratic moral psychology.[7] But this does not seem to have been the way they saw themselves. They saw Socrates as an example of the philosophical life, but in moral psychology they aligned themselves with what we see as Platonic rather than Socratic. Not only later Stoics, but the second founder of Stoicism, Chrysippus, tried to interpret the account of the Platonic tripartite soul in Stoic terms—a project to which we return.

Moreover, the ancient Platonists, in their accounts of Plato's doctrines, did not see two successive stages of Plato's moral psychology here.[8] Alcinous,[9] for example, gives an account of virtue which patently draws on the *Republic*. There are four virtues, namely the four which Plato made canonical there: wisdom, courage, self-control, and justice.[10] The accounts which are given of them clearly draw on the *Republic:*

Wisdom is the knowledge of what is good and evil, and what is neither,[11] while self-control is a sense of order in relation to desires and impulses and their submission to the ruling element, which is the reason. When we speak of self-control being a kind of order and submission what we mean to convey is that it is a faculty in virtue of which the impulses are brought to order and submission in relation to that element which is their natural master, that is, the reason. Courage is the maintenance of a law-abiding opinion as to what is and is not to be feared, that is to say, the capacity to maintain a law-abiding doctrine. As for justice, it is a kind of harmonization of these three with one another,

---

[7] But cf. Gosling 1987, p. 198: "[The Stoics'] view of the development of reason is nearer to that of Plato's *Republic* than to that of the *Protagoras*."

[8] We shall see later that the Platonists do not all speak with one voice here.

[9] *Handbook,* chaps. 29 (on virtue) and 30 (on good natural dispositions and progress toward virtue). Chaps. 31 (on the involuntariness of vice) and 32 (on the emotions) are also relevant.

[10] Although Alcinous deals with them "in the normal Stoic order of the virtues": wisdom, self-control, courage, and justice (Dillon, p. 179).

[11] This is a standard Stoic definition, which Alcinous does not find out of place in a Platonic account of the virtues.

being a capacity in virtue of which the three parts of the soul agree and harmonize with one another, while each of them fulfils the function which is proper to it and falls to it as its due.[12]

And yet Alcinous at once goes on to say that the virtues are all reciprocally entailing, and proceeds to defend the view that nobody is voluntarily wicked. Clearly, he sees these elements of what is for us a "Socratic" view as consistent with what is for us a "Platonic" view. Further, this is not an idiosyncratic view; Middle Platonists all adopt not only the tripartite soul but the position that the virtues are all mutually reciprocal.[13]

It is always possible, of course, that the Platonists were confused, or too eager to produce a synthesis, at the cost of rigor and consistency of detail. After all, they also ascribe to Plato the view that the virtues are means, a clearly Aristotelian idea, and this may seem like hopeless anachronism. But it is also possible that we might gain from laying aside the developmental assumption for a while, and trying to see things from the perspective of Platonists who took it that what appears to us as "Socratic intellectualism" is simply an understated view, which is not trying to abolish parts of the soul other than the rational, but simply saying nothing about them, and giving us a position which is compatible with the account of the soul we find in the *Republic, Phaedrus,* and *Timaeus.* If so, the idea that we find a clear shift here between "early" and "middle" dialogues receives a setback. And we shall even see that there is more to be said than we might imagine for the idea that Plato thinks that virtues are means.

Crucial to the way that Alcinous gives us his account of virtue is a distinction between "perfect virtues" and virtues in the everyday sense. These are "homonymous," or have the same word used for them,[14] and are said to have some similarity (otherwise, we would hardly use the same word) but are different kinds of thing. Virtues in the ordinary sense are identified with the Stoic notions of "good natural dispositions" and "ways of progressing"; they are what Aristotle called natural virtues,[15] being natural behavioral tendencies to act and feel in certain ways. "It is in this sense," says Alcinous, "that we call

---

[12] Dillon's translation, except that I have substituted "knowledge" for "science" in the definition of wisdom. Dillon in his comments on this passage lists parallels from relevant texts. Although the definition of wisdom is Stoic, it is paralleled, at least for "knowledge of good and evil things," from the *Platonic Definitions* (411d). The definitions of the other three are recognizably from *Republic* 442–444.

[13] See Lilla 1971, chap. 2, esp. pp. 60–84.

[14] Alcinous, opening of chap. 30 (183.17 ff.), and already brought in at the end of chap. 1 (152.32–39).

[15] *Nicomachean Ethics* 1144b1–17.

certain soldiers brave, and even on occasion say that some people who are fool-ish are brave."[16] This is the kind of virtue that we identify by types of action, regardless of the person's overall state; we firmly say that the person who fights doggedly is brave, even if he afterward reveals himself to be lacking in judg-ment in other areas. Such a condition needs education and the right sort of nur-ture if it is to become "perfect" virtue.[17] What we find here is a distinction pro-duced to avoid a difficulty that arises in the Socratic dialogues, where Socrates urges his interlocutors to give an account of a virtue such as courage, and then points us toward an account of courage in terms of knowledge which makes it appear incomprehensible how we ever attributed courage in the first place on the basis of performances such as fighting in battle. On the later Platonist ac-count, we are not wrong to judge, as Laches does, that someone who holds the line and does not retreat in battle is brave,[18] as long as we are aware that this is not "really" bravery, because this state can occur in isolation from other virtues, in an agent who lacks education and habituation in virtuous ways, and who thus may lack other virtues such as self-control, and go and rape and pillage after the battle.[19]

Perfect virtues are the product of education, and the growth of an under-standing of what the virtue in question is, and why one should, on each occa-sion, act in accordance with it. In the Socratic dialogues Socrates tends to re-gard the understanding in question as being knowledge of the kind which an expert such as a skilled craftsperson has. But even without this, we can see the point of the idea that what matters, for a virtue, is the aspect of it which is not isolated from other virtues, and is not independent of education and the achieve-ment of understanding of the agent's whole life. Perfect virtues imply one an-other, because to have even one, you have to have the kind of overall under-standing or practical wisdom which is a part of all the others also. Each virtue can't come with its own little practical wisdom, since practical wisdom is a global understanding of the person's life.

In the Socratic dialogues the virtues not merely imply one another; they are

---

[16] *Handbook* 183.19–22. This suggests the *Laches*. It is also interesting that in the *Protagoras* (as Dan Russell has pointed out to me) Protagoras thinks that a natural dispo-sition for one skill is specific to that skill (327B–C), which fits with his thesis that the virtues are distinct.

[17] *Handbook* 152.23–29.

[18] *Laches* 190D–E.

[19] The Anonymous Commentator on the *Theaetetus* twice discusses *euphuiai*, or "good natural dispositions," commenting that they are not mutually reciprocal whereas perfect virtues are (9.39 ff., 11.16 ff.). (The context is a discussion of Theaetetus's unusual com-bination of qualities at *Theaetetus* 143E–144B.)

all identified with the global understanding of the agent's life which is practical wisdom. Alcinous, however, is also working with the picture of the virtues of the *Republic,* specified in terms of different parts of the soul, and so he claims only that the virtues are inseparable, although they remain distinct, since each is the perfection of a different part of the soul. This might seem at first to give us an un-Socratic picture. Wisdom is the perfection of the rational part; courage, of the spirited part; and temperance, of the desiring part; justice, which involves all three, involves the perfection of all three of the other virtues, and thus all the parts.[20] Alcinous argues that "courage, then, being the 'maintaining of law-abiding opinion,' is thereby also the maintaining of right reason; for law-abiding opinion is a sort of right reason, and right reason arises from wisdom. But wisdom in turn is involved with courage; for it is knowledge of what is good, but no one can see the good if his view is obscured by cowardice and the feelings that follow upon cowardice."[21]

This might seem to establish *a* connection between the virtues, but one which falls short of showing that they imply one another on the basis of sharing a common understanding or practical wisdom, which is employed in different areas. Alcinous is using the scheme of the *Republic,* according to which courage is the virtue of the spirited part. If we understand this via the model of the ideal state, we find that courage in the state is the virtue of the Auxiliaries, who do not have knowledge—only the Guardians have that—but rely on true belief, as long as it is the product of the right sort of training, and thus stable, like a dye which is not easily washed out.[22] If courage requires only true belief, however, whereas wisdom is a kind of knowledge, then wisdom and courage will be mutually interdependent in the way suggested—courage will require some firm cognitive state, and wisdom will require conditions in which it is not annoyed and upset by factors which it requires courage to face down— but they will not be mutually entailing virtues in the way envisaged in the Socratic dialogues, for they will not share a global wisdom or understanding which is one and the same whether exercised in cases of wisdom or in cases of courage.

It might be, however, that the virtues have this stronger relationship, and we

---

[20] Dillon in his comments (p. 180) points out that *panteleia,* the word used here for the way justice stands to the other three virtues, is not Platonic, and is "a rare and interesting word." Alcinous is also unsubtle in regarding temperance simply as the perfection of the desiring part, unless the perfection of a part already involves a correct apprehension of the relations of that part to others. He certainly makes temperance more dissimilar to justice than appears in the *Republic.*

[21] *Handbook* 183.10 (trans. Dillon).

[22] *Republic* 429B–430C.

find that they do when we look at another distinction Alcinous introduces, one perhaps designed especially to cope with this issue:

> It must be noted also that, among the virtues, some have a predominant role, others a subsidiary. Predominant are those which belong to the reasoning element in the soul, from which the rest also take their perfection, while those are subsidiary which pertain to the appetitive element. The latter achieve noble acts when they are in accord with reason, not, however, reason inherent in themselves (for they have none) but in accord with that which wisdom grants them, and which they acquire through habituation and practice. And because there exists neither knowledge nor skill in any other part of the soul than the reasoning element, the virtues that relate to the appetitive part are not such as to be teachable, because they are neither skills nor kinds of knowledge (for they have no proper object of study). Indeed wisdom, in its capacity as knowledge, bestows on each of the other virtues their proper objects, even as the helmsman instructs the sailors about certain things that are not visible to them, and they obey him; and the same applies to the soldier and the general.[23]

This gives us a rather different picture, one in which the rational part of the soul is dominant in the perfection of the other parts. Rather than robustly independent parts developing each in its own way and with its own goal, turning out merely to need one another, we find one in which the other parts are trained and developed through habituation, but in accordance with a cognitive structure for which they are dependent on the rational part. Desire, that is, is seen not as a part which has the capacity on its own to reflect on its own ends; we just fulfill a desire and gain gratification, whatever that might be. And desire, as a part of the soul, lacks the capacity to develop on its own in the way a skill or expertise does. It cannot on its own come to an understanding of the general principles underlying its own practice, and so come to understand what its own practice is. To the extent, then, that desire can be trained to function according to principles and not at random, this is the work of reason supplying the necessary goal and structure to the desiring part, which on its own supplies merely the capacity to be habituated and trained to work in some ways rather than others.

This, of course, raises the issue of what the parts of the soul other than reason actually are. On one picture, they are "non-rational" in being different in kind from the rational part, deaf to reason in that reason has no internal hold on them and can control them only externally, by coercion. On another picture, they are receptive to reason in that reason has an internal hold on them, and can

---

[23] *Handbook* 183.37–184.10 (trans. Dillon, with "knowledge" substituted for "science," "kinds of knowledge" for "sciences," and "skill" for "art").

control them from the inside, by changing and restructuring them. Alcinous gives us the latter picture: desire has a goal and an internal structure, but these are due to reason and not to the nature of desire itself taken as a non-rational phenomenon. On this view, reason informs our desires quite fundamentally. Insofar as desire is a force that can be trained to have a goal and to respond to the structure of our reflection, it is itself rational.

When Alcinous denies that the parts other than reason have reason "in themselves," it might at first look as though he were promoting the view that reason controls them in a way external to them. However, in saying that they lack reason "in themselves," he is making the point that he is defending a Platonic rather than a Stoic view. A Platonist has to hold, contra the Stoics, that there *are* parts of the soul other than reason, and he also has to hold that they do not have *their own* little reasons. Thus, any way in which they develop rationally, such as when the appropriate virtue is developed in systematic and reliable ways, is owed to reason, rather than to their own nature; for it is reason, rather than their own nature, which supplies the required goals and cognitive structure. Reason thus has an internal hold on the other parts of the soul because it gives them their internal structure. Hence, even if we recognize parts of the soul distinct from reason, they do not stand in substantial opposition to reason, since their virtues are developed in accordance with reason. The virtue of another part of the soul cannot develop in opposition to reason, since for the virtue to develop just is for that part to develop in accordance with the aim, and in the structured way, which reason provides for it. Hence the virtues of the other parts are subordinated to the virtue of the rational part; it provides what is needed for them to develop as virtues.

We can now see what was wrong with the picture of courage as relatively independent of wisdom, even granted that they needed one another. For a virtue to be courage is just for the spirited part of the soul to have developed in accordance with wisdom, the virtue of the rational part. Thus by the time the person genuinely is courageous, the cognitive state that underlies courage will be practical wisdom, and not just an indoctrinated opinion (even if it has been dyed into the person by less than fully rational means). For if the latter were the case, then courage would not be a subordinate virtue, taking its perfection from wisdom. Courage is a subordinate virtue just because it cannot develop into a perfect virtue without coming to have as its basis practical wisdom, the virtue of the rational part, which it owes to the rational part.

Thus we can see that for us to develop any of the virtues, including the virtues of the parts of the soul other than reason, is for us to become more rational; all the virtues have practical wisdom as their basis, and thus we find, after all, the Socratic-looking conclusion that the virtues are inter-entailing, that to have one is to have them all. The *Republic*'s parts of the soul complicate this picture, because now it emerges that there are aspects of the person which need to be trained and habituated to achieve virtue, and cannot become virtuous just by teaching, as the rational part can. But the virtues of these parts other than reason are subordinate to its virtue, practical wisdom; they cannot achieve virtue without achieving the goal supplied by reason, and doing so in a way structured by reason, so that by the time the person is in fact courageous, or temperate, she has not only habituated the relevant parts of the soul; she has acquired practical wisdom, the virtue of the rational part. Otherwise, the other parts of the soul would not have developed in the right direction.

Can this be the right interpretation of the *Republic?* One problem looms straight away; when we began with the model of the state, we found that courage, for example, was the characteristic virtue of one of the classes, the Auxiliaries, and that these lack the wisdom of the Guardians; in the state it looks as though, if the Auxiliaries can be said properly to have courage, then courage does not, after all, require practical wisdom, but merely a "law-abiding opinion" which may be held in a less than fully rational way. If we deny that courage can be had with anything less than practical wisdom, then the Auxiliaries are not really courageous. But this seems absurd; in the state they are the people who paradigmatically have courage. Since it is obviously unattractive to deny that the paradigmatically courageous people in the ideal state are really courageous, and since the structural analogy of state and soul is prominent in the *Republic,* many have thus been moved to hold that in the *Republic* Plato has given up the reciprocity of the virtues, and no longer holds that practical wisdom is essential for the virtues of the parts of the soul other than reason. If so, the parts of the individual's soul will themselves be relatively independent of reason in that they can achieve their perfection (the development of their respective virtues) independently of the rational part of the soul, by habituation and practice rather than by rational reflection and understanding.

Should we, however, accept this line of reasoning? If the virtues of the *Republic*'s individuals are mutually reciprocal, then, by the soul–state analogy, not all the citizens of the ideal state will be fully virtuous, only the Guardians. But should we be afraid of this conclusion? Some have tried to avoid it because of the elitism involved. Plato will on this view be committed to the thought that not all the citizens of the state can participate in virtue, and hence in happiness, to the same extent. For the Guardians will be the only ones who are fully virtuous, and thus happy, and they spend their time directing others who are not fully either. However, is Plato really developing as a serious proposal the idea of one set of virtuous, happy people ordering around another set of people who are neither virtuous nor happy? Only if we ascribe to the political part of the dialogue the status of a developed piece of political philosophy, setting out in detail how society should be run. If we prefer the view that the political part of the

Republic should be read as a model or illustration for the structure of virtue in the individual, then the apparent elitism is not a problem, since we do not have to read the details of it in a literal-minded manner. The Auxiliaries'are not second-rate people; they are a model for the spirited part of the soul, which needs training through habituation.

Thus Alcinous, after introducing the *Republic's* virtues, the perfections of the distinct parts of the soul, argues that they are in fact mutually reciprocal. The virtuous person will be just, and justice is a kind of harmony of the three parts with one another, so that justice requires each part to do what is proper for it; hence reason rules, while the other parts of the soul are ordered by reason, each in the appropriate way, and become obedient to it, and we get the mutual reciprocity of the virtues.[24] Courage requires wisdom, since the "law-abiding opinion" it holds must come from right reason if the state is to be truly *courage;*[25] and wisdom requires courage, since one has not achieved *right* reason if one's view is clouded by cowardly thoughts.

Is it plausible to read the *Republic* as maintaining this subordination of the virtues of the soul's other parts to the virtue of reason, practical wisdom?

In book 4 the argument from conflict which establishes that there are three parts of the soul focuses, not surprisingly, on their distinctness. The desiring part in particular is characterized in ways which appear to set it up as something completely non-rational. Thirst, the desire for drink, we are told, is just desire for drink, not for a particular kind of drink, and in particular does not bring with it a thought that drink is good.[26] In the case of a conflict between reason and desire, we find on the one hand the part that reasons, and on the other the part "with which [he] loves and hungers and thirsts and is upset about the other desires, a part which is irrational and desiring."[27] The spirited part is introduced,

---

[24] *Handbook* 185.37–186.16. In this sentence I think that Dillon's translation lays too much weight on the idea of reason forcing the other parts to give way; for example, he translates *katestalmenon* (lines 183.1–2) as "brought into submission." Whittaker notes, on this word's earlier appearance at 152.14, that although widely used, it has Stoic suggestions, which would indicate that here reason is responsible for internally ordering the other parts, rather than making them submit.

[25] Is Alcinous implying that the Auxiliaries in the state really do have knowledge after all? Perhaps he means that courage turns out to be a virtue only if the "law-abiding opinion" turns out to be a case of knowledge, rather than mere indoctrination.

[26] *Republic* 437B–439E. See the comments on this passage in Annas 1981. Cf. also 442A4–B3, and the violent restraining of the lowest part of the soul by the other two in the image of the soul as a two-horse chariot with charioteer in *Phaedrus* 253D–254E.

[27] *Republic* 439D4–8. The word for "being upset" in the case of other desires, *eptoētai*, recurs in Stoic discussions of the emotions. Cf. the claim just before that the desiring part struggles against reason "thanks to afflictions and diseased states" (Waterfield's

via the story of Leontius, as a part which can take the side of reason, and so would seem to be open to the suggestions of reason, but also as existing in animals and children, and so as lacking an essential connection to reason.[28] Moreover, the language of the relationship of the parts, in this section, is mainly that of dominance and control; the reasoning part prevents the desiring part by mastering it, and the spirited part is isolated in a passage dominated by metaphors of conflict and full-scale war.[29] Significantly, when the spirited part rebels against reason and is finally calmed down, it is compared to a sheepdog calmed down by the shepherd.[30] We shall return to this idea that the parts other than reason stand to it as an animal stands to a human, and to the importance of this for Plato's overall view.

Even in book 4, however, we find that when Plato describes the unified soul of the virtuous person, the language of control is joined by the language of agreement and harmony; the parts agree among themselves and so produce an integrated whole.[31] Moreover, it is now the *person* who is said to "rule himself" and "not to allow" any of the parts to function in an improper way. The relationship of the parts of the soul is now seen in terms of the person's having (or not having) a unified personality in which different and potentially conflicting sources of motivation have been integrated.

The long passage in books 8 and 9 in which we find the successive breakdown of defective characters and the (allegedly) corresponding types of state presents us with parts of the soul which contain extremely complex sets of beliefs and desires which go wrong in complicated ways. The decline to the various types of timarchy, "oligarchy," "democracy," and "tyranny" (conditions to which Plato strangely applies political terms which are used in a way quite foreign to their

---

translation—*pathēmatōn kai nosēmatōn*). This would be congenial to Stoics familiar with their own discussions of the emotions, which tend to cast them as pathological.

[28] *Republic* 439E–440C.

[29] See *Republic* 439C5–7 for reason mastering the desiring part. For the language of domination in the discussion of the spirited part, see 440A5–6, A8–B4, C7–D3. Even in the passage where Homer is quoted for the difference between reason and the spirited part (441B–C) and Odysseus addresses his spirit as though it were something that could understand, we find harsh rebuke and forcing, rather than attempt to persuade.

[30] *Republic* 440C7–D2.

[31] *Republic* 442C–D, 443C9–444A2. Later passages in the dialogue suggesting the same idea are 485D6–E5 (when someone is intent on one kind of thing, her desires tend naturally to flow toward that rather than other kinds of pursuit); 554C11–E5 (the parts of the virtuous person's mind are in harmony, with no conflict, unlike the oligarch's); 586C7–587A5 (the spirited and desiring parts achieve their proper pleasures when guided by reason, with no conflict; they fail to get this only when one of the other parts is in control, for they force all parts to seek unsuitable pleasures—here the language of coercion is used only of the situation where reason is not in control).

normal sense),[32] does not correspond to any simple change of power relation between the three parts of the soul. Rather, we have people who are dominated
by various clusters of concerns which are related to the three parts of the soul in
a complex way. Moreover, the changed types of people are not presented as
merely the result of power struggles between the parts of the soul. Rather, it is
the person himself, under various kinds of pressure, who is said to produce the
changes. The "timocratic" man, for example, "hands over the power within himself" to his spirited part;[33] the oligarchic man "dethrones" it and "installs" the
desiring part;[34] the "democratic" man loses control over his overall personality
and drifts into following one desire after another, but retains enough control to
"refuse to admit" the idea that desires should be distinguished as good and bad;[35]
the "tyrannical" man is the only one to have lost all overall control, once a master desire has been implanted within him. No adequate account of the progress
from virtue to vice can be produced just by citing dominance of one or another
part of the soul; the progress looks more like a person making a series of increasingly catastrophic decisions as to which kinds of motivation to prefer. The
parts of the soul look simply like loci of competing motivations within the person, all of which are capable of being structured by reason and following reason's goals when the person makes the right decisions, but which can become
increasingly dissociated from them when the person is tempted by circumstances
into making the wrong decisions.

As I remarked above, it is notable that even the early Stoics displayed an interest in the tripartite model of the soul and its potentialities. Chrysippus, notably
hostile to Plato on other issues, discussed the tripartite soul of the *Republic,
Timaeus,* and *Phaedrus,* as we find from Galen, who repeatedly criticizes him for
not arguing against the tripartite soul, as he would "officially" have been expected to do, given that Stoic psychology held that the soul was uniform and
rational, with no irrational parts.[36] Chrysippus appears to have regarded Plato's

[32] Cf. D. Frede 1996.

[33] *Republic* 550A4–B7, esp. B5–6.

[34] *Republic* 553B7–C7.

[35] The change from the oligarchic to the democratic condition is complicated by a
lacuna (559D10–E2), but it does not seem to be anything that the person actively decides upon. This is because the democratic condition is envisaged as one of passive drift
among desires, with the overall authority only to refuse the idea that this is a bad way to
be (561B7–C4).

[36] Galen discusses the Stoic view of the emotions and compares it with his own account of a divided soul, which he identifies with Plato's, in *On the Doctrines of Hippocrates
and Plato,* books 4 and 5. Galen has frequently been criticized for his unfairness to Chrysippus and his interpretation of Posidonius. Christopher Gill, in an outstanding article
(1997), shows that Galen's understanding of Plato is likewise one-sided, tending to the
view that the parts other than reason give reason no internal hold and are thus to be

tripartite soul as a way of talking about the soul that could be interpreted as compatible with a Stoic psychology.[37] Indeed, he co-opted language recognizably from the *Phaedrus* in giving his own account of the emotions, so he must have thought this language harmless, in that it would not derail a Stoic understanding of his own theory.[38] Chrysippus might well have been attracted to Plato's account of the tripartite soul because of its combination of the language of agreement of the parts and integration of the whole person with a stress on the tension and feeling of conflict attending on cases where we fail to follow reason in the sense of right reason, the reason that ideally should control the person as a whole.

The Stoics, of course, cannot accept the idea that there is such a thing as a part of the soul which is distinct from reason in being itself non-rational; for them, the entire soul is rational. But this is consistent with the soul's not being all equally responsive to reason in the normative sense of good reason; emotions, for example, are impulses which are rational in the sense of being beliefs which embody a reason, but which give us bad reasons, and which can thus be described as impulses which are excessive, and which are disobedient to reason in the normative sense. For them, Plato's parts of the soul other than reason can be understood as loci of bad reasoning in the soul which have to be brought into conformity with normative reason for the person to be an integrated and rational whole.

Here we find a point on which later Platonists, however much they may have agreed with the Stoics about reason in the person, refused to go along with them. For the Stoics, the result of the person's conforming to reason is that the emotions, or *pathē,* are eradicated; indeed, this follows from their position that to

---

dominated or coerced rather than persuaded. He also points out Chrysippus's apparent acceptance of the idea of Platonic tripartition as not necessarily objectionable. The passages in *On the Doctrines of Hippocrates and Plato* (PHP) are 3.1.16–21; 4.1.5–7 (referring to the *Timaeus*), 14–15; 4.3.6; 5.7.43, 52.

[37] Gill (1997) suggests that "Chrysippus might have seen in Plato's account of spirit, embodied in the heart, an anticipation of his own (psychophysical) account of the *pathos* of anger, and, more generally, of the heart as the centre of the psychophysical communication-system."

[38] At PHP 4.2.27 Medea's anger is said to "throw off the reins" (*aphēniazein*); the same word recurs at PHP 4.5.18, used of emotions rebelling against reason. In both passages Galen is summarizing Chrysippus, and must be doing so accurately, for he at once accuses Chrysippus of self-contradiction in saying this and also saying that the emotion is also rational. The image suggested is, of course, that of the soul as a two-horse chariot in the *Phaedrus*. Many scholars have suggested that Galen must be introducing the idea into a discussion of Chrysippus, from either Plato or Posidonius, but, unfair though Galen is, this would be self-defeatingly unfair. See Price 1995.

have a *pathos* is already to have gone wrong, since all *pathē* involve faulty beliefs. For the Stoics, this does not imply that the person is left affectless, since there is an acceptable form of feeling which does not amount to a *pathos*. But the ancient Platonists insisted on regarding *apatheia*, absence of the emotions, in its common-sense meaning of being affectless, and hence insisted that in the virtuous person the result of the completely successful integration of the personality in a way that answers to the demands of reason still leaves moderate emotions—the state of *metriopatheia*.[39] In fact, the dispute with the Stoics is almost entirely a verbal one, since neither side thought that the virtuous person would be affectless.[40] The only controversial point is that the virtuous person will feel not just some feeling but a *moderate* amount;[41] but there are passages in Plato which suggest that the reasonable response to events involves moderation,[42] and we can see how this would have led later Platonists to take what was perceived as Aristotle's side against the Stoics on this particular point.[43]

We can see nonetheless how someone paying attention to the passages where the relations between Plato's parts are described in terms of cooperation and persuasion, and are also described in terms of what *the person* does and decides, might well think that these passages could be read in Stoic terms. This seems to have been a project of Posidonius, a later Stoic who modified Chrysippan psychology about reason and the emotions. Our evidence about this is dis-

[39] This is a standard view among Middle Platonists; see Lilla 1971, pp. 99–103.

[40] See Dillon 1983.

[41] The pseudo-Pythagorean ethical writings contain an interesting defense of *metriopatheia* against Stoic *apatheia* on the grounds that the former, but not the latter, does justice to the weak and needy side of our nature (pseudo-Archytas *On Moral Education* 41.9–18 Thesleff).

[42] For example, *Republic* 431C, where the desires, pleasures, and pains of the minority of the city are said to be "simple and moderate, those that come along with intelligence and are led by the reasoning of correct belief," as opposed to the many and various desires, pleasures, and pains of the many. Such passages, however, demand only the weaker of the two interpretations of *metriopatheia* distinguished in the next note.

[43] The obvious relevant passage in Plato is *Statesman* 283D–284D, where the Eleatic Visitor insists that there is mutual dependence between the existence of expertise and there being a way in which excess and defect are relative not just to each other but to the due mean. This point is taken up by Aristotle at *Nicomachean Ethics* 1106b8–16, where virtue is said to aim at the mean on the grounds that expertise and knowledge do so. It is thus surprising that Alcinous ascribes to Plato a position on *metriopatheia* which appears to ascribe to him the implausible idea that the virtuous person has a degree of feeling which is moderate in being between the defect (*apathes*) and the excess (*huperpathes*). We would expect the idea, which would fit both Plato and Aristotle better, that the virtuous person has the degree of feeling appropriate to hitting the mean in her practical judgment (an amount which might be moderate or extreme, depending on the circumstances).

putable, since it comes mainly from Galen, who claims in a tendentious way that Posidonius was abandoning Stoic psychology and returning to the true, Platonic way of looking at things. Posidonius certainly introduced one innovation; he thought that in making emotions rational, presenting inadequate reasons which set themselves up against normative reason, the Stoics had given themselves inadequate resources to explain why it is that emotions can ever win against the preponderance of reason against them. If anger is an impulse embodying a weak, bad reason, why do we ever succumb to it? Posidonius argued that we have "passionate (or affective) movements" (*pathētikai kinēseis*) which are not themselves emotions but explain why we react to appearances in a way that seems to outrun the reach of reason. Emotions get their hold on us through certain tendencies that we have to react emotionally—that is, in a way which is not responsive to the appeal of right reason.[44] He may well have thought that he was allowing for the idea that Plato expressed by saying that there are parts of the soul other than reason.

Posidonius was interested in something which occupies Plato's attention in the *Republic,* namely education and the development of character. He seems to have tried to restate this in Stoic terms, taking into account factors which make it difficult for us to become and stay rational.[45] Posidonius made, however, a quite large, and possibly misguided, concession to Plato, to which we shall return.

So great a degree of convergence between Stoics and the moral psychology of the *Republic* is a further indication that that psychology need not be seen as standing in conflict with the idea that virtue requires practical wisdom, and that all the virtues thus imply one another. Rather, it can be seen as filling a gap left by the Socratic dialogues. The *Republic* raises the question of those aspects of us, not treated in the Socratic dialogues, which require habituation and training before we can come to have knowledge, and which appear to make it difficult for us to accept the results of right reason. But this does not deny the claim of the Socratic dialogues, that virtue requires knowledge; it merely shows that achieving knowledge is more complex than the Socratic dialogues allowed. To achieve

[44] See Gill 1997; Cooper 1997; Price 1995, 175–78. Modern scholars tend to concur that Galen is misguided in assimilating Posidonius's view to Plato's, and that he does not give way on the basic issues of Stoic psychology, notably the point that we are responsible for our emotions and the way we deal with them; we cannot appeal to the emotions to shed responsibility for what we do. See Annas 1992, chap. 5.

[45] *PHP* 5.5.30–35. Posidonius admired Plato on the treatment and education of babies and children, and in the first book of his *Emotions* wrote a summary of Plato's views on child-rearing. A quotation shows that Posidonius did so in terms of a rational and a passive aspect of the soul, and he even co-opted the *Phaedrus*'s charioteer image (as Chrysippus had done). Cf. also *PHP* 5.6.9–22, where Posidonius uses his own analysis to criticize Chrysippus's characterization of our final end and how we achieve it.

knowledge, the virtuous person has had to bring all aspects of himself into agreement and conformity with the rational part; only thus has he acquired the integrated personality of the virtuous person who exhibits practical wisdom and is never led to act against it. And thus we can see the accounts of later Platonists such as Alcinous as entirely legitimate attempts to see Plato's ethical thought as a whole, not differentiated into stages by the partial or fuller accounts of our moral psychology which accompany it.

Many readers, however, will have been made impatient by this synthesizing of different theories which not only employ very different terminology but seem divergent in some of their basic aims. Doesn't reinterpreting the *Republic*'s moral psychology in a way making it consistent with Socratic and Stoic views of the soul lose the *point* of what is different in the *Republic?* There are many things one could have in mind here; I discuss three of them.

Surely part of the point of the idea that the soul is composite is to give recognition to mental *conflict*. This is the point of the vivid description of the thirsty person refraining from drink, and Leontius's agonized reaction to recognition of the shamefulness of his desires. This, however, is describing conflict in us as we unregenerately are, and is not something that Socrates has to be denying. All of us except the perfectly virtuous recognize conflict between the way we should be and the way we are. The question is how this is to be explained—whether the recalcitrant elements of the personality are taken to be fundamentally irrational in the sense that reason has to force them into line, having no internal hold on them, or whether they can be brought into line with reason in a deeper way, in which they can be said to listen to reason and come to agree with it. On the second picture, reason has, in the fully virtuous person, removed the conflicts that were so vividly described. Only on the first picture has reason tamped them down without being able to remove their sources.

It is sometimes thought that the account of Leontius's self-division is a recognition of the reality of *akrasia,* or weakness of will, something which the Socratic dialogues seem to leave no room for.[46] But the existence of *akrasia* in everyday life is hardly news; the problem in the Socratic dialogues is rather how anybody could act against *knowledge,* and this problem has hardly altered in the *Republic;* indeed, that dialogue puts the standards for knowledge which the virtuous person must reach so high that it seems harder, if anything, to see how anybody could act against it.[47]

Second, it may be thought that the distinctness of the parts of the soul has im-

[46] The *Protagoras*'s denial of *akrasia* is based on hedonistic premises which are unparalleled in Plato (whether or not we hold that the hedonism is seriously held by Plato, or defended dialectically).

[47] Kahn (1996, chap. 8) deals with this point at length.

plications for the moral theory of the work. Virtue can be seen as sufficient for happiness, goes this thought, as long as virtue is identified with the wisdom of the virtuous person, and other aspects of the personality are ignored. But when we bring these into the picture, we can see that they also need to achieve their own satisfactions, so that happiness for the person would involve not merely virtue but some at least of the conventional goods which form the aim of the spirited and desiring parts. This is too quick, however. In the virtuous person, all the parts of the soul have been brought into harmony with reason, and Plato notes that where this happens, desires that go in other directions weaken accordingly;[48] so someone in whom the parts of the soul other than reason were clamoring for their own satisfaction, over and above that of the rational part, would simply be someone who was not, or not yet, virtuous. In the virtuous person all the parts get their own proper satisfaction,[49] something quite compatible with the thought that virtue is sufficient for happiness. There is, then, no change in moral theory signaled by the fuller moral psychology of the *Republic*.[50]

Finally, however, we must admit that, even if the theory that there are parts of the soul other than reason can be explained, or explained away, consistently with Stoic and Socratic views of virtue and the soul, there is something which Plato sometimes has in mind in using this idea which Socrates and the Stoics cannot take over. We have seen that, as well as the language of agreement and integration between the parts, we sometimes, especially in the passage of book 4 where they are introduced, find the language of dominance and coercion, with its suggestion that reason has only external control over the other parts, and cannot give them internal structure. It is in this passage that the reasoning part is said to control the spirited part as a shepherd controls his dog.[51] This idea, that there is a part of me which is not fully human and can be characterized as an animal, is one that sometimes has unfortunately powerful appeal to Plato. It reappears in the *Phaedrus* in the idea that the tripartite soul is like a chariot with two horses, driven by a charioteer. The charioteer, of course, is reason; the horses

[48] *Republic* 485D–E.

[49] *Republic* 586E–587A.

[50] Dillon (1996) argues that Plutarch and Calvenus Taurus were Platonists who rejected the Stoicizing interpretation of Plato as holding the sufficiency of virtue for happiness, on the basis of their holding that the soul could not be completely "rationalized" in the way the Stoics thought. However, this does not follow (on 195 Dillon recognizes that the "duality of the soul" could be combined with a Stoic position in ethics), so Plutarch's *On Moral Virtue* does not seem relevant to this issue. Plutarch elsewhere (*On Common Conceptions* 1060c ff.) commits himself to the anti-Stoic position that conventional goods such as health, beauty, and strength help make up "our natural fulfillment," and Taurus holds a similar position.

[51] *Republic* 440C–D.

(one of which is ugly and violent) are the other parts of the soul. In the *Republic* this idea that a human is something human controlling two subhuman parts reappears in a most surprising place, after the long discussions of the inharmonious souls in books 8 and 9.[52] We are told to picture the person as a human being containing a little human, a lion, and a many-headed, shape-changing beast.[53] Of course, it is clear that we are to identify with the human aspect of us, not the parts represented as animals; these are the parts of us which we, the humans, have to keep down and keep under control.

This idea, that something is part of me but not really me, not really human, is an unattractive and dangerous way of looking at myself. When I think that *I* am rational but it is not, I am externalizing part of myself, looking at it as something over which I have only the kind of control that I might have over an animal—that is, external control; I can get it to do some things and refrain from others, but I can never get it to understand my deliberations. It is thus not an accident that we find in this context the most extreme form of the language of coercion in the *Republic*—the view that the lowest part, or the person following it, should be enslaved to the best part, the reason—either his own, or, if this is inadequate, the reason of somebody else in whom reason does dominate.[54] It would be hard to find a more direct indication of how thinking of part of yourself as external to the real you leads to thinking of your relation to it as one of power—the most one-sided kind of power relation that there is.

It seems obvious to us that Plato's agent who is supposedly unified in this kind of way is in reality profoundly self-alienated. To regard part of yourself as external to the real you, and to project onto it characteristics which you reject, is obviously to live with a profound self-*division,* which talk of control does not abolish. It is at any rate clear that this is far different from the Stoic view of the integrated rational personality, in which the person is responsible for all she does. There is, then, a residue of the *Republic*'s moral psychology which resists assimilation to Stoic and Socratic views, and Plato can be seen to be tempted by two quite distinct models of the composite soul.

Moreover, the suppressed-beast model unfortunately attracted some later philosophers, such as Galen, who relentlessly insists on Plato's parts of the soul as though they were chronic irrational forces that reason can control only by domi-

---

[52] It might be argued that in the progressive dissolution of rational unity, we get a similar split between the self (the person who hands over control to one of the non-rational parts) and the not-self (these parts, which then control his soul). The picture seems to be rather of a progressively more disunified self, however, not of a growing conflict between a self and something dissociated from that (there is no animal imagery).

[53] *Republic* 588B–591A.

[54] *Republic* 591C–D.

nance. Some later Platonists also find this a compelling model. Plutarch, who dislikes the Stoics, argues that they are wrong to see mental conflict as a case of the person oscillating between two courses of action. There is not a change in one thing, he says, but battle and struggle between two. It is like supposing the hunter and his prey to be one thing which oscillates between being a human and being an animal.[55] Here again the animal image and the language of violence go together; the hunter obviously cannot persuade, or become harmonized or integrated with, the animal he hunts. And Posidonius, though in other respects he was probably interpreting Plato in ways congenial to Stoics, made a big concession in holding that the cause of giving in to emotions, and thus of living a discordant and unhappy life, was "that men do not follow in everything the divinity in themselves which is akin and by nature similar to the divinity that rules the whole universe, but sometimes they turn aside in the company of that part of them which is inferior and beastlike and let it carry them along." This beast-like part, he repeats, is "irrational, unhappy and godless."[56]

This division in the Platonist ranks indicates that Plato is not here, as we and Arius both say, speaking with one voice. There are two ways in which Plato regards the divided soul, especially in the *Republic*. In one he is trying to do justice to the way in which some aspects of us may fail to go along with right reason, and may need habituation and training to develop in rational ways and in pursuit of ends sanctioned by reason. The ideal here is the harmonized, integrated person all of whose motivations are, without conflict, in line with reason. This is the side of the *Republic*'s moral psychology which later Platonists and Stoics rightly thought compatible with the reciprocity of the virtues and the kind of importance of practical wisdom for virtue that we find in the Socratic dialogues. But Plato also sees the idea at times in a different way, one in which the person isolates his "true self" in his reason and then externalizes the parts other than reason as something subhuman, rejected and kept under harsh external control. We can agree that this is a new idea in the *Republic* (and *Phaedrus*). It is an idea which does not fit the rest of the moral psychology, which can be, as we have seen, so interpreted as to be thoroughly consistent with the claims of Stoics and of the Socratic dialogues. And we can also agree that the Platonists who ignored Plato's vivid metaphor of a human as a little animal tamer were being true to those of Plato's thoughts that were consistent with his views on virtue and knowledge in Socratic dialogues—and also with those of his views that are better, and more in accordance with the truth of things.

---

[55] Plutarch *On Moral Virtue* 447b–c.
[56] Posidonius ap. Galen PHP 5.5.4–5 (trans. de Lacy).

[VII]

ELEMENTAL PLEASURES:
ENJOYMENT AND THE GOOD IN PLATO

In various places in Plato's work we find passages which express what looks, at least at first, like hedonism. The *Protagoras* discusses hedonism as a theory, but the passages I have in mind go beyond discussing it; they seem to accept it. Here are a couple:

> If someone declared that the most just life was happiest, everyone who heard him, I suppose, would ask what was the good and fine in it superior to pleasure, which the lawgiver praises. What good could come to a just person separated from pleasure? For example, is fame and praise from gods and men good and fine, but unpleasant? . . . The argument that does not separate the pleasant from the just and good and fine is, if nothing else, plausible for getting someone to be willing to live a pious and just life . . . for nobody could willingly be persuaded to do something unless more pleasure than pain followed it.[1]

"By nature what is human are especially pleasures, pains and desires, from which every mortal creature is necessarily so to speak suspended and dependent by the greatest influences." Thus the virtuous life is recommended as bringing the most pleasure, if followed properly; and to determine this we have to see what kind of life is natural for us. We choose pleasure, reject pain, and welcome a neutral state only as a relief from pain, not as a loss of pleasure. "We choose less pain with more pleasure, do not choose less pleasure with more pain and when they are equal find it hard to be clear about what it is we want." Pleasure and pain influence our wishes, and hence our decisions, because of their "num-

---

[1] *Laws* 662E8–663B6.

ber, size, intensities, equalities and the opposites." "Since things are necessarily thus ordered," we desire a life in which pleasure predominates over pain, whether both kinds of feeling are frequent and intense or few and weak. The equally balanced life, in which neither preponderate, is like the neutral state; we welcome it if it has more of what we like and not if it has more of what we dislike.[2] "We should regard our lives as all being naturally bound up in these; and therefore if we say that we wish for anything beyond these, we are speaking as a result of some ignorance and lack of experience of lives as they are."[3]

These passages, both of which come from the *Laws,* certainly look as though they are endorsing some version of hedonism. Yet it is hard to accept that this is what they are doing. Hedonism is not a position that we expect to find Plato holding, not just because it seems a departure from his usual lofty and demanding views about virtue and happiness, but because he does not seem to have room for it. If virtue is sufficient for happiness, what space is left for pleasure to be our aim in everything that we do?[4] Of course, we can say that Plato is tempted by hedonism in some dialogues, but in others he rejects it. And on many developmental views, hedonism is a view to which he inclines in the *Protagoras* but rejects in other dialogues, notably the *Gorgias.* We get a story of Plato changing his mind, a story with many variants as to how he changes it. But the *Laws* passages cannot be explained in this way, unless we think that Plato could cobble together a work full of self-contradictions. The first of the passages above immediately follows a firm endorsement of the sufficiency of virtue for happiness; the second follows the great preamble to the law code, which stresses the crucial importance of honoring one's soul and following virtue in all things, culminating in an attack on self-love as the root of most human evils. These are not the contexts in which we would expect an introduction of hedonism. Nor can development explain a switch to or from hedonism within two Stephanus pages.

The problem deepens when we notice that there are discussions of pleasure in five of Plato's dialogues—*Protagoras, Gorgias, Republic, Philebus,* and *Laws*—but it is very difficult to find a single theory of pleasure in all of them. Indeed, it is so difficult that many scholars hold that in these five dialogues we find, in effect, five different theories of pleasure. There is nothing necessarily faulty in this; pleasure is a very difficult topic, and it would not be surprising (or count for or against a theory of overall development) if Plato, like Aristotle, returned

---

[2] In the sentence 733C6–D2 I accept Ritter's emendation *hyperballonta* for *hyperballontōn.*

[3] *Laws* 732E4–733D6.

[4] Virtue might guarantee pleasure, and so be a reliable if roundabout way to pleasure, but this idea, though arguably in Epicurus, is alien to Plato's conception of pleasure and virtue (this is argued more fully below).

to the topic at different times with different thoughts. One ancient writer, Aulus Gellius, says that Plato wrote about pleasure in such a variety of ways, both because of the complex nature of pleasure and because of his having different aims in different places, that his works can be seen as the source of later, mutually contradictory theories of pleasure.[5] Even if we think this exaggerated, the differences between the dialogues where pleasure is discussed obviously complicate the question whether Plato ever does accept hedonism in some form.

Once again, if we are looking for an account which tries, as far as can be done, to unify the various accounts of pleasure that we find in Plato, it is interesting to turn to the Middle Platonists. Moreover, the account which they contain is suggestive in another way. Modern discussions of Plato on pleasure tend to proceed in what is usually deemed to be chronological order, going from *Protagoras* and *Gorgias* through *Republic* and ending with *Philebus* and *Laws*. Moreover, most of the scholarly work has focused on the first two dialogues. The ancient accounts, however, see the issue thematically rather than chronologically, and the analysis they give directs us first to the dialogues that we now usually consider last. Looking at the ancient take on Plato's views on pleasure, then, can give us a fresh perspective on a peculiarly recalcitrant part of Plato's thought.

Alcinous, in his *Handbook,* discusses pleasure under the heading of the emotions (*pathē*).[6] "An emotion is an irrational motion of the soul, in response either to something bad or to something good." "There are just two simple and elemental emotions, pleasure and distress; the others are compounds of these."[7] Desire and fear (which the Stoics count as basic) are not equally "basic and simple," nor are other emotions, "for in these pleasure and pain can be seen, as if they were compounds of these." Alcinous goes on to make further comments on pleasure, taken from various dialogues. He concludes that pleasure cannot be good absolutely. "It seems, in fact, to be precarious and without value, being by its nature supervenient, and containing nothing proper to true being or primary, and coexisting with its opposite."

---

[5] Aulus Gellius *Attic Nights* 9.5. He claims, implausibly, that Plato can be seen as the source of the views of Epicurus, Antisthenes, Speusippus, Zeno, and the Peripatetic Critolaus. It would be interesting if this view of Plato's variety of positions on pleasure were that of a Platonist—Gellius immediately afterward cites his Platonist teacher, Calvenus Taurus. But Taurus is cited for a different point, and Tarrant (forthcoming) has argued convincingly that the source, if there is one, for Gellius's view is likely to be somebody else, perhaps Favorinus, who saw himself as a skeptical Academic and thus would take a non-doctrinal interpretation of Plato, seeing different views of pleasure as required by different argumentative contexts.

[6] In chap. 32.

[7] I use Dillon's translation of the chapter, but have substituted "elemental" for "basic" as a translation of *stoicheiodēs*.

At first glance this analysis seems to be more puzzling than helpful. How can pleasure be both a basic emotion and something supervenient? There is a similar puzzle with the Stoic account of pleasure, to which we return later. First, however, it is helpful to look at another later writer, Arius Didymus, who though not a Platonist at least shares some of his sources with Alcinous. Arius finds an extensive point of comparison between Plato and Democritus.[8] Both of them, he says, place happiness in the soul—that is, in the virtue that we can achieve, rather than the external goods which are not up to us to gain or keep. Democritus "makes happiness consist of distinguishing and discriminating pleasures, and says that this is the finest and most advantageous thing for humans." Plato is in agreement with this, says Arius, when he writes in the *Timaeus*[9] that happiness depends on our spirit, or *daimon,* reinterpreting this to mean our mind. "Of this good [happiness] the origin is the emotions (*pathē*), while the definition and limit are reasoning. At any rate, we can read, '[Pleasure and pain] are the two fountains let loose by nature to flow; the person who drinks from them ‹whence he should, and where and how› is happy, while the person who does not, is the reverse.'[10] So, in naming pleasure and pain, he establishes the origin of happiness from the emotions; and in saying 'the person who drinks from them whence he should, and where and how, is happy' he ascribes to reasoning the distinguishing element in happiness. On this point, therefore, Plato and Democritus agree, inasmuch as Plato places in excellence of reasoning the good which is primary and sought for its own sake, and in pleasure that which supervenes, which he also supposes as a consequence to be called by the same words as 'joy' and 'tranquillity.'"[11]

Here we find the same point, that pleasure is characterized both as an emotion and as something which supervenes, but we also find a clue helping us make sense of it. As an emotion, or *pathos,* pleasure is the origin of happiness in that it is what we begin with, but it emerges that reason plays a crucial role in what is called "distinguishing" pleasure, so crucial that reason turns out to be the more impor-

---

[8] Arius ap. Stobaeus *Eclogae* 2.52.13–53.20. (This is an important point about Democritus, which cannot be followed up here.)

[9] *Timaeus* 90A, which Arius abbreviates, as Stephen White points out. I am very grateful to Stephen White for allowing me to see his translation and notes on this passage of Arius.

[10] The quotation is from *Laws* 636D–E. In Arius's text the crucial phrase in brackets has dropped out here, but is discussed a couple of lines later. Plato's text is a little fuller—the point applies not just to individuals, but also to states and "any living creature"; but the passage is brief and Arius gets the gist of it.

[11] Presumably, Plato is said to do this as well as Democritus, and the final clause refers to the latter's use of these terms. I follow White in rejecting Wachsmuth's addition, from Meineke, of ‹*allēlois diapherontai*›.

tant element in happiness, and pleasure, as a result, turns out to be something which supervenes (however that is to be understood). It is also important that in the passage from Alcinous the emotions, or *pathē,* were emphatically said to be irrational responses to good and bad. We have here, then, a picture of reason taking the lead with regard to the part of us which is irrational, and which seeks pleasure and avoids pain, so as to put it in a state in which we achieve happiness.

Even at this point, we can see that the passages with which I began, with their apparently strange emphasis on the inescapability of our seeking pleasure, need not be taken as expressing a position that we would call hedonistic, namely that pleasure is our final end, that which we seek in order to be happy. It is the thought that this is what is going on which makes these passages so odd in their contexts. But all they need be taken as doing is insisting that to begin with, originally, we all seek pleasure, since pleasure is what we seek with the irrational aspect of ourselves. This is worth insisting on given that the Athenian is emphasizing realism about human motivation, one important thing stressed in these passages. But in them we also find the claim that the nature of this motivation can be affected by reasoning. This is the point which the later Platonist passages fill in for us, enabling us to get a fuller picture of what is going on. Pleasure, it appears, is an elemental response to good; we cannot but be affected pleasurably by what we perceive as good and painfully by what we perceive as bad. But Plato does not go on to conclude from this that pleasure must be our final good, or *telos* (at least not in these passages; the *Protagoras* comes into the discussion later). For we see, in the brief extract where pleasure and pain are called two springs from which we drink, that it is not just taking them that leads to happiness, but doing so as and when one should. And clearly it is the function of reason to lead us to do this.

Another passage, again from the *Laws,* shows us, in a fairly vivid manner, how we are to understand the way that reason can lead us to the happy life, given pleasure and pain to work on as the basic responses of our irrational nature. It comes early in book 1, in a discussion of the importance of education.[12] The Athenian reminds his interlocutors that they have agreed that self-mastery is a good thing, giving in to oneself, bad, and says that he will clarify this by an image. Each of us is a single thing, but contains internal complexity; for we have two internal advisers, pleasure and pain. Unfortunately, these are stupid and mutually antagonistic. Other psychological phenomena are built upon these; when we have beliefs about the future, for example, if these involve pain they take the form of fear, whereas if they involve pleasure they take the form of confidence. (Pleasure and pain are thus basic among the *pathē,* or emotions, that we have.) We also, however, have reasoning as to which of these other things is better or

---

[12] The most important section runs from *Laws* 643D6 to 645C6.

worse; and the reasoning which is the common resolution of a state is called the law.[13] The Athenian proceeds:[14]

> Let's think about it in the following way. Let's think of each of us living things as a puppet of the gods, either as one of their toys or as constructed for some serious purpose, for that we don't know. But this we do know, that these emotions (*pathē*) in us are like cords or strings which drag us along. Being opposed to each other, they pull us in different directions to opposite kinds of action, and this is where the division between virtue and vice lies. Reason says[15] that we should all follow along always with one of these pulling forces and in no way leave go of it, pulling against the other strings. This is the directing[16] of reasoning, and is golden and holy, and is called the common law of the state. The others are hard and like iron, but it is soft, being golden, while the others are like forms of all sorts. We must always co-operate with the directing of the law, which is the finest; for since reasoning is fine, but gentle and not violent, its directing needs helpers so that the golden kind in us will win over the other kinds. In this way our story of virtue, which is about us as though we were puppets, would be a success, and the idea of being "self-master" or "giving in to oneself" would become somewhat clearer, as would the point that an individual must grasp the true reasoning within himself about these pulling forces, and live following it, and a state must grasp the reasoning (whether from a god or from a human with knowledge), establish it as law, and live by it both internally and with other states. In this way both vice and virtue would be more clearly articulated for us.

At first this appears to be a horrifying passage. If we are the puppets of the gods, then not only do we have a very discouraging relationship with the gods,

---

[13] Since this section is concerned with public education, it is not surprising that we frequently find references to public reason, in the form of the law. In the present context they are of less relevance than the references to the individual's reason.

[14] *Laws* 644D7–645C1.

[15] *Ho logos* at E4–5 is here, I think, "reason." However, Saunders and Bury translate "our argument." Presumably, this is to avoid having reason tell the person to cooperate with an element in her which turns out to be reason. I agree that this is awkwardly phrased at this point, but I argue that part of the point of the image is to show us that the whole person should in fact identify with one aspect of herself, namely reason, and thus it is consistent for the virtuous person to do what reason tells her to do; in doing this she is identifying with reason rather than pleasure and pain. (In this respect the image is very like the more famous image of the person's inner complexity represented as a little person, a lion, and a changing beast, at *Republic* 588B–591C.)

[16] This translates *agōgē*, which has a variety of applications; it refers to directing, leading, and guiding, but can also be used for a way of life.

we appear to have no freedom; what looks like freedom of action is merely the greater strength of one rather than another of the cords pulling us. It is not clear how this picture of us can help clarify the ideas of self-mastery and giving in to oneself, unless by showing that these are no more than fictions.

In the passage, however, it is clear that the person and his decisions are not reduced to a battle between the tugs of pleasure and pain. The cord of reasoning is special in two ways. First, it is soft whereas they are hard and inflexible. Perhaps this is a confusing development of the image of a puppet, but the softness of the gold cord makes the point that reason can deal with pleasure and pain in ways that they cannot deal with it. They simply yank and pull, whereas it can manage and manipulate them; its greater flexibility gives it greater power over them than they have over it. Second, the person can be encouraged to cooperate with and follow the gold cord; it needs help, but the person can follow it and thus be able to withstand the pullings of pleasure and pain, inflexible though these are. The picture here of how the person is a puppet is in fact rather complex. One very important aspect of us—desire to get pleasure and to avoid pain—is simply given; we cannot choose to be without it. Insofar as we just yield to this, we will do the actions which answer to the pullings of the strongest desire at any time. However, our susceptibility to pleasure and pain, though we cannot get rid of it or wish it away, is not completely intractable. For we are also able to reason and thus to reflect on and pass judgment on our urgings toward pleasure and away from pain; we can, by reasoning, judge which are better and which worse—that is, judge them by an independent standard which cannot itself be reduced to the result of the strongest desire. Reasoning is not only independent of the outcome of the pleasure-pain struggles within the person, and capable of judging the result; it is also capable of leading and manipulating the feelings, even though they are strong and stubborn and it is comparatively weak. It can do this because it is adaptable and flexible where they are not, and thus can lead and direct them in ways that change them, whereas they are incapable of changing themselves. Reason, then, is the part of us which can lead and mold the other part, our susceptibility to pleasure and pain, which would not of itself ever produce anything other than the winner of a battle for the strongest desire. Hence, insofar as the person identifies with reasoning, and consciously and as a matter of policy tries to go along with it and strengthen its effects, he is acting to change himself, and thus initiating action, rather than acting mechanically as a result of the strongest pull.

It is thus the person who just drifts and yields unthinkingly to the pulls of pleasure and pain who is like a puppet, jerked about by forces that are not under her own control. Susceptibility to pleasure and pain is genuinely part of her nature, but in simply giving in to this she is abdicating any attempt to alter or guide the way she is, and losing any attempt to control her own life. The person who tries to live by reasoning, and encourages the control which it exercises on our susceptibility to pleasure and pain, on the other hand, is doing the controlling herself. Instead of pleasure and pain just getting her to do things, she is in control of how desires for pleasure and to avoid pain are directed. She is controlling herself as a person controls a puppet; part of her needs to be controlled by the other part in order to function properly. The moral of the image seems, then, to be not that human action is always at the mercy of intractable internal forces, but rather the opposite, namely that it is open to us to control and direct internal forces that might have appeared to be intractable.

But, it might be claimed, this is going too fast. For, in the image, we are *all* puppets of the gods, perhaps nothing more than their toys. Does it then matter which string does the controlling—the hard strings of pleasure and pain or the flexible manipulative string of reason? It does not look as though within the image *any* of the puppets can be said to have real control over what they do.

It is hard to know how much of this idea Plato wants to suggest—the idea that both those who control their own actions and thus illustrate "self-mastery" and those who "give into themselves" and abdicate decision to the victory of the strongest desire are equally playthings of the gods. Certainly it has been often noted that in the *Laws* we find a far more pessimistic picture than before of the relation of humans to the divine; we should obey them gladly and be "lowly and ordered" as we follow God.[17] But here it is surely equally important that the golden cord is reason, and that our reason is the divine element in us. If we are puppets of the gods, one reasonable interpretation of this is that insofar as we identify with and encourage reason, the divine element in us, we achieve control over the other aspects of us, which are not rational. This is what it is to be controlled by the divine, namely to control ourselves by reason, and not be at the mercy of the non-rational aspects of ourselves. Thus the message of the puppet image is meant to be inspiring rather than depressing: insofar as we identify with reason, the divine in us, we can control and change ourselves.[18]

We can now see that the passages I began with, in which Plato insisted on the unavoidability of our pursuing pleasure and avoiding pain, do not contradict their contexts, in which he insists on the all-importance of virtue for happiness. The fact that we always desire pleasure rather than pain is just a basic fact about human motivation. However much we succeed in living according to a rational ideal, we all still have to begin from the substrate of human motivation—the given, non-rational appeal of pleasure and the fact that we reject and flee from pain. In fact, all non-rational motivations, such as fear and hope, come down,

[17] *Laws* 716A. See Chapter 3, n. 15.

[18] This is obviously related to the idea of "becoming like God," discussed in Chapter 3.

in the end, to variants on seeking pleasure and avoiding pain, which are thus basic or elemental in our non-rational motivation. But we are more than the result of the mutual struggles of desires and aversions which we cannot help having; our reason enables us to guide and channel these, and thus to change and mold ourselves.

In the *Laws* Plato pays a great deal of attention to the ways in which we can change ourselves and develop in some ways rather than others; this is why he insists on having so many social sanctions and such an extensive system of education and training. Nothing will do short of an education which leads the person to understand that virtue is sufficient for happiness, and that external goods are irrelevant to it.[19] Reason guides us to the point of seeing that we achieve happiness by seeking to be virtuous, whatever the cost in external goods or worldly success. As we have seen,[20] this has a transformative effect on the person; reason takes us in a totally different direction from that in which we mindlessly seek pleasure and avoid pain, and our values and priorities become profoundly changed. This is achieved not simply by intellectual reflection, but by an extended education and training of character, in which our tendencies to go for and take pleasure in certain things are appropriately encouraged or discouraged by a number of factors.[21] The Athenian later[22] says, simplifying somewhat, that all human motivation depends on the three basic drives, for food, drink, and sex. In their irrational form they are actually called *nosēmata,* or diseased states. They must, the Athenian says, be turned toward what is best, rather than what is said to be most pleasant, by the three greatest forces—fear, the law, and true reason, backed up by the Muses and the gods of competition. Here Plato envisages an entire process of socialization, relying not just on reason but also on non-rational factors such as stress on competition, led by reason to be directed toward what is best.

The result of valuing virtue in this way is not that we come to reject pleasure, or to have none. Plato assumes that the happy life must be a pleasant one. The pleasure in question, however, is not the same as the pleasure that the non-rational part of us is bound to seek in a mindless way. The pleasure of the virtuous life can be had only by the virtuous, and, of course, it takes enormous efforts of both intellectual reflection and education of character to become virtuous. In the *Laws* most people are said to have the wrong perspective, and to be in a fog, as far as concerns the pleasures of the virtuous life.[23]

[19] See Chapter 2.
[20] Cf. Chapter 2.
[21] See Chapter 6. This is of course particularly stressed in the *Republic* and *Laws.*
[22] *Laws* 782D–783A.
[23] See Chapter 2, pp. 46–47.

Thus the virtuous have a pleasant life, but there is no neutral position from which one can evaluate this pleasure; it and its correct evaluation are available only to the virtuous. It is only from within the transformed life that the nature of pleasure is properly discerned. Plato continues to insist that the virtuous life will bring what he calls the most, or greatest, pleasure, which might suggest at first sight that it can be compared for amount of pleasure with the non-virtuous life (and given the prize). But he cannot be understood as holding the position that the virtuous has more of the very same thing which the vicious person is mindlessly going for. The greatest pleasure, for Plato, is to be found in the life in which the person aims not at pleasure but at virtue, and indeed trains his desires so thoroughly that he values only virtue, even when accompanied by all conventional evils. This is not more of what the ordinary pleasure-seeker is aiming at.

Pleasure thus comes, we may say, only when not directly sought, and it comes as a result of what *is* sought, namely virtue. It is this idea, I think, which later Platonists and others tried to express by the idea that pleasure "supervenes." The idea here is no relation to modern complex and technical conceptions of supervention in the philosophy of science; it seems simply to be the idea that A supervenes on B if A could be directly aimed at, but is not, but instead accompanies B when B is aimed at, and aimed at successfully. (This idea of "successfully" of course requires further exploration.) Aristotle's second analysis of pleasure in the *Nicomachean Ethics* suggests this idea; pleasure supervenes on an activity if certain success conditions are fulfilled, but this is different from aiming directly at pleasure in performing the activity. Aristotle has been criticized for the elusive and difficult nature of his analysis of pleasure as something that supervenes, but he can certainly be held to have located, at least, a resolution of the problem. The happy life, characterized as the virtuous life, has to contain pleasure, but pleasure cannot be the goal aimed at, or we do not have a properly virtuous life. (Aristotle is clearer than Plato on why the virtuous life must be pleasant; his account of virtue and virtuous activities shows why taking pleasure in what you do indicates that you are achieving virtue, rather than a merely self-controlled state.) The idea of supervention captures the point that pleasure must accompany the virtuous life but is not the goal of the virtuous person.

Plato has no word that corresponds to the later philosophical term "supervenes" (*epigignesthai*), but we can see why this might be thought a good term to describe his position if we draw together the different strands we have seen in the *Laws*. The desire for pleasure is the most basic motivation that we have, but rational reflection can so educate and train the person that they aim in an appropriately uncompromising way at being virtuous. The person who succeeds in becoming virtuous, and who does not aim directly at pleasure, in fact gets pleasure as a result of his virtue. Thus pleasure is an elemental motivation for everyone, but the highest pleasure supervenes only on the life of the virtuous. The best pleasure comes only to those who don't seek it.

The ancient Platonist understanding of Plato's position about pleasure thus is well grounded in the texts of at least the *Laws.* It also, interestingly, resembles the Stoic position on pleasure. In some Stoic texts pleasure is said to be a *pathos,* or emotion—and thus, for the Stoics, to be bad, since all emotions already embody faulty beliefs.[24] But elsewhere it is said to be a "supervention"[25] in a passage which explicitly denies that pleasure is what all living things naturally go for. Rather, their primary impulse is to self-preservation, and pleasure comes, if at all, as something which supervenes when nature is successfully fulfilled. Again, we find that pleasure comes to those who don't seek it—even more strikingly for the Stoics, since, for them, to seek pleasure as a feeling or emotion is already to have gone wrong. Indeed, we can note a difference of tone between the Stoics and Plato. The Stoics are notably unenthusiastic about pleasure; they veer between calling it a preferred indifferent, natural but not valuable, and neither natural nor valuable.[26] Plato, despite his obvious puritanism in some respects,[27] is readier to allow that there is some force in the way most people consider pleasure to be a good. He thinks it worthwhile, as the Stoics do not, to show that our intuition that happiness involves pleasure is satisfied even if virtue turns out to be sufficient for happiness; indeed, one can regard his various grapplings with the notion of pleasure as an attempt to come out with an account of pleasure which will account for this—that is, will allow the happy to have a pleasant life even when happiness has been drastically rethought as a result of a radical reevaluation of the goods whose attainment brings us happiness.

There is one notable corollary of this theory, in both Plato and the Stoics. Pleasure is natural to us, as the kind of beings we are; this is one major aspect of

---

[24] Arius ap. Stobaeus *Eclogae* 2.88.8.–90.6. For the Stoics, desire and fear are the basic elemental emotions, and pleasure and pain are derivative. The later Platonists follow Plato's lead in reversing this.

[25] Diogenes Laertius 7.85–86. In 7.149 nature is said to aim at advantage and pleasure, but presumably the way nature does this is just by allowing pleasure to supervene when natural processes are working well.

[26] See Sextus Empiricus *M* 9, para. 73: the Stoics in general say that pleasure is indifferent and not preferred, but Cleanthes says that it is neither natural nor has value in life, having no natural being, like a cosmetic. Archedemus says that it is natural, like hairs in the armpit, but has no value, and Panaetius says that it is partly natural and partly not. The analogies of cosmetic and armpit hair are clearly meant to produce an austere effect.

[27] He is always notably unenthusiastic about the processes of eating and drinking and the pleasures most people derive from them. He shares with the historical Puritans a horror of sleep, as being a waste of time, and a strong desire to stop people from sleeping much (*Laws* 807E–808C).

the fact that desire for pleasure and to avoid pain is characteristically human. Plato insists on the naturalness of pleasure,[28] which is the accompaniment of the process back to our natural state when this has been disturbed by need or interference. But Plato, like the Stoics, also thinks that what is natural for us as humans does not stop there, but continues in our progress as ever more rational beings, who learn to live according to the conclusions of reason, and hence to acquire the virtues, and so to acquire a radically different attitude from our original one to our initial feelings of pleasure.

The upshot of such a theory of pleasure, of course, is that the virtuous person's conception of pleasure is very different from that of the ordinary person with whose given tendency to seek pleasure we began. The second passage I quoted at the beginning[29] starts with an emphatic statement that we are talking to humans, not gods, and thus must focus on what humans are like; a student of human nature must learn to cope with the fact that humans always go for more pleasure and less pain overall. Someone who thought that this was heading in the direction of an ethics based on maximizing pleasure would be grievously disappointed to find that the product of education in the best-run state would be a life aimed uncompromisingly at virtue. The pleasure you get from *that*, it might be complained, is not what was meant in the observation that everyone always goes for pleasure and away from pain.

Plato is quite open about the need to educate and transform our basic urges for pleasure and to avoid pain. In a long passage in the second book of the *Laws*[30] the Athenian comments that children's first perceptions are of pleasure and pain, and that it is "in these" that virtue and vice first come to the soul. A program of education is sketched, which establishes that it is the properly educated person who is the norm for what is truly pleasant.[31] Perhaps the most radical note is struck in book 8,[32] where we find the claim, recognized to be controversial and implausible, that people can be brought to think of homosexual sex as utterly taboo, in the way they think of incestuous sex; if society presents homosexual sex in a consistently negative and repulsive light, people will cease to think of it as pleasant and will actually cease to feel desire for it.[33] The extent to which Plato here takes our desire for pleasure to be plastic is astonishing. Ideally, the Athenian comments, people should desire none but marital, reproductive sex, but perhaps

[28] Cf. *Timaeus* 64C–65B.

[29] *Laws* 732D ff.

[30] *Laws* 653A–671A; cf. esp. 663A–D.

[31] In the *Laws* we find the depressing claim that when it comes to cultural displays it is the old whose judgment about pleasure is the normative one (658D–E).

[32] 830B–841E.

[33] 838B; see also 838C, 841A–C.

this is an unattainable ideal; but he is fairly confident that the desire for male homosexual sex can be got rid of.[34]

It is obvious enough by now that Plato's is not the familiar modern conception of pleasure as something which is always the same kind of thing whatever its sources, and which reason can serve to provide but not to alter. Plato is manifestly not telling us that the virtuous life is a good bet to get the pleasure which you were originally getting mindlessly from sensual pleasures. It is only when you give up aiming at pleasure and aim at virtue instead, in the most uncompromising way, that you get true pleasure, and *that* is not at all the kind of thing that you were aiming at before. What of the ordinary person applauding Plato's apparent realism in recognizing pleasure as a basic human motivation but feeling let down when she discovers that the best kind of pleasure requires the lengthy and demanding process of becoming virtuous? We can now see that this states the situation wrongly, for by the time the person becomes virtuous she appreciates that the pleasure accompanying virtue is, in fact, the best pleasure; and if she fails to achieve the requisite change of viewpoint, then she simply fails to understand what true pleasure is. This is just the fact that there is no neutral viewpoint on pleasure here.

Pleasure, then, is a basic element in our non-rational motivation, but it does not survive unchanged as an element in the rationally ordered virtuous life. Reason does not function merely as the instrument to provide efficiently the pleasure which the non-rational part seeks anyway. Rather, the reflections of reason and the way they have directed the life have produced a whole in which the drive for pleasure has been thoroughly transformed. Reason has transformed a human life to the extent that the non-rational element no longer fixedly seeks pleasure, but has been trained to fall into line with reason, which seeks virtue; and the whole life as a result achieves true pleasure, which accompanies virtue without being directly sought.

So far, this idea has been illustrated from the *Laws*, which is not usually stressed in modern discussions of Plato's views of pleasure, but which has been seen to reward investigation which reflects the emphasis of the ancient Platonists. However, the position of the *Laws* can reasonably be seen as similar to that of the more

[34] Such attention as this passage has attracted has mostly focused on the unexpectedly harsh attitude to male homosexuality, unexpected in the light of dialogues such as the *Symposium, Phaedrus,* and *Lysis,* and this is certainly problematic. It is equally important, however, for the assumption that a drive for pleasure which Plato recognizes as exceptionally strong can be not merely repressed but actually transformed by social and cultural pressures. Plato is right in thinking that contemporary Greek culture encouraged homoerotic relationships; his mistake lies in thinking that a change in that culture would eliminate them.

familiar *Republic,* notably in that both dialogues explicitly defend the idea that the virtuous life is pleasant. They do this, moreover, in the context of a eudaimonist framework. We all seek happiness, and find, when we investigate properly, that happiness is to be found in the virtuous life. But it is part of our conception of happiness that it involves pleasure, and so the virtuous life must be shown to be a pleasant one. Plato undertakes to show not only this, but also that the virtuous life is a better candidate for bringing pleasure than the life of the vicious. In the *Laws* the argument to show this is brief.[35] In the *Republic* we find extensive argument in book 9 to show not merely that the virtuous life is pleasant but that, notoriously, the virtuous person's life is 729 times more pleasant than that of the vicious.[36] These arguments are part of the overall argument to show that the virtuous life is happy; Plato is showing us that he can account for the pleasantness of the happy virtuous life by showing us that it is the virtuous who have real pleasure, while the vicious do not.

The *Republic* has a more theoretical discussion of pleasure than does the *Laws,* and three new ideas appear. Pleasure is characterized as a movement, or *kinēsis,* whereas mere absence of pain is a state of rest (*hēsuchia*). Lack or need is also characterized as an emptying, and pleasure as the subsequent filling or replenishment. And the virtuous person's pleasures are said to be real, whereas the vicious person's are unreal, in a way that rests directly on a metaphysical theory about the nature of the real and the illusory.[37]

These differences are, however, minor when we bear in mind the many overall similarities between the two dialogues about pleasure in the virtuous life, and the importance of reason in the argument. Both dialogues, as already stressed, argue that the happy life, which has turned out to be the virtuous life, is the most

---

[35] *Laws* 661–63. This is the only passage where virtue, happiness, and pleasure are brought together, but the connection is clear. The young person persuaded to be virtuous, if he were to discover that this life were not after all the most pleasant, would complain to his preceptors; they wanted him to have the happiest life he could, and persuaded him that this would be achieved by being virtuous. If this life turns out not to be the pleasantest life then, it is taken for granted, his complaints would be reasonable.

[36] The whole passage goes from 580D to 588A. At 581E and 588A it is stressed that we are comparing lives for pleasure and not for some other kind of advantage; but the arguments are not establishing an independent measure for pleasure, which virtue will happily chance to meet. Rather, the arguments are best seen as establishing a conception of pleasure which Plato takes to be correct and which enables him to show that the virtuous life is the happiest, since he can account for the deep-seated assumption that happiness involves pleasure.

[37] These points all emerge in the second of the two arguments, that which runs from 583B to 588A. The first argument relies only on the idea that the virtuous person's judgment about the superior pleasantness of his own life is authoritative in a way that the judgments of the honor- and money-lovers are not.

pleasant. The *Republic* argues, as vigorously as the *Laws,* that reason must rule in the person for her life to be pleasant. This is the explicit conclusion of the second *Republic* argument;[38] when reason rules, then the rational part obtains its own pleasures, and so do the other two parts, the honor-loving and the money-loving; thus all the soul's parts get what is appropriate and the person's life as a whole is pleasant. When, however, reason does not rule, none of the parts gets the pleasure that is appropriate to it, and the whole life goes askew and fails to be pleasant overall.

The *Republic* assumes, moreover, as does the *Laws,* that our desire for pleasure is plastic, and can be educated and drastically changed and transformed by social and cultural forces, particularly education. The extensive passages on education in the early books of the *Republic* assume that education results in the person's taking pleasure in different kinds of thing, and that this is a part of the virtuous person's development. The virtuous person, who by the end of book 9 is said to have a far more pleasant life than the vicious, is also said by the end of book 9 to care for external goods only insofar as they support and enable his virtuous condition. And finally, in the *Republic* as much as the *Laws* we find the idea that there is no neutral viewpoint from which a rational decision can be made between the virtuous and vicious lives with a view to the pleasure in them. The virtuous person has a life which contains what is called the greatest, or most, pleasure; but there is no scale on which this can be measured for quantity against the pleasure of the vicious life. The virtuous person's judgment, that she has the pleasantest life, is the correct, authoritative one; just this is the conclusion of the first *Republic* argument.[39]

The major difference between *Republic* and *Laws* in their treatment of pleasure is that in the *Republic* reason has its own pleasures, and so for reason to rule in the person's life is for reason to ensure the other parts' proper pleasures in a way that also achieves its own. In the *Laws* the tripartite account of the soul has been dropped, and reason is simply opposed to the non-rational part of the soul as a whole. Reason does not have its own pleasures; the virtuous life is achieved by reason's molding and controlling our desires for pleasure. This is not as major a difference as we might expect at first. Both dialogues hold that the happy, and so pleasant, life is achieved by the person's reason achieving its proper ends—

[38] *Republic* 586E–587A.

[39] At *Republic* 582E–583A the virtuous person's judgment is preferred because it is based on "experience, intelligence, and reason" (*empeiria, phronēsis, logos*). But these are themselves not neutral; the non-virtuous types have some kind of experience and reason, but these are not authoritative, since they do not take into account the whole soul and its perspectives on the different parts, merely the interests and perspective of one of the parts.

that is, subordinating and molding the non-rational aspects of the person. The *Republic* allows that in doing this, reason achieves its own pleasures; but this does not make pleasure the goal of the person.

The *Republic* and *Laws,* then, differ here in tone rather than substance; both see a non-rational drive for pleasure being transformed by reason into a part of a life which is virtuous and happy, and so pleasant. But does this idea transfer to other dialogues? No other dialogues contain ideas which are closely or directly comparable. The *Philebus* and *Gorgias,* two dialogues in which pleasure is a major theme, differ considerably from *Laws* and *Republic,* and not merely in being concerned with the individual's pleasures rather than with questions of social training and education. In them we do not find any idea which could easily be transposed into the schema we have seen so far, of pleasure as a basic element in human motivation, transformed by reason in such a way that pleasure accompanies the virtuous life without being sought. Nonetheless, we find ideas which are in an obvious way comparable. *Republic* and *Laws* can be compared with the other two dialogues only at a high level of generality, much higher than that at which they can be compared with one another. Still, it is, I think, worth bearing even high-level similarities in mind as we look at *Philebus* and *Gorgias.*

The *Philebus* opens with a dispute as to whether the happy life is constituted by pleasure or by knowledge; which of these is the good that we all seek?[40] It is surprising that we find no mention of virtue here, and very little of virtue and happiness elsewhere.[41] Plato's concern in the *Philebus* is not with virtue, the importance of which is taken for granted, but with the kind of contribution that pleasure and reason make to the life which renders the agent happy. That this is the virtuous life is not here argued.

The good life, we are told, must be complete and self-sufficient, and so can be constituted by neither pleasure nor reason alone. Pleasure alone, with no reason or thought, would provide the life of a clam; reason, with no pleasure, that of a god. For humans, the happy life must involve a combination of both.[42] The question is, of course, what kind of combination? We then get a famously obscure passage in which all beings are distinguished into four classes—unlimited, limit, mixture, and cause. Pleasure belongs in the class of the unlimited, reason in that of cause, and the good life in that of mixture. The point of this abstract discussion seems to be to insist that the good life is not a combination of reason and pleasure in which they are both simply ingredients—a life in which we have

---

[40] *Philebus* 11B–E.

[41] The occurrence of *ton bion eudaimona* at 11D6 is the only significant one in the dialogue (occurrences at 22B8 and 47B7 are trivial). Similarly, of the six occurrences of *aretē* (45E6, 48E9, 49A1, 55C1, 63E5, 64E7), only the last three are significant.

[42] *Philebus* 20C–22B. See Chapter 2, pp. 36–38.

now one and now the other. Rather, it is a combination in which pleasure is raw material which enters the combination in a way determined by reason. Reason dominates the mixture in that it determines what the limit is that is to be imposed on pleasure for pleasure to be able to contribute to the happy life.

Why should reason be thus dominant? The idea is that the pursuit of pleasure in itself can never organize a life in the way that is necessary for the achievement of happiness; a life built around the pursuit of pleasure is bound to be a life with no overall organizing principle. This point is made vividly in the *Gorgias,* where the overall organizing power of reason is connected to the possession of the virtues. "It looks as though anyone who wants to be happy must seek out and practice self-discipline, and beat as hasty a retreat as possible away from self-indulgence. The best course would be for him to see to it that he never had to be restrained, but if he or anyone close to him (whether that's an individual person or a whole community) does ever need it, then he must let justice and restraint be imposed, or else forfeit happiness. . . . We should devote all our own and our community's energies towards ensuring the presence of justice and self-discipline, and so guaranteeing happiness. . . . We shouldn't refuse to restrain our desires, because that condemns us to a life of endlessly trying to satisfy them. And this is the life of a predatory outlaw." [43] The happy life must be the rationally ordered life, one which contains organizing principles with the complexity and degree of rationality that a skill possesses; in the *Gorgias* the practice of skills provides an analogy which Plato takes to have persuasive force (whereas in the *Philebus* the need for the happy life to be rationally ordered emerges rather from a metaphysical account).

To live a life of pleasure-seeking is, according to the *Gorgias,* to live a life which is mindless, the life of what is in the *Republic* and *Laws* called the non-rational part of us. Callicles, who (ineffectively) defends this life, claims that the life of pleasure is one in which you aim at satisfying desires, without regard to restraint by other factors. Socrates objects to this on the grounds that it makes the good that is sought dependent on the pain or discomfort that is removed as the pleasure is achieved. The pleasure of eating requires hunger; the pleasure of scratching requires an itch; and so on. We may wonder why this is supposed to be an objection; in the *Laws* Plato insists that pleasure and pain are characteristically human motivations; they are important to us just because of the characteristically needy and ever-changing beings that we are. So we would expect Plato to accept the idea that pleasure requires a preceding felt discomfort or pain; indeed, when he discusses pleasure, he tends to see it as essentially a repletion or restora-

---

[43] *Gorgias* 507C8–E3, trans. Robin Waterfield, World's Classics Series (Oxford: Oxford University Press, 1994).

tion of a lack.[44] For Plato, however, this—restoring lacks as they come along—is never enough for a good human life. Reason must control and transform the non-rational aspects of us for us to achieve the kind of happiness that humans need. Merely seeking pleasure cannot provide what is needed for the living of a human life; for we do not just seek pleasure, we also realize the need for rational organization of our life as a whole, as the life of a rational being.

A life spent pursuing fulfillment of desires is, Socrates claims in the *Gorgias,* like a leaky jar which constantly needs replenishment, or a bird that excretes while it eats;[45] we are meant to recoil from the idea that this is all a human life amounts to. The two arguments with which Socrates crushes Callicles' position also depend on this idea, that pleasure cannot be a final end in life which amounts to happiness. Pleasure cannot amount to happiness, since happiness is found over an entire life, whereas pleasure can coexist with its opposite, pain. Seeking pleasant experiences, then, falls far short of a structured attempt to achieve happiness over one's life as a whole.[46] Moreover, if achieving pleasure is our sole aim, we will not be able to make sense of our admiration for the traditional virtues; we despise cowardice, even if the coward achieves far more pleasure than the brave person, but the pursuit of pleasure cannot generate this attitude simply from within itself.[47] Plato retails this last argument in both the *Gorgias* and the *Philebus,*[48] and seems to regard it as especially forceful against the idea that pleasure alone can generate what we regard as necessary parts of the good life.

A great deal of the *Philebus* is taken up with further, often much more subtle, arguments for the inadequacy of pleasure to constitute happiness on its own.

[44] This is especially prominent in the *Philebus,* as it is in Aristotle's account of pleasure in *Nicomachean Ethics,* book 7.

[45] *Gorgias* 493D–494E.

[46] *Gorgias* 494B–497A. This argument has been criticized on the ground that it unfairly pits happiness, as a state holding over one's lifetime, against the pleasure of a single moment. But Callicles commits himself at 491E–492C and 494C to saying that pursuing pleasure through the untrammeled fulfilling of desire just is what it is to live happily, so it is fair for Socrates to take him to be putting forward an account, but an inadequate account, of happiness, and to press the point that pursuing pleasant experiences cannot amount to what we reasonably expect of pursuing happiness. Pleasure-seeking cannot fill the conceptual role required of happiness. In this point, as in the discussion of the *Gorgias* and *Philebus* more generally, I am indebted to the work of Daniel Russell.

[47] This argument holds even against a theory which (like that of the *Protagoras*) identifies happiness with the long-term, prudent pursuit of pleasure over one's life as a whole. I thus agree with those who claim that the *Gorgias* contains arguments which hold against a theory of the *Protagoras* type, and thus that we cannot argue that the former must predate the latter. (In fact, the *Protagoras* is so different from all the other dialogues that consider pleasure that *any* chronological hypotheses would be unwise.)

[48] *Gorgias* 497D–499B; *Philebus* 55A–C.

The main drift of the *Gorgias* and *Philebus* is quite similar: the pursuit of pleasure and avoidance of pain on its own cannot generate the ordered and organized life which happiness requires. Pleasure must fit into a reasoned structure, dominated by the virtues, before it can become part of the good life. The *Philebus,* for example, distinguishes four kinds of pleasure which are "false"; one thing that unites them is that they all involve either a failure of reasoning or something which interferes with reasoning, and thus they are all excluded from the good life as not being compatible with the overall organizing rule of reason. Pursuit of pleasure unrestrained by the virtues turns out to be a kind of floundering, a pursuit of local satisfaction at the cost of overall coherence.

In one respect the two dialogues give the impression of being more opposed than they in fact are. The *Gorgias* appears hostile to pleasure, and is often regarded as anti-hedonistic, whereas the *Philebus* is more sympathetic to the extensive discussion of pleasure, and finds it a place in the good life. But the *Gorgias* is not so against pleasure as may appear from passages where Socrates contrasts the self-sufficient life to Callicles' unrestrained pursuit of pleasure. Callicles spurns this life as that of a stone or a corpse, and it appears to be a life of freedom from disturbance rather than one containing pleasure.[49] However, Socrates then develops the idea of the rationally ordered life in a way that takes off from the admission that there are good pleasures[50]—indeed, we need the rationally ordered life so that we can reliably obtain good rather than harmful pleasures—and it explicitly does not reject pleasure, but rather produces the right attitude to pleasure on the agent's part.[51] Plato does not seem to have thought through the relation of the self-sufficient life to the rationally ordered life. The *Gorgias* seems at any rate to reject the presence of intense, disruptive pleasures in the good life, without specifying which pleasures would find a place in it.

The *Philebus* discusses these, in a way which could reasonably be seen as filling a gap rather than signaling a change of position. Although it is more interested, and more detailed, in discussing pleasure, it is not notably generous in its allowance of pleasure into the good life at the end of the day. At the end of the

---

[49] *Gorgias* 492D–E is the passage where Callicles rejects Socrates' suggestion that the life without needs would be happy. 493D–494A puts forward the idea that happiness could be a matter of filling one's jars and keeping them filled; Callicles retorts that the pleasure just is the filling of the jars, so that the pursuit of pleasure requires the jars to be leaky. These passages certainly suggest that the self-sufficient life contrasted to the life of Calliclean pleasures (whether or not it is identical to the "philosophical life" at 500C) is a life without pleasure.

[50] *Gorgias* 499D ff.

[51] At 507B we find it as part of the characterization of the virtuous person that he will flee and pursue the things, people, pleasures, and pains that he should.

dialogue[52] Socrates allows that the good life will contain all kinds of knowledge, practical as well as theoretical. How will pleasures fit in? The question is raised in an imaginative way. Pleasures are asked whether they would prefer to live with or without reason, and reply that it is neither possible nor a good thing for them to be separated from reason. "We would prefer to live side by side with that best kind of knowledge, the kind that understands not only all other things but also each one of us, as far as that is possible."[53] Pleasure, that is, understands its own inadequacy to provide happiness on its own. Reason, however, has a stricter line, refusing to have anything to do with intense pleasures. The only pleasures allowed in to the happy life are those that have been called true and pure, that is, pleasures which do not rely on awareness of a previous lack or need for their pleasantness; and the pleasures of health and of virtue.[54]

What kind of pleasure will the happy life contain, then? Again, it will be far from the kind of pleasure which ordinary people have in mind. In the *Philebus* Plato seems wedded to the idea that all pleasures are in some way fulfillments of lacks or needs, and so even true pleasures, and the pleasures of being healthy and virtuous, depend for their pleasantness on their being some kind of need which is being met. In their case, however, the lack or need is not one that we are aware of, so we do not appreciate these pleasures by contrast with a previous pain or discomfort.

This conclusion is awkward in some ways. The pure pleasures, acceptable in the good life, are illustrated by restricted pleasures of the senses, and the pleasures of learning; there is a brief and rather offhand reference to the pleasures that "attend on virtue," but if we are to be consistent with the model so far, these must be the pleasures of becoming virtuous—that is, those involved in the process of becoming virtuous as the pleasures of learning are involved in the process of learning. But then it turns out, rather strangely, that the virtuous, happy life does not involve the pleasures of *being* virtuous.[55] The virtuous, happy person will

---

[52] *Philebus* 59D ff.

[53] *Philebus* 63C1–3, trans. Dorothea Frede (Indianapolis: Hackett, 1993).

[54] *Philebus* 63E3–7.

[55] This is a vexed question of *Philebus* interpretation. At 63E we find, apparently in addition to the pure pleasures already mentioned, pleasures that are "together with" health and temperance, and "all those that commit themselves to virtue as to their deity and follow it around everywhere" (Frede translation). Yet in the final ordering at 66C–D (repeated at 67A) no place seems to be made for them, suggesting that they should after all be understood to be examples of the pure pleasures, and thus the pleasures of becoming healthy, or virtuous, with no previous felt lack. Many have understandably found this simply implausible, but even if 63E is read so as to commit Plato to regarding the pleasures of virtue as a different kind from the previous pure pleasures, it must be admitted that he says very little about them and appears to neglect them in the final summing-up.

take pleasure in smells and some other sensory experiences, and in learning and other examples of intellectual and moral progress; but virtue at the end of the day does not seem itself to involve pleasure.

Many have thought, not surprisingly, that the conclusion of the *Philebus* makes a disappointingly minimal concession to pleasure. It does not in the end recommend a life which seems by ordinary standards markedly more enjoyable than that recommended in the *Gorgias*. But this should not really be surprising. As in the *Laws*, Plato realizes that pursuit of pleasure and avoidance of pain are basic to human nature; but the good life for humans, as is familiar by now, is one in which this element has been so thoroughly transformed by reason that the resulting pleasure of the happy life can be appreciated, as pleasure, only from the perspective of the happy life. The ordinary person would think that such a life was not enjoyable at all, but this is not seen as an objection.

The *Gorgias* and *Philebus* are not easily amenable to the idea that pleasure is something that supervenes on the happy life, as we find that in the *Laws* (and related ideas in the *Republic*). However, they express an idea which can reasonably be seen as related, namely that pleasure cannot be the overall goal of the happy life; it can at best be a minor and thoroughly transformed part of it, given the role that is assigned to it by reason, which in its uncompromising commitment to virtue transforms the person's life overall. In all cases, pleasure is seen as something that can have a place in the happy life only if it accepts the organizing role of reason, and aiming at pleasure is taken to be essentially short-term; aiming at pleasure can at best produce a string of gratifications, but never generate a rationally ordered whole, still less generate any concern for virtue.

The ancient Platonist analysis of Plato's position on pleasure has, then, pointed the way to a reasonable account of four dialogues. Pleasure is a basic element in human nature, but it is a mistake to think that pleasure could be our final end. It is only when we recognize virtue as the aim that constitutes happiness for us that we get the kind of pleasure that the happy life involves, and by then our perspective has been so transformed that we recognize, as being the highest and best form of pleasure, something which the unregenerate pleasure-seeker would scarcely count as pleasure at all. In all these dialogues reason plays a role in ordering the virtuous life which can thoroughly transform the non-rational part of the soul and what it goes for. And our urge for pleasure, though basic to us, is taken to be plastic, something that can be so transformed that as we move from living mindlessly to living in accordance with reason, we take pleasure in entirely different kinds of activity, and find the highest pleasure without directly seeking it.

Even on a more generous construal of the dialogue than I have given, the pleasures of virtue get strikingly little attention.

To nobody's surprise, the standout here is the *Protagoras*. Most of this dialogue is occupied by discussions about the nature of expertise, and the relation of what we take to be the separate virtues. In a short passage at the end, however, Socrates uses a thesis about pleasure to show that knowledge cannot be overcome by other factors, such as pleasure, pain, love, or fear. The thesis is not introduced very clearly, but Socrates claims that "good" is interchangeable with "pleasant," and that when we ask about the goodness of things, it is merely their pleasantness that we bear in mind; so it seems reasonable to call the thesis hedonism, that is, the idea that it is pleasure that is our final good, with reference to which we estimate which things are good and benefit us.[56]

In this passage two things are remarkable. One is that the ordinary conception of pleasure is taken at face value and remains unchallenged; our desires for pleasures are not treated as plastic, or in need of education before pleasure could be our final end. Second, reason is, amazingly, treated as having a purely instrumental role with regard to pleasure. For we find that we fail to achieve pleasure through making quantitative, and recoverable, mistakes; we think immediate pains are to be avoided and immediate pleasures taken, for example, and underestimate the consequences of so doing. What we need, we are assured, is an "expertise of measurement" to deal with pleasures, and this will enable us to weigh and measure pleasures in a way unaffected by proximity; it will give us an objective calculus of pleasures and thus enable us to pursue pleasure in a rational and objective way. "Since it has been shown that our salvation in life depends on the right choice of pleasures and pains, be they more or fewer, lesser or greater, farther or nearer, then doesn't our salvation seem primarily to be the art of measurement, which is the study of relative excess and deficiency and equality?"[57]

Nowhere else in Plato is the function of reason, in shaping the happy life, taken to be that of playing a purely instrumental role in enabling us to maximize pleasure as that is ordinarily conceived. Nowhere else is pleasure, as that is ordinarily conceived, taken to be something which can be taken up uncriticized and untransformed into the happy life. In all the other four dialogues pleasure is an element which appears greatly altered in the final product. The *Protagoras* passage, in which the ordinary notion of pleasure becomes our final end and has reason to serve it, is thus exceptional. However, it has chanced to fit in well with post-utilitarian theories of pleasure to such an extent that its eccentricity as a Platonic position tends to escape us. Many scholars have found in the *Protagoras* passage a satisfying account of pleasure and reason, in part because it fits in with

---

[56] *Protagoras* 351A–361D.

[57] *Protagoras* 357A5–B3, trans. Stanley Lombardo and Karen Bell (Indianapolis: Hackett, 1992).

modern views that limit reason to an instrumental role and assume pleasure to be something uniform whatever its sources.

But does this hedonist thesis represent Plato's own view? Or does he present Socrates as arguing on its basis in a dialectical spirit, testing its consequences while remaining uncommitted to it?[58] It may not be significant which position we take here; since the *Protagoras* passage is so out of line with Plato's other treatments of pleasure, it may not matter so greatly exactly *why* it is so out of line. Nonetheless, if the passage indicates a change of mind on Plato's part, it is a change of mind so fundamental, especially on the role of reason, that it is more charitable to suppose the passage to be discussed dialectically.

First, if it expressed Plato's own view, this would suit a modern preoccupation with finding a definite and quantifiable specification of what our final end is; this has appealed to scholars with otherwise utterly different methodological assumptions.[59] But this is, precisely, a modern preoccupation; it has no echo in the ancient world, and is quite foreign to ancient ethical theory. To see the *Protagoras* passage in these terms is to run an obvious risk of anachronism.

Moreover, if the hedonist thesis is Plato's answer to a substantial philosophical problem, it is strange that it is arbitrarily tacked on to the end of a long dialogue most of which, on this view, is about something else. If, however, the thesis is one which Socrates is considering without being committed to, this fits with a conception of the dialogue as teaching a philosophical lesson about methodology, something done throughout the dialogue. Protagoras appears throughout as someone who, though he has a big reputation, fundamentally dislikes argument and is no good at it; his attempts to meet Socrates' arguments

[58] The "dialectical" interpretation is put forward by Michael Frede, in his introduction to the Hackett translation (see n. 57); however, he does not support it in detail from the text.

[59] That the *Protagoras* gives us an interpretation of *eudaimonia* which is definite and quantifiable and thus gives us a decision-procedure for working out what to do is a view shared by Grote (1888), Nussbaum (1986), and Irwin (1995). See Grote's chapter on the *Protagoras,* and also his chapter on the *Euthydemus,* where he complains of the alleged vagueness of Plato's account of happiness. "There is only one dialogue in which the question [What is the Good?] is answered affirmatively, in clear and unmistakeable language, and with considerable development—and that is, the Protagoras: where Sokrates asserts and proves at length, that Good is at the bottom identical with pleasure, and Evil with pain: that the measuring or calculating intelligence is the truly regal art of life, upon which the attainment of Good depends: and that the object of that intelligence—the items which we are to measure, calculate and compare—is pleasures and pains, so as to secure to ourselves as much as possible of the former, and escape as much as possible of the latter" (pp. 540–41). See Nussbaum 1986, chap. 4, and Irwin 1995, chap. 6. Irwin (p. 88) endorses Grote's claim that the questions about happiness raised in the *Euthydemus* can be answered with pleasure as a "more determinate and specific" conception of happiness.

founder because of vanity and inability to argue. In the context of the dialogue Socrates has no motivation suddenly to espouse a position about pleasure and reason which runs sharply up against every other treatment of the issues that we find in Plato. But he does have the motivation to force Protagoras to argue properly.[60]

We thus end up finding no completely overall view about pleasure and reason in Plato; though the *Laws* and *Republic* can usefully be considered together, and the *Philebus* and *Gorgias,* although in some ways different, fit in with this picture, the *Protagoras* gives us a view which cannot be harmonized with them. Does this matter? When we look at the entire picture of Plato's treatments of pleasure, it can be seen to matter less than might appear from recent scholarly concentration on the *Protagoras.* Whether Plato puts forward the view as one that he is committed to at the time, or merely has Socrates put it forward for dialectical discussion, the *Protagoras* examines a view of pleasure in a way that has no analogue elsewhere in Plato. Why should Plato not have tried out a different view on a difficult matter?

It might appear, however, as though I have taken too unifying a view on the remaining four dialogues. They differ, after all, in style and method quite considerably. I have tried to follow as far as I reasonably could the track of the ancient Platonists, who thought that Plato had a single view on pleasure. I have shown that this view has much to commend it, and that it directs us to a more fruitful interpretation than the usual approach through contrasting *Protagoras* with *Gorgias.* Clearly, however, much remains to be explored. Some may feel that the level of description uniting all four dialogues is too general; perhaps what links *Philebus* with *Gorgias* renders them both substantially different from the *Laws* and *Republic,* complicating the comparison I wish to make here. It is also, of course, startling to us to link the *Philebus* more closely with the *Gorgias* than with the *Laws,* to which it is closer in the standard developmental story. Some may also object to the idea that the *Protagoras* treats pleasure dialectically, whereas we find Plato discussing pleasure in a committed way in the other four—since the *Gorgias,* at least, has some features linking it to discussions in the *Protagoras* and other Socratic dialogues.[61]

It has never been part of my claim, however, that the ancient Platonists should always have the last word. Their claims are in any case too broad to satisfy mod-

---

[60] See Appendix for an extended defense of the dialectical reading of Socrates' position about pleasure in the *Protagoras.*

[61] I am grateful to Brad Inwood for pressing this point. I remain convinced, however, that the *Protagoras* is dialectical in a stronger sense than other Socratic dialogues, since the practice of question and answer is the subject of the dialogue to a greater extent in it, and accordingly its Socrates is more methodologically self-conscious.

ern standards of scholarship. In the case of pleasure, the helpful texts fit the *Laws* best, and little or nothing is said to show how the account should be extended to other dialogues. Nor do we have any idea how the *Protagoras* was brought into their picture. Nonetheless, the ancient Platonist account serves, I think, to move us forward in many ways. It directs us to crucial texts that have been neglected because of developmental emphasis. It directs us to an interpretation which offers the hope of finding an overall account in dialogues which also treat pleasure rather differently. And it indicates that the kind of account we find in Plato is one quite remote from modern theories of pleasure, but is, like Aristotle's theory of pleasure, philosophically interesting in its own right. Once again, the ancient Platonists turn out to point us down an old road which leads us in new directions.

CONCLUSION

I hope that the reader has come to share my thought that the ancient Platonists point us in an illuminating direction, and that modern Plato studies—at least in the area of ethics, which is all I have tried to cover here—would benefit from a greater readiness to see them as partners in the interpretation of Plato. Certainly it seems quite inadequate to regard them as merely fitting Plato into an anachronistic mold.

Of course I have not tried to argue that Plato's ancient interpreters are right on all points. There are obvious reservations that we are in a position to make about their approach to Plato. For a start, since they are not a unified school, they do not always agree on a crucial matter. We have seen that Alcinous's approach to the moral psychology of the *Republic* is utterly different from, and at odds with, that of Galen and Plutarch. Alcinous sees the tripartite soul as compatible with the moral psychology of the Socratic dialogues, including the reciprocity of the virtues, and in the process works out an account of the tripartite soul which gives reason a role of persuasion and agreement in the development of the other parts and their integration into a whole. Galen and Plutarch, on the other hand, see the tripartite soul as a combination of elements which are robustly separate and always in a state of struggle and conflict, in which the winner dominates by force and violence. Finding two such disparate interpretations, however, obviously should not lead us to lose confidence in the ancient Platonists as interpreters—for here the two different approaches alert us to a tension in Plato's own writings. Later writers pick up on one or the other side of a debate sharpened by the development of Stoic moral psychology. As we have frequently seen, a later debate or development clarifies an issue for ancient inter-

preters of Plato more than it was clarified for Plato himself.[1] In this way the ancient Platonists, by their divergencies within a common set of assumptions, may
direct us to real problems in Plato.

The ancient Platonists, as is clear by now, were more unitarian in tendency than
all but a few modern interpreters are. I have argued that despite their currently
unfashionable status, unitarian interpretations deserve to be taken seriously. The
current dominance of the developmental paradigm for interpreting Plato has
frequently blinded us to the idea that it is merely one among alternatives, not the
only serious option.

Moreover, there are many different kinds of unitarian interpretation. Sometimes we cannot but feel that the ancient Platonists tried to find a unified system
of ideas at too high a level, passing over problems of detail. When they look for
Plato's account of our final end, they emphasize an idea which modern scholars
have ignored, of virtue as "becoming like God." But they assume that this can
be read into Plato's work as a whole, as though Plato always has a single account
of virtue and happiness which can accommodate this. As we saw in Chapter 3,
this assumption is too optimistic; although the idea of aiming to become like
God plays an important role in Plato's thought, it also appears to go with an unworldly streak which turns out to be in considerable tension with his more usual
view of virtue as the practical skill of working on the materials of this world, that
is, putting external goods to use. Also, though the ancient accounts of Plato's
position on pleasure direct us to a more helpful place than modern developmental views, they too pay little attention to the ways in which this account
might be fitted on to a number of dialogues with rather disparate views on pleasure. As to how a possibly conflicting piece of evidence, such as the *Protagoras,*
might be dealt with, they are silent. Again, this does not seem to be a good reason for ignoring or rejecting the ancient Platonists, but rather is a reason for following up in greater detail than they do the interpretations they propose.

Sometimes we may also feel that the later Platonists imposed on their reading
of Plato more precision on an issue than Plato's own writings warrant. When
they read Plato's dialogues in terms of the three parts of philosophy, we may
sometimes feel that this imposes a degree of self-consciousness about method
and treatment not always appropriate to Plato. But once again this does not in-
validate their approach; it merely shows that we must be cautious in our own

---

[1] The same may be true for the sufficiency of virtue: most ancient Platonists hold that
this is Plato's view, whereas Plutarch and Calvenus Taurus denied it. Unfortunately, we
know nothing of their grounds for holding this. It is tempting to think that they ascribed
to Plato an "Antiochean" view on the basis of the passages discussed in Chapter 2, but
this is speculation.

employment of it. Analyzing Plato philosophically in terms of the three parts of philosophy is not so dissimilar to the approach of modern books and articles on Plato, which divide his works up in ways that are familiar and congenial to us; no such approach implies that we should simply disregard the dialogue form and its implications. However, the ancient approach may warn us against a common and influential reading of the *Republic* in particular. Because in it we find ethics, metaphysics, and politics mixed together, we may wrongly infer that they are more closely linked than they are—that the ethics depends on the metaphysics or the politics, or both, for its content. It has been argued at length that such inferences are mistaken. Worse, we may, because of the central role that the *Republic* has come to have for us, think that this mixture is either typical of Plato or presented as a solution to problems that arise for dialogues where the issues are treated separately. The ancient thematic approach is here useful in directing us away from a mistaken emphasis on the *Republic* and a mistaken interpretation of its contents.

Despite reservations such as this, however, the ancient Platonists have proved to be useful partners in the project of interpreting Plato. We would, after all, expect eudaimonists to have an edge in interpreting a eudaimonist theory, and this proves to be the case. We would expect them to take advantage of the greater precision and clarity about the issues achieved through lengthy debate, and this is what we find. If we are inclined to be dismissive about, for example, the tendency to see Plato in Stoic as against Aristotelian terms, we are dismissing the viewpoint of philosophers within a debate in favor of our own, although we are outside the debate and may not be sensitive to the development of the issues. Indeed, it is surprising that as a resource for discussing Plato's ethical theory the ancient Platonists have been relatively neglected in scholarly discussion.

One final reservation has already been noted. In the twentieth century unitarianism has often been associated with an approach to Plato which is dogmatic in the pejorative sense: insensitive to the arguments on which positions are based and to which they answer. We need to recover the idea of a unitarian approach which allows for the arguments to have due weight. Here the ancient Platonists are particularly interesting. Some take Plutarch's quite open position, welcoming the skeptical Academy, while others take the narrow, dogmatic line of Numenius and reject it.

The people we call Middle Platonists were aware of following a tradition which identified Platonic philosophy with Socrates' practice of ad hominem arguing and refusing to be committed to his own philosophical position. In taking Plato to hold a system of doctrines, they could choose to turn their back on that tradition, as Numenius did, or else to look to it for support and continuity. Even those of them who do not explicitly raise the matter could find it open to them to accept their own historic tradition. For doctrine can coexist alongside the practice of ad hominem argument. Even if the latter does not directly support the former, it alerts us to the importance of clearing away false opinions before adopting others taken to be true, and also the importance of adopting a position solely as the result of a reasoned conviction that it is true—a conviction that can come only from thorough personal reflection and argument.

Accounts such as those we find in Alcinous's *Handbook of Platonism* could and can be used as compendia of views to be learned and parroted. But they can also serve as the basis for discussion and argument, leading the reader to question her own position as to what Plato thinks and how well based it is. Used as a stimulus to reflection in this way, such works get the reader to question her own views as to the truth of the matter in engagement with Plato. We cannot, for example, properly answer the question whether Plato holds that virtue is sufficient for happiness, without reflecting for ourselves on the grounds for this view. In this book I have tried to take the ancient Platonists as partners in something like this way. So taken, they contribute to the ongoing relationship between Platonic doctrine and Platonic argument which forms part of most modern interpretative practice.

If this makes the ancient Platonists sound like modern interpreters of Plato, this seems to me a vindication of my approach rather than an objection to it; for it has been my aim all along to show that where Platonic ethics is concerned, we can learn from the old, mainly by seeing how it can contribute more than we might think to the new. Of course, we do not have to read Plato as the ancients did. But we do not have to read him as the Victorians did, either. And it is Victorian assumptions about how to read Plato (particularly with respect to the *Republic*) which linger unremarked in our practice, not ancient ones. And hence it is, perhaps surprisingly, the ancients who are best fitted to wake us from our developmental slumbers.

APPENDIX:

HEDONISM IN THE *PROTAGORAS*

Is the hedonist thesis in the *Protagoras* Socrates' own position, or is it a position adopted ad hominem against Protagoras? This view of the options informs much recent work on the dialogue, but perhaps the idea that these are exclusive alternatives does not do justice to them, or to ancient views of the issue.

Certainly the thesis is presented, in the argument we find in the dialogue, in an ad hominem manner. It is worth tracing the interaction of Socrates and Protagoras in the dialogue to bring this out.

Protagoras is introduced to us as someone who holds forth at length and makes an evasive answer to a straightforward question (318A–B). When he is forced to be precise, claiming that he teaches the expertise of citizenship (319A), Socrates points out that this is inconsistent with Athenian democratic ideology, leaving Protagoras with a problem, since he hopes to find customers in Athens for his supposed expertise. Protagoras responds with a story and discussion (320C–328D) which, rather than clarifying his position, bring out vividly the difficulties for it. The ability in question, now called justice, is something that everybody has an aptitude for, and picks up from their cultural surroundings, like learning one's native language. Protagoras claims that his teaching merely furthers this; if so, however, his notion of an *expertise* of virtue seems to be a feeble one, falling far short of the standards which Socrates assumes when he is talking about expertise. The bulk of the dialogue consists of Socrates' attempts to show Protagoras that, in thinking of virtue as made up of unconnected "parts," he is thinking of it in a way that implies that it is not teachable in the way implied by Protagoras's claims to be an expensive teacher. However, it is also a continuing lesson in the contrast of method; Socrates persistently tries to get Protagoras to engage in argument, unsuccessfully, since Protagoras (like many pretentious lecturers) turns out to be useless at argument, handicapped by a combination of ineptitude and ego. Protagoras retains his superiority at continuous speeches, but by the end of the dialogue his claims to be an intelligent teacher have been very thoroughly undermined.

Socrates' method of argument is called *dialegesthai*. The conversation at 335B–338E reveals that, alongside a broad sense of *dialegesthai,* meaning discussion or argument in general (335D, 336B), the audience recognizes a narrower sense in which it refers to the method of argument that Socrates uses, and can be described as "dialectical argument" (335B, 336C–D). In the *Protagoras* this requires that the interlocutor defend a thesis and answer Socrates' questions honestly (331C), but, in contrast to other Socratic dialogues, it does not require that the thesis defended be what the interlocutor is personally committed to (333B–C). The interlocutor must agree to be the respondent and to defend the thesis against Socrates' questions; the point of doing that is not, here, directly to test the interlocutor's beliefs, and hence his life, but to test the thesis, as a way of discovering whether it is true. It is indirectly a test of both respondent and questioner in that it serves to clarify what they are committed to, and enable them to discard false beliefs (333C, 348C, 360E–361A).

So, throughout the dialogue, Socrates makes Protagoras be the respondent. In the first argument (330B–332A) he introduces Protagoras to this idea by joining him as the respondent against an anonymous questioner. Thus he gives the answers, but then forces Protagoras to see that he, Protagoras, is committed to the answers, since it is his thesis that has been questioned and he has gone along with Socrates' answers (330E–331B). Protagoras, however, balks. Forced into answering yes or no to a question, where the answer yes clearly commits him to an assertion conflicting with his original one, he refuses to say either, trying to disengage from the argument and changing the subject by drawing a distinction (331C–E). Unable to think of a move to make if he says no, and unwilling to be committed to contradicting himself, he dodges the issue. It is the first, but not the last, time in the dialogue where he makes a move familiar on the part of people who find argument threatening and uncongenial.

Socrates drops the argument and then walks Protagoras firmly through the second argument (332A–333B), allowing no irrelevance, pointing out the options, and forcing Protagoras unwillingly to admit that he cannot hold to his original statement. Protagoras, clearly worsted, henceforth tries to avoid dialectical argument, but is not allowed to (though there is no doubt that Socrates' method is the one that Plato approved of, Socrates is not, and perhaps is not meant to be, an endearing figure in this dialogue).

In the third argument Protagoras, anxious to avoid a repetition of what happened in the second, takes the first opportunity to go off on an irrelevant speech

(334A–C), and the argument is aborted. Socrates, seeing that Protagoras is unwilling to persist with dialectical argument (335A–B), washes his hands of the discussion, and has to be prevailed on by the audience to stay, and to accept a kind of quid pro quo whereby he and Protagoras discuss a poem by Simonides before the argument is resumed. Socrates' outrageous interpretation of the poem is not directly relevant to the main argument (though it is worth noting that Simonides, the poet whose work he treats so cavalierly, is traditionally the first poet to compose for money, and the reference to Prodicus and Simonides at 340E–341A links the poet with the Sophists, probably because of their commercial attitude).

When the argument resumes, Socrates makes Protagoras clear about the position he is to defend as respondent: the earlier thesis is dismissed, and Protagoras undertakes to defend the claim that courage is distinct from the other virtues, and in particular from wisdom (349D). Socrates first tries to get Protagoras to defend this directly, but Protagoras yet again evades the argument by going off in his own direction (350E–351A). This time Socrates switches the argument very abruptly; at 351B he brusquely introduces another idea, the first appearance of the hedonist thesis, which Socrates tries to get Protagoras to defend, though Protagoras rejects it as his own personal position (351D). Socrates introduces hedonism as an idea of his own (351C), but when at 351E Protagoras, still failing to grasp that he is the one supposed to be defending the thesis, treats the idea as a thesis Socrates is defending, Socrates abruptly rejects this, insisting rather rudely that he is in charge of the argument, and tries yet a third tack to get Protagoras to face the argument.

This time he focuses on the existence of *akrasia*. Despairing of getting Protagoras to defend it, however, he reuses the tactic of the first argument; he joins Protagoras against a fictional third party, in this case "the many." This time the third party is cast as the respondent, and Socrates (and notionally Protagoras) asks the questions. Protagoras, still confusing the importance of querying a thesis with the matter of who holds it, has to be persuaded of the point of examining views ascribed to "the many" (353A), but thereafter introduces no more irrelevancies, and at the end of the long argument Socrates insists that the existence of *akrasia* has been disproved (358E). This argument depends on the respondent ("the many") accepting not only the existence of *akrasia* but hedonism; it is pointed out at 355A that the argument can be rejected if the respondent is willing to give up hedonism. This point makes it clear that hedonism is being defended as a position in argument by a respondent who does not accept it in person, since it was made clear at 351C that in fact "the many" do not accept hedonism. Since Protagoras has notionally joined with Socrates in the argument, he cannot dissent, and with this in hand Socrates ruthlessly makes Protagoras defend the distinctness of courage and wisdom, which predictably leads to Protagoras's being forced to admit a conclusion inconsistent with his initial claim (360D–E). Protagoras is ungracious and tries to personalize the dispute, but in the end concedes defeat more politely (362D–E).

Hedonism, as we have seen, is not the actual position of the many, though they are made to defend it in argument. Is hedonism Protagoras's position? Personally, he rejects it, but it appears as part of the position which he is assuming in the final argument (360A), and he makes no argumentative moves to reject it, so he is left in the potentially embarrassing position of having accepted a position in argument which he was unwilling to take on.

Finally, is hedonism Socrates' own position? On the one hand, it is introduced as a position which Socrates unsuccessfully tries to get Protagoras to accept, and which is rejected by the many. Socrates is the only one discussing it, and at 351C4 it is marked as what Socrates says (*egō gar legō*). As soon as Protagoras starts treating it as Socrates' own position in the argument, however, Socrates drops it abruptly and tries a different tack. We thus have unambiguous indications both that Socrates introduces the position and that it is not his position in the argument. He has, after all, spent much of the dialogue trying to explain, guide, and bully Protagoras into being the respondent. It would make no sense at all for him, so late in this project, to start defending any position in his own person.

The dialogue, then, gives us clear evidence that hedonism is not Socrates' own position, if by that we have in mind a position defended in argument. But the careful explication of dialectical argument in the dialogue makes it clear that this provides no evidence at all either for or against the idea that it is Socrates' position in the sense of a thesis which he personally holds. In the *Protagoras* what you personally believe and what you defend in argument are two quite different things, as is illustrated by Protagoras's various inept confusions of them.

Is the fact that Socrates explicitly introduces the idea himself evidence that he personally accepted it, despite refusing to defend it in argument? No, as we can see from the briefest reflection on actual argumentative practice. Philosophers often introduce theses into the argument which they do not themselves personally accept, and for precisely the reason which Socrates lays out in the *Protagoras*: they are interested in finding out the truth about the thesis, not in the issue of who personally believes what. That this is what Socrates is doing is indeed strongly suggested by the fact that it crops up in his third attempt to get Protagoras to understand how to argue about courage and wisdom.

Thus all we can reasonably infer is that Plato thought hedonism in this form worth formulating and discussing, and so introduced it into Socrates' argument. At a minimal level, then, he takes it seriously. Is this position an exclusive alternative to the standard doctrinal interpretation? It depends on what the doctrinal position is. Since the hedonism of the *Protagoras* is so different in kind from the forms of theory about pleasure which occupy Plato elsewhere (pleasure being taken at its face value and set up as our final end, and reason subordinated to an instrumental role in obtaining it), perhaps there is not so much difference be- tween an interpretation holding that Plato commits Socrates to hedonism only in the *Protagoras* and one holding a position like the above, that he introduces it as a thesis worth discussing and using in an argument about the unity of the virtues. (An important difference would remain in that on the standard doctrinal view, Plato is indicating a way of explicating the unity of the virtues which he himself, if only temporarily, accepts, whereas on the view sketched above, Plato would be, in this dialogue, raising problems about the unity of the virtues rather than giving his own solution to it.) However, an interpretation according to which Plato takes hedonism seriously as a thesis worth introducing into argu- ment is scarcely strong enough to sustain the idea that the hedonism in the *Protagoras* is an important aspect of a whole segment of Plato's thought, serving to explain Platonic thesis outside the *Protagoras* itself. There is little evidence as to how the *Protagoras* was read in the ancient world, but, although the kind of in- terpretation given here is clearly in the spirit of ancient skeptical interpretations of Plato, we find no trace of the modern view that hedonism of this sort can serve to give a good answer to questions arising outside the dialogue. Perhaps this is connected to the fact that at any rate the Platonists were more interested in Plato's accounts of pleasure elsewhere, which make pleasure transformable by reason, than in an account of pleasure which turns reason into an instrumental means to achieve pleasure as an unquestioned goal.

CAST OF CHARACTERS

Brief biographical notes are provided on authors referred to in the book. The notes refer only to what is relevant for this book; for fuller information, see the *Oxford Classical Dictionary* (3d ed., 1996) or the Garland *Encyclopaedia of Classical Philosophy* (ed. D. Zeyl).

ACADEMY   Plato's school, originally in the grounds of a gymnasium. After Plato's death the Old Academy (Speusippus, Xenocrates, Polemon, Crantor, and Crates) for a time developed original metaphysical and possibly ethical ideas, and seem also to have argued about the interpretation of Plato's works. With the headship of Arcesilaus (around 268 B.C.) the Academy took a different turn, to emulating the ad hominem and negative argumentative style of Socrates, and continued, the most famous successor being Carneades, as the New or Skeptical Academy. We know little of institutionalized attention to Plato's work at this date. The Academics principally argued against their main dogmatic rivals, the Stoics, in ever more organized and familiar ways. From the accession of the last head, Philo of Larisa, around 110 B.C., the Academy's tradition was under stress. Philo himself held a modified position: views reached as a result of systematic argument are not established as true, but warrant some reasonable confidence. Against this Antiochus broke away to found a frankly dogmatic, eclectic school, and Aenesidemus broke away in the other direction, to found a new form of radical skepticism named after Pyrrho. After the sack of Athens in 88 B.C. the Academy petered out as an institution. From the first century B.C. we find various "Platonists" who interpret Plato as holding doctrines and are committed to these, but they are not continuous with the Academy and do not form a unified school or institution.

ALBINUS A Platonist philosopher, pupil of Gaius. Galen heard Albinus lecture at Smyrna in A.D. 151–52; his date and place are otherwise unknown. The only work of his preserved is a short preface to Plato's dialogues (*Prologos* or *Eisagōgē*) (text in Hermann's Teubner edition of Plato). Extensive notes on Plato, based on lectures by Gaius, and probably commentaries on *Phaedo* and *Timaeus* have been lost. In 1879 the German scholar Jakob Freudenthal proposed that Albinus was the author of the *Handbook of Platonism* that we have, the author's name "Alcinous" being a corruption of Albinus. Until recently, Albinus has been treated as the author of the work, but recent scholarly work has thoroughly undermined the identification, and with it the assumption of a Platonist "School of Gaius."

ALCINOUS Author of a *Handbook of Platonism,* otherwise unknown. In 1879 the German scholar Jakob Freudenthal proposed that "Alcinous" was a textual corruption for "Albinus," thereby identifying the author with the Platonist Albinus, who has a place and date. Until recently, Albinus was treated as the author of the work, but the identification is now generally rejected. As a result, Alcinous has reverted to having no fixed date (the work could have been written between the first century B.C. and the second century A.D.) and to being for us no more than a name. There are correspondences, one major, with the account of Platonism in Arius Didymus. While the author of the *Handbook* was identified with an author in the second century A.D., this was taken to imply that the Platonist author copied from an earlier non-Platonist history of ideas; but now that the date of the *Handbook* is once more regarded as uncertain, no conclusions about date or dependency are secure. All we can say is that Alcinous and Arius share some of their sources.

ANONYMOUS COMMENTATOR ON THE *THEAETETUS* Author of a commentary on papyrus, preserved only in its first part, on Plato's *Theaetetus*. The author knows and rejects the position of the skeptical Academy, and writes as a doctrinal Platonist, but cannot be identified with any other Platonist known to us. The commentary's date is disputed; suggestions range from the first century B.C. to the second century A.D. (the date of the papyrus).

APULEIUS Platonist philosopher from Madaura, born around A.D. 125. He also wrote works of rhetoric and a novel, *The Golden Ass*. His work *On Plato's Doctrines* in two books is in some ways comparable with Alcinous's *Handbook,* particularly in the ethics. When the *Handbook* was ascribed to Albinus, this gave rise to the idea of a Platonist "School of Gaius." But careful comparison shows that, though in some respects they may rely on a common tradition, the works are not similar overall or in detail.

ARISTOCLES   An Aristotelian philosopher of the first or second centuries A.D. Nothing is known about him, unless he can be identified with the "Aristoteles" who was the teacher of Alexander of Aphrodisias, the great Aristotelian commentator. Long extracts of Aristocles' history of philosophy are quoted in Eusebius's *Preparation for the Gospel.* They are generally of a high standard when compared, for example, with Diogenes Laertius.

ARISTOTLE   of Stageira, 384–322 B.C. Plato's most famous pupil, who eventually founded his own school, the Lyceum. Aristotle in several of his own works engages with Plato's ideas, but he also devotes much attention to other philosophers, and the account he gives of Plato's place in the history of philosophy is in many ways puzzling and unconvincing. Later Platonists either tried to harmonize away divergences between Plato and Aristotle (for example, Arius) or regarded them as essentially opposed (for example, Atticus).

ARIUS DIDYMUS   First-century B.C. philosopher, probably to be identified with Arius the court philosopher of Augustus; possibly a Stoic. Fragments survive on philosophers' views about physics (edited by Diels); also three long passages on ethics, preserved in the anthology collected by John Stobaeus in the fifth century A.D. Two are long accounts of Stoic and Aristotelian ethics. The third is a condensed and confused introduction to ethics, which contains material on Plato. Correspondences between Arius and Alcinous were thought to show Alcinous's dependence on Arius, as long as Alcinous was identified with the later Platonist Albinus. But without this identification it is not clear which author is the earlier (especially as the identification of Arius Didymus with Augustus's court philosopher is not certain). We can safely say only that Arius and Alcinous share some sources.

ATTICUS   Platonist philosopher, ca. A.D.150–200, possibly at Athens. Passages survive from his works, attacking Aristotle and the idea that Plato's ethical ideas are similar to Aristotle's. He took a literal view of the creation of the world in Plato's *Timaeus.*

CHRYSIPPUS   Ca. 280–208 B.C., from Soli in Cilicia. Third head of the Stoa, and its most influential philosopher; he restated Zeno's positions and strengthened them by copious argument and organization.

DEMOCRITUS   Philosopher from Abdera, fifth to fourth century B.C. The second and more influential philosopher of atomism. Plato never mentions him, though his ideas are clearly in view in *Laws* book 10; but his ethical views are represented by Hellenistic authors as eudaimonistic in form, as are Plato's, and his views on pleasure are coupled by Arius with Plato's view of pleasure in the *Laws*.

DIOGENES LAERTIUS   Second- to third-century A.D. author of a ten-volume *Lives of the Philosophers*, which combines chatty gossip with accounts of their philosophy. Diogenes is uncritical and is only as good as his sources, which are very mixed. The account of Plato's philosophy is comparable with other "Middle Platonist" accounts.

GALEN   A.D. 129–ca. 210, from Pergamon. Doctor with philosophical interests. His work *The Doctrines of Hippocrates and Plato* defends a radical position about parts of the soul which he claims to find in Plato, particularly the *Republic* and *Timaeus*. He pits this against the Stoic view and claims Posidonius as an ally.

NUMENIUS   of Apamea, second century A.D. A Platonist, sometimes referred to also as a Pythagorean. His work *On the Revolt of the Academy from Plato* belittles the skeptical Academy and claims that it was an aberration from the true Platonic tradition, which he holds to be Pythagorean, converging with ancient wisdom from India, Persia, Israel, and Egypt.

PHILO OF ALEXANDRIA   Ca. 20 B.C.– A.D. 45. Jewish philosopher, whose works take the form of commentary on the Pentateuch. Philo's philosophical education is extensive, and he makes use of Stoicism as well as Platonic themes. He can be counted as a "Middle Platonist" if due allowance is made for the fact that his own self-conception is as a student of Scripture rather than as a member of a Greek philosophical school.

PLATO   of Athens, ca. 429–347 B.C. Plato wrote a large number of dialogues throughout his long life. We know little about the audience or audiences for these dialogues, or about the relation between the dialogues, especially the more technical ones, and Plato's own teaching in the Academy. Plato's school went through different stages after his death (see Academy), but his works seem to have been continuously popular because of their literary appeal. After the end of the skeptical Academy the rise of "Platonism," with Plato's ideas treated as a set of doctrines, could take the form of commentaries on dialogues, or handbook accounts of his major ideas.

PLOTINUS   of Lycopolis, A.D. 204–270. Platonist philosopher of great originality, generally considered the first "Neoplatonist," since his work (arranged by his follower Porphyry in six sets of "enneads," or groups of nine treatises) breaks with previous Platonists in its intense philosophical focus on a set of abstract issues arising from Plato's works, but developed in a distinctively new way.

PLUTARCH of Chaeronea, ca.A.D. 45–125. Platonist philosopher, who also wrote numerous *Lives* of famous Greeks and Romans. His hostile works against Stoics and Epicureans almost certainly use arguments from the skeptical Academy, which he respects. His own version of Platonism, however, is that of a set of doctrines, though supported by and answerable to argument. He is personally more interested in the metaphysical and religious aspects of Platonism than in the ethics.

POSIDONIUS Ca. 135–51 B.C. Stoic philosopher from Apamea. Although he defended Stoicism, his interests ranged beyond those of his predecessors, and he was interested in natural phenomena and their explanations more than was typical for a Stoic. In psychology he made some important innovations, the exact nature of which is difficult to determine because of the bias of Galen, our major source.

SOCRATES of Athens, 469–399 B.C. Socrates devoted his life to philosophizing, and was put to death by the restored democracy. He wrote nothing, and his philosophical legacy was immediately and continually disputed. Several writers as well as Plato wrote "Socratic dialogues" in which he was represented as a figurehead for different ideas. The appropriation of Socrates continued into the Hellenistic period, with the skeptical Academy and the Stoics both regarding him as a founding figure. Socrates was agreed to be the ideal figure of the philosopher, but the content of his ideas continued to be interpreted in mutually conflicting ways.

ZENO of Citium, ca. 334–262 B.C. Founder of Stoicism, he laid its basis in all major areas, and was an influential teacher.

EDITIONS USED

Albinus

    Eisagōgē eis tous Platōnos dialogous. In *Platonis dialogi secundum Thrasylli tetralogias dispositi,* vol. 6, ed. C. F. Hermann. Leipzig: Teubner, 1853, 147–51.

Alcinous

    J. Whittaker. *Alcinoos: Enseignement des doctrines de Platon.* Les Belles Lettres. Paris: Budé, 1990.

Anonymous Commentator on Plato's Theaetetus

    Text, translation, and commentary by G. Bastianini and D. Sedley. In *Corpus dei papiri filosofici greci e latini,* vol. 3. Florence: Olschki, 1995, 227–562.

Apuleius

    J. Beaujeu. *Apulée: Opuscules philosophiques (Du Dieu de Socrate, Platon et sa doctrine, Du monde).* Les Belles Lettres. Paris: Budé, 1971.

Aristotle

    Nicomachean Ethics. Ed. I. Bywater. Oxford Classical Texts, 1894.
    Politics. Ed. W. D. Ross. Oxford Classical Texts, 1977.

Arius Didymus

    Stobaeus. *Eclogae* 2. Ed. C. Wachsmuth. Berlin: Weidmann, 1884.

Atticus

    E. des Places. *Atticus: Fragments.* Text and translation. Les Belles Lettres. Paris: Budé, 1977.

Cicero

    De finibus. Ed. J. N. Madvig. Copenhagen, 1876.
    De officiis. Ed. M. Winterbottom. Oxford Classical Texts, 1994.
    Tusculan Disputations. Ed. T. Dougan and R. Henry. New York: Arno, 1979.

Diogenes Laertius
H. S. Long. *Diogenis Laertii Vitae Philosophorum.* Oxford Classical Texts, 1964.

Galen
P. de Lacy, ed. and trans. *Galeni De Placitis Hippocratis et Platonis.* Corpus Medicorum Graecorum 5.4.1, 2, 3. Berlin: Akademie Verlag, 1978, 1980, 1984.

Numenius
E. des Places, ed. and trans. *Numénius.* Les Belles Lettres. Paris: Budé, 1973.

Philo
On Flight and Finding. Ed. F. H. Colson and G. H. Whittaker. Philo, vol. 5. Loeb Classical Library. Cambridge: Harvard University Press, 1934.

Plato
Platonis Opera. Vol. 1, ed. E. A. Duke et al., 1995. Vols. 2–5, ed. J. Burnet, 1901–7. Oxford Classical Texts.

Plotinus
Plotini Opera. Ed. P. Henry and H. R. Schwyzer. 3 vols. Oxford Classical Texts, 1964–83.

Plutarch
Platonic Questions. In Plutarch's *Moralia,* vol. 13, part 1, ed. H. Cherniss. Loeb Library. Cambridge: Harvard University Press, 1976.

Pseudo-Pythagorean ethical writings
The Pythagorean Texts of the Hellenistic Period. Trans. H. Thesleff. Acta Academiae Aboensis, Humaniora 30.1. Abo, 1965.
Pseudopythagorica Ethica. Ed. B. Centrone. Naples: Bibliopolis, 1990.

Sextus Empiricus
Sexti Empirici Opera. 3 vols. Ed. H. Mutschmann and J. Mau. Leipzig: Teubner, 1914–58.

BIBLIOGRAPHY

Annas, Julia. 1981. *An Introduction to Plato's Republic*. Oxford.
——. 1992. *Hellenistic Philosophy of Mind*. Berkeley.
——. 1993. *The Morality of Happiness*. Oxford.
——. 1994. "Virtue as the Use of Other Goods." In *Virtue, Love, and Form*, ed. T. Irwin and M. C. Nussbaum. Edmonton, 53–66.
——. 1995. "Reply to Cooper." *Philosophy and Phenomenological Research* 55, 600–610.
——. 1996. "Happiness Then and Now." Taft Lecture. University of Cincinnati conference on *eudaimonia* and well-being.
——. 1997. "Virtue and Eudaimonism." *Virtue and Vice*. Social Philosophy and Policy Center. Cambridge.
——. Forthcoming. "Platonist Ethics and Plato." In a Festschrift for Jacques Brunschwig, ed. M. Canto-Sperber and P. Pellegrin.
Armstrong, John. 1998. "The Politics of Virtue in Plato's Laws." Ph.D. dissertation. University of Arizona.
Barker, E. 1906. *The Political Thought of Plato and Aristotle*. London.
Barnes, J., ed. 1995. *The Cambridge Companion to Aristotle*. Cambridge.
Boas, G. 1948. "Fact and Legend in the Biography of Plato." *Philosophical Review* 67, 439–57.
Boyancé, P. 1971. "Cicéron et les parties de la philosophie." *Revue des Etudes Latines* 49, 127–54.
Brickhouse, T., and N. Smith. 1994. *Plato's Socrates*. Oxford.
Brunt, P. 1993. "Plato's Academy and Politics." In Brunt, *Studies in Greek History and Thought*. Oxford, 282–342.
Burkert, W. 1971. "Zur geistesgeschichtlichen Einordnung einiger Pseudopythagorica." In *Pseudepigrapha*, vol. 1, *Entretiens sur l'Antiquité classique* (Fondation Hardt), ed. K. Von Fritz. Vandoevres-Genève, 25–55.

Bussanich, J. 1990. "The Invulnerability of Goodness: The Ethical and Psychological Theory of Plotinus." *Proceedings of the Boston Area Colloquium in Ancient Philosophy* 6, 151–94.

Cooper, J. 1995. "Eudaimonism and the Appeal to Nature in the Morality of Happiness." *Philosophy and Phenomenological Research* 55, 587–99.

———. 1997. "Poseidonius on the Emotions." In *Hellenistic Theories of the Emotions,* ed. J. Sihvola and T. Engberg-Pedersen. Florence.

Crossman, R. 1937. *Plato Today.* London.

DeFilippo, J. G., and P. Mitsis. 1994. "Socrates and Stoic Natural Law." In *The Socratic Movement,* ed. P. Vander Waerdt. Ithaca, N.Y., 252–71.

Demetriou, K. 1996. "The Development of Platonic Studies in Britain and the Role of the Utilitarians." *Utilitas* 9, no. 1, 15–37.

Dillon, J. 1977. *The Middle Platonists.* Ithaca, N.Y.

———. 1983. "Metriopatheia and Apatheia: Some Reflections on a Controversy in Later Greek Ethics." In *Essays in Ancient Greek Philosophy* 2, ed. J. Anton and A. Preus. Albany, N.Y., 508–17. Reprinted in Dillon 1990, chap. 8.

———. 1990. "Plotinus, Philo, and Origen on the Grades of Virtue." In J. Dillon, *The Golden Chain: Studies in the Development of Platonism and Christianity.* Aldershot, chap. 16.

———. 1993. *Alcinous: The Handbook of Platonism.* Clarendon Library of Later Philosophy. Oxford.

———. 1996. "An Ethic for the Late Antique Sage." In *The Cambridge Companion to Plotinus,* ed. L. Gerson. Cambridge, 315–35.

Donini, P. L. 1990. "Medioplatonismo e filosofi medioplatonici: Una raccolta di studi." *Elenchos* 11, 79–93.

Dörrie, H., and M. Baltes. 1990–96. *Der Platonismus in der Antike.* Vols. 2–4. Stuttgart/Bad Cannstatt.

Edelstein, L. 1966. *Plato's Seventh Letter.* Leiden.

Festugière, A. J. 1954. *Personal Religion among the Greeks.* Berkeley.

Field, G. C. 1924–25. "Socrates and Plato in the Post-Aristotelian Tradition." *Classical Quarterly* 18, 127–36; 19, 1–13. Reprinted in *Classical Philosophy: Collected Papers,* vol. 2, ed. T. Irwin (New York: Garland, 1995), 297–319.

———. 1930. *Plato and His Contemporaries.* London.

———. 1949. *The Philosophy of Plato.* Oxford.

Fortenbaugh, W. W., ed. 1983. *On Stoic and Peripatetic Ethics: The Work of Arius Didymus.* Rutgers University Studies in Classical Humanities, vol. 1. New Brunswick.

Frede, D. 1996. "How Sceptical Were the Academic Sceptics?" In *Scepticism in the History of Philosophy,* ed. R. H. Popkin. Dordrecht, 1–26.

———. 1997. "Die ungerechten Verfassungen und die ihnen entsprechenden Menschen (Buch VIII 543 a–IX 576 b)." In *Platon: Politeia,* ed. O. Höffe. Berlin, 251–70.

Frede, M. 1987. "Numenius." In *Aufstieg und Niedergang der Römischen Welt,* ed. W. Haase and H. Temporini, part 2 (Principat), 36.2, 1034–75.

Gill, C. 1973. "The Death of Socrates." *Classical Quarterly* 23, 25–28.

———. 1977. "The Genre of the Atlantis Story." *Classical Philology* 72, 287–304.

———. 1979. "Plato's Atlantis Story and the Birth of Fiction." *Philosophy and Literature* 3, 64–78.

———. 1997. "Did Galen Understand Platonic and Stoic Thinking on Emotions?" In *Hellenistic Theories of the Emotions,* ed. J. Sihvola and T. Engberg-Pedersen.

Glucker, J. 1987. "Plato in England: The Nineteenth Century and After." In *Utopie und Tradition: Platons Lehre vom Staat in der Moderne,* ed. H. Funke. Würzburg, 149–210.

———. 1996. "The Two Platos of Victorian England." In *Polyhistor: Studies in the History and Historiography of Ancient Philosophy,* presented to Jaap Mansfeld, ed. Keimpe Algra, Pieter van der Horst, and David Runia. Leiden, 385–406.

Göransson, T. 1995. *Albinus, Alcinous, Arius Didymus.* Studia Graeca et Latina Gothoburgensia. Göteborg.

Gosling, J. 1987. "The Stoics and *Akrasia.*" *Apeiron* 21, 179–202.

Grote, G. 1888. *Plato and the Other Companions of Sokrates.* London.

Grube, G. 1935. *Plato's Thought.* London.

Hadot, P. 1979. "Les divisions des parties de la philosophie dans l'Antiquité." *Museum Helveticum* 36, 210–23.

Hahm, D. E. 1990. "The Ethical Doxography of Arius Didymus." In *Aufstieg und Niedergang der Römischen Welt,* ed. W. Haase and H. Temporini, part 2 (Principat), 36.4, 2935–3243.

Ierodiakonou, K. 1993. "The Stoic Division of Philosophy." *Phronesis* 38, 57–74.

Inwood, B. 1996. Review of *Albinus, Alcinous, Arius Didymus,* by T. Göransson. *Bryn Mawr Classical Review* 7.1, 25–30.

Ioppolo, A.-M. 1993. "The Academic Position of Favorinus of Arelate." *Phronesis* 38, 183–213.

———. 1994. "Accademici e Pirroniani nel II secolo d.C." In *Realtà e Ragione,* ed. A. Alberti. Florence (Accademia Toscana di Scienze e Lettere "La Colombaria"). *Studi* 140, 85–103.

———. 1995. "Socrate nelle tradizioni accademico-scettica e pirroniana." In *La tradizione socratica,* ed. G. Giannantoni et al. Memorie dell'Istituto Italiano per gli Studi Filosofici. Naples, 89–123.

Irwin, T. 1995. *Plato's Ethics.* Oxford.

Jenkyns, R. 1980. *The Victorians and Ancient Greece.* Oxford.

Kahn, C. 1981. "Did Plato Write Socratic Dialogues?" *Classical Quarterly* 31, 305–20.

———. 1983 "Arius as a Doxographer." In *On Stoic and Peripatetic Ethics: The Work of Arius Didymus,* ed. W. W. Fortenbaugh. New Brunswick, N.J., 3–13.

———. 1988. "On the Relative Date of the *Gorgias* and the *Protagoras.*" *Oxford Studies in Ancient Philosophy* 6, 69–102.

———. 1996. *Plato and the Socratic Dialogue: The Philosophical Use of a Literary Form.* Cambridge.

Keyser, P. 1991. Review of *Recounting Plato,* by G. Ledger. *Bryn Mawr Classical Review* 2.7, 402–27.

———. 1992. Review of *The Chronology of Plato's Dialogues,* by L. Brandwood. *Bryn Mawr Classical Review* 3.1, 58–74.

Konstan, D., and P. Mitsis. 1990. "Chion of Heraclea: A Philosophical Novel in Letters." In *The Poetics of Therapy,* ed. M. Nussbaum. *Apeiron* (special issue) 23, 257–80.

Lefkowitz, Mary. 1981. *The Lives of the Greek Poets.* London.

Lilla, S. 1971. *Clement of Alexandria.* Oxford.

Long, A. A. 1988. "Socrates in Hellenistic Philosophy." *Classical Quarterly* 38, 150–71. Reprinted in *Stoic Studies,* ed. A. A. Long (Cambridge, 1996), 1–34.

Merki, H. 1952. *Homoiosis theoi: Von der platonischen Angleichung an Gott zur Gottähnlichkeit bei Gregor von Nyssa.* Freiburg.

Morgan, M. 1990. *Platonic Piety.* New Haven.

Nussbaum, M. 1986. *The Fragility of Goodness.* Cambridge.

Price, A. 1995. *Mental Conflict.* London.

Richard, C. J. 1994. *The Founders and the Classics.* Cambridge, Mass.

Riginos, Alice. 1976. *Platonica: The Anecdotes Concerning the Life and Writings of Plato.* Leiden.

Roberts, J. 1994. *Athens on Trial: The Antidemocratic Tradition in Western Thought.* Princeton.

Rue, R. 1993. "The Philosopher in Flight: The Digression (172c–177c) in the *Theaetetus.*" *Oxford Studies in Ancient Philosophy* 10, 71–100.

Schofield, M. 1984. "Ariston of Chios and the Unity of Virtue." *Ancient Philosophy* 4, 83–96.

———. 1991. *The Stoic Idea of the City.* Cambridge.

Sedley, D. 1996. "Three Platonist Interpretations of the *Theaetetus.*" In *Form and Argument in Late Plato,* ed. C. Gill and M. M. McCabe. Oxford, 79–103.

———. "The Ideal of Godlikeness." In *Oxford Readings in Plato: Ethics, Politics, Religion and the Soul,* ed. G. Fine (Oxford, 1999).

Shorey, P. 1904. *The Unity of Plato's Thought.* Decennial Publications of the University of Chicago 6, 129–214. Reprint. New York: Garland Press, 1980, 1–88.

Stopper, M. 1981. "Greek Philosophy and the Victorians." *Phronesis* 26, 267–85.

Tarrant, H. 1983. "Middle Platonism and the *Seventh Epistle.*" *Phronesis* 28, 75–103.

———. Forthcoming a. "Platonic Interpretation in Aulus Gellius."

———. Forthcoming b. "*Politike Eudaimonia:* Olympiodorus on Plato's *Republic.*"

Turner, F. 1981. *The Greek Heritage in Victorian Britain.* New Haven.

Vander Waerdt, P., ed. 1994. *The Socratic Movement.* Ithaca, N.Y.

Vlastos, G. 1991. *Socrates, Ironist and Moral Philosopher.* Cambridge.

Von Fritz, K. 1971. "The Philosophical Passage in the Seventh Platonic Letter." In *Essays in Ancient Greek Philosophy,* vol. 1, ed. J. Anton and G. Kustas. Albany, N.Y. 408–47.

Waldron, J. 1995. "What Plato Would Allow." NOMOS 37, *Theory and Practice,* 138–78.

White, J. L. 1986. *Light from Ancient Letters.* Philadelphia.

Whittaker, J. 1990. *Alcinoos: Enseignement des doctrines de Platon.* Les Belles Lettres. Paris.

INDEX LOCORUM

INDEX OF NAMES
AND SUBJECTS